The Cypress Tree

The Cypress Tree

A LOVE LETTER TO IRAN

Tree

KAMIN MOHAMMADI

BLOOMSBURY

LONDON • BERLIN • NEW YORK • SYDNEY

First published in Great Britain 2011

Copyright © 2011 by Kamin Mohammadi
Map by John Gilkes

Bloomsbury Publishing Plc
36 Soho Square
London W1D 3QY

www.bloomsbury.com

Bloomsbury Publishing, London, New York and Berlin
A CIP catalogue record for this book is available from the British Library

ISBN 978 0 7475 9152 8 (hardback)
ISBN 978 1 4088 1701 8 (trade paperback)

10 9 8 7 6 5 4 3 2 1

Typeset by Hewer Text UK Ltd, Edinburgh
Printed in Great Britain by Clays Ltd, St Ives plc, Bungay, Suffolk

For my parents

and in memory of Firooz

'Somewhere beyond right and wrong is a garden. My Friend,
I will meet you there.'

Rumi

'Call it [the tree] of Paradise, if you do not know why you
should call it the Cypress . . .'

Ferdowsi, *Shahnameh*

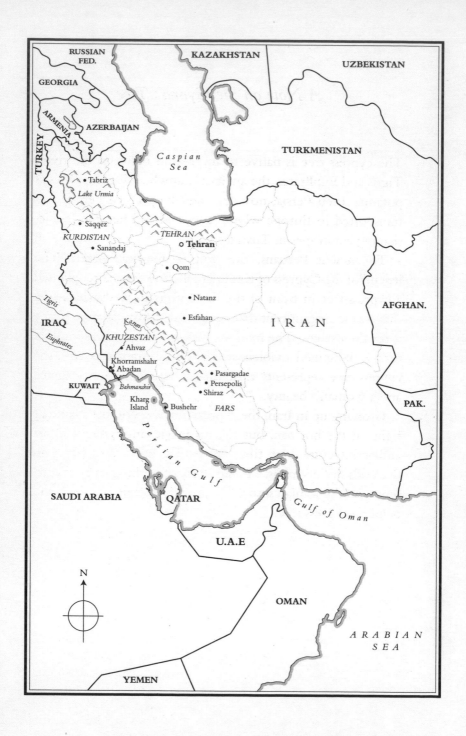

A Note on the Cypress Tree

The cypress tree is native to the region between the rivers Tigris and Euphrates, the ancient land which was first Mesopotamia, then Persia, now Iran and Iraq. From here it was transported to Europe where it thrived and became iconic, shaping landscapes in Tuscany.

To ancient Persians, the cypress tree was sacred. The legend of the Cypress of Kashmar tells how Zoroaster planted a cypress tree in front of the fire temple in Kashmar, a tree that was so magnificent that people came from all over to see it for themselves. The man – a Muslim Caliph – responsible for its felling died a violent death. Within Iranian poetry, the cypress tree represents truthfulness, freedom, purity, grace and a woman's beauty.

Growing up in Iran, the cypress tree was not just a familiar sight on the horizon, but also an image omnipresent in art and architecture – on tiles, on textiles, on carpets, even on the walls of Persepolis. I could think of nothing so perfect to represent the Iranian soul as the pure flexible line of the ever-bending cypress tree.

Dramatis Personae

Mother's side (Persian)

Sedigheh	my mother
Fatemeh Bibi	my grandmother/Sedigheh's mother (Maman-*joon*)
Mirza Esmael Khan	Fatemeh Bibi's father/Sedigheh's grandfather
Abbas Abbasian	Fatemeh Bibi's husband/Sedigheh's father

Fatemeh Bibi's children

Ali (Shapour)	m. Ashraf, children: 5, including Ebby
Parivash	m. Jahanzadeh, child, Alireza
Mahvash	m. Jamshid, children: 4, including Mahnaz
Mina	m. Abdolhossein Busheiry
Sedigheh	m. Bagher Mohammadi
Hossein	
Pardis	m. Shirin, children: Cyrus (Koochooloo), Nazanin
Mostafa	
Ahmad and *Reza*	Fatemeh Bibi's twin sons
Mohammad (Mamaly)	Fatemeh Bibi's last son
Yassaman (Yassi)	m. Seini, children: 4, including Amin and Ali
Ebby	my cousin, son of Shapour
Alireza	my cousin, son of Parivash, m. Shahnaz: child, Maryam

Mahnaz	my cousin, daughter of Mahvash
Noosheen	my cousin, daughter of Reza
Haydeh	Mina's friend

Father's side (Kurdish)

Bagher	my father
Shokrollah	my grandfather/Bagher's father. Widower when he married
Kowkab	my grandmother/Bagher's mother. Widow of the Tailor
Akhtar-khanoum	Shokrollah's third wife
Ebrahim	Kowkab's son from her first marriage to the Tailor. Bagher's half brother m. Sa'adat-*khanoum*, their children:

Firooz	my cousin
Mehry	my cousin
Guity	my cousin
Behrooz	my cousin. m. Firoozeh, one child
Parviz	my cousin

Prologue

'NOTHING. I FEEL nothing,' the old man declared, his expression inscrutable.

Here he was, the saviour of the Iranian people, the architect of the Islamic Revolution: Ayatollah Khomeini, returning triumphant to his country after fifteen years in exile, Mohammad Reza Shah Pahlavi toppled and fled, two and a half millennia of monarchy interrupted. And Iran was waiting, holding its breath to hear what he would say – this old man whose words had undammed rivers of blood to wash through the streets – on being asked how he felt to be returning to his country after all this time.

This had been his answer.

This response, squeezed dry of any feeling, provoked silence from the disenfranchised, poor, illiterate citizens who had brought this man back on a tide of violence and chaos and longing. There was a pause in homes across the land: in the sprawling detached houses of the middle classes, smart families wearing Europe's latest fashions gathered around state-of-the-art televisions, and in the mud villages where the population thronged round the ancient set belonging to the local landowner's estate manager. For the space of one heartbeat, the country was stunned.

I was a chubby child of nine addicted to reading and chocolate, sitting on the floor, a book in my hands. Underneath me lay a carpet of silk and wool flowers spun into meadows of colour. I hadn't been to school in weeks, and I could sense the tension radiating from my parents. I knew that the shah had left the country and I knew that I had to be careful of what I said when I was out of the house – my mother had said that there were ears everywhere and though I had not understood how that was possible, it had silenced me none-theless. I had felt the violence on the streets moving ever closer to our home and I knew that every night more of our friends and neighbours vanished from their beds where they slept, never to be seen again.

Despite this, I was more bewildered by this thing called a revolution than scared by it. I thought I understood what was happening: the shah was gone and the joy emanating from this penetrated even the compound that protected us and our modern, middle-class lives. Iran would be free! *Estegh-lal, azadi, jomhooriy-e Eslami.* I had heard the chants on the streets, their insistent rhythms echoing through the walls: independence, freedom and an Islamic Republic! I under-stood even less what this meant but I felt the excitement of it anyway. But as I watched this man, the author of so much destruction in my world, the cause of so many murders and disappearances, and listened to him say those words – 'I feel nothing' – for the first time in my young life, true fear entered my heart.

HOME

My tongue, every atom of my blood, form'd from this soil,
this air,
Born here of parents born here, from parents the same, and
their parents the same . . .

Walt Whitman, 'Starting from Paumanok'

I

Longing to Go Back

M Y FATHER HAS never spoken much of Kurdistan.
Most Kurdish people, even those without any nationalistic fervour, are so steeped in their own culture, language
and environment that they cannot help but fill their talk with
the mountain air of their land. Without direct mention of
Kurdistan, my Kurdish friends and family – even those who
have lived away for over fifty years – seem to sigh rushing
streams and the pleasure of lying dappled with light under a
walnut tree in fields of gold.

But my father has never shared these memories. He has
never talked much of his extended family either, of all those
weddings where he must have perfected complicated Kurdish
dance steps. He was known for the accuracy and nimbleness
of his dancing and I see this still as he trips about the sitting
room in north London leading us, his women, unrhythmi-
cally in his wake, the *choupi* in his hand a white napkin from
the table, unable to break down the steps adequately so I
can learn them, and equally unable not to dance when the
music is playing. My mother, an anarchic Khuzestani with
fire in her veins, gets bored and breaks the circle, whirling
like a dervish in the middle as she creates the chaos which my
father, with his precise steps, tries to contain. Of course, he
does not succeed. He cannot succeed. The Abbasian women
have always been driven by fire and the Mohammadi passion
for order has only ever, at best, imposed a loose structure on
my mother. She continues to be the nucleus of our family,

our little tribe, just as her mother was before her and her sisters continue to be in Iran, our lost paradise.

My parents didn't share much of their past with us, but they did try to share their culture; it was me who wanted none of it. I was nine years old when we moved to London and as I grew up I turned my back determinedly on Iran and all things Iranian. I realise now that the things I regret – the loss of fluency, the ability to read and understand our greatest poets in my native tongue, my ignorance of Persian epithets, songs and dances – are not just the result of estrangement from our land, but also of the gap that opened up between us children and our parents, the abyss that yawned between us, separating their Iranian culture from our adopted English one. On their side were poems quoted liberally at parties, traditional songs sung as their friends gathered around the piano, jokes and a litany of teasing and banter that flew between them all in poetic Farsi. On our side were Duran Duran and the Famous Five, my passion for ponies and pop music. Disappearing into the gap between us fell my parent's entreaties for us to speak to our extended family in Iran, threats to send us to Farsi school on Saturdays and pleas for us to stop running away from their friends and parties.

I had no idea why I was turning my back on Iran, except that I was angry. Angry and ashamed; such a complex cocktail of shame I was carrying – shame for the revolution, shame for the hostage crisis, shame that we had had to leave, shame for the austere looks of Ayatollah Khomeini and the radical images and ideals of the Islamic Republic. In some strange way, I was ashamed of standing among these reasonable English people and of not being like them. I sought to erase the shame by fitting in and ignoring Iran as if just by willing it, by denying its existence, I could cease to be Iranian, cease to be from a place that had dealt my young heart such a shattering blow.

Iran would not be willed away. It was there on our screens, a collage of familiar elements made unfamiliar by their juxtaposition; there were the plane trees of Tehran's Pahlavi Boulevard, but they were providing the background for a march of revolutionaries, there were the familiar American cars like the one we had owned, but instead of driving down the street, they were on fire by the roadside. Iran was also inside me, our rose garden, noisy family gatherings and balmy nights spent sleeping on the rooftop of my grandmother's house in Abadan. The memories and the longing for my country seeped inexorably through me until one day the knowledge had risen to the surface, undeniable, and I knew that I had to go back.

It still took me years. The pull back to Iran was easy to resist when all the pleasures of the Western world were at my disposal. Finally, I found myself outside the Iranian consulate in a quiet square behind Kensington High Street, resentfully adjusting a makeshift headscarf as my father led me inside to apply for my Iranian passport. I was apprehensive, even of the bearded man behind the counter, but contrary to my expectations these representatives of the revolutionary government were charming, not impassioned and angry but smiley and full of *ta'arof*, the elaborate Persian form of courtesy whose deciphering has dogged my life.

Over tea at Barkers afterwards, as my father filled out the piles of forms, I was overwhelmed by twin feelings that have become familiar companions on my travels to Iran: anxiety and inadequacy. Anxiety because my last memories of Iran were of streets full of angry unshaven men punching the air, shouting, rioting, of a bloodlust that every night claimed the lives of our neighbours. Inadequacy because despite my degree in literature and burgeoning career as a journalist, I could not read or write well in Farsi, and could only speak it hesitantly and with an English accent. In my mother tongue, I

was practically illiterate, an uncomfortable space for an intellectual snob to occupy.

The drive back to Iran continued almost in spite of me
and finally, one day I found myself fiddling again with my
headscarf as my mother and I started the journey back to the
land of my birth and my forefathers. I was twenty-seven and
it was eighteen years since I had last been in Iran.

2

Metamorphosis

M Y METAMORPHOSIS INTO a citizen of the Islamic
Republic of Iran started at Heathrow airport, October 1996. Shrouded in a long, loose coat and wearing one of
my mother's slippery Hermès scarves on my head, I hoped
I wouldn't be spotted as the impostor I felt. Travelling with
IranAir may have meant (as I discovered later) the world's
most delicious airline food, but it also meant that from the
moment of check in, you had to adhere to sharia, the Islamic
law that governs Iran and so I was already clad in a *hejab* in
London.

For many, Iran conjures up the Green Wave and the haunt-
ing stare of Neda as she died on camera, the axis of evil, the
US hostage crisis or Ahmadinejad's innocuous sports jacket
and his less innocuous comments on the Holocaust. For me
it is simply the country of my birth. Home both to one of
the world's greatest ancient civilisations and the most shock-
ing revolution seen in modern history, mine is a country so
contradictory that even its children are divided as to what
they call themselves and how they present themselves to the
world. Iranians living outside the country and having to deal
every day with the reactions that being from there provokes,
fall into two camps as to what they call themselves: Iranian
or Persian. Some of us remain stridently and unashamedly
Iranian, although for many Westerners this recalls images
of revolution, fanaticism and black-robed women; others
choose instead to call themselves Persian, an exotic word that

brings to mind splendid carpets, fluffy cats and the griffin-topped towers of ancient Persepolis.

I have, over the thirty years I have been exiled from my country, made the transition from calling myself Persian to calling myself Iranian. For me it is now merely a matter of accuracy – to call myself Persian while I am in fact half Persian, half Kurdish would be like a Scotsman calling himself English. He may call himself British but never English and similarly, Persia does not contain the whole picture for me.

It was the Islamic Republic of Iran that I was going back to. To me, Iran was not just the Islamic Republic as glimpsed on the television, the almost monochrome society depicted as repressed and joyless. Iran, to my mind, was still a place of golden memories of building sandcastles by the Caspian Sea, beloved cousins coming to visit, snuggling under the *korsy* in my Kurdish uncle's house in the winter, my grandmother's jet-black plaits hanging over earlobes elongated by heavy gold earrings. I also had darker memories of death and fear, of a time when my mother had no patience, the tense cab ride through Tehran when she had chided me for mentioning the shah's name – ('That's not a name you can say in public any more,' she had hissed) – and the day we ran away from our house without saying goodbye to any of my friends. There they all were, jostling with each other for space, fragrant memories infused with jasmine and orange blossom and terrible ones weighed down with dead neighbours and lost friends.

Fear gnawed at me as I boarded, adjusting the scarf that slid forward over my forehead, just one of a million adjustments I was to make to this innocuous piece of fabric over the next few weeks. I was not the first Iranian woman to discover how much a little square of silk can rule your life, though later I found it an unexpected ally when I flicked it across my face to deter the unwelcome attentions of one of the male stewards.

To try to calm myself I imagined Iran's birth unfolding beneath us; a large plateau riven by faults in the earth's crust, one of the most earthquake-prone zones on the planet, the soil piled on some of the world's richest natural resources, oil as yet undiscovered, huge reserves of gas fizzing under the surface, giving it an explosive, volatile nature, liable to go off at any moment.

To the south is the long, languid stretch of the Persian Gulf, a lapis sea of fever and pearls, and up to the north, carried on the back of the sitting cat that is the map of modern Iran, is the Caspian Sea, foaming with oil and caviar. Ranges of mountains ruck up to the heavens, snowbound and magnificent, permanently cloaked in clouds. Full forests and fecund valleys, wild places stalked by wolves, bears and lions, lie carpeted in a weave of wild flowers. And then deserts, seas of sand and scrub holding in tight embrace oases of green palm plantations and rivulets of water, underground springs that are channelled by the inhabitants into *qanats*, underground reservoirs that conjure up gardens from the bare desert, lush groves of towering trees – cypress, juniper, linden, pine – and orchards of pomegranate, pear, apple and peach, all cut through by straight canals of water, gurgling into rectangular turquoise pools, delighting the senses and reflecting the beauty all around. The ancients called this *pairadiza*, and it's still our vision of paradise.

For every Iranian the vision of paradise encompasses our land. The very soil of the place feels familiar to us, we are tied to it, to the changes that have befallen us and have formed us, so many thousands of years of bloodshed, violence and uncertainty that have coded themselves into our genes. Our roots go deep in Iran – we are exiles with a lost paradise forever swimming in our eyes, steeped in the culture of our lost land while living in foreign countries, following every beat of news, perusing the opinions of the young on the blogosphere, anything so as not to let go of Iran – ours is not just romantic love for an idealised country but also an expression of the loss each of us feels on being physically separated from the land.

We have been here a long time; Iran is the longest continuously inhabited land by a single race. First we were great: the mighty Achaemenid Empire of Cyrus the Great was consolidated by Darius the Great, the man immortalised in the Bible for freeing the Jews. He built great palaces at Persepolis in marble and gold, black stones polished to a mirror-like sheen, set amidst a chequerboard of *pairadiza* – dream gardens rising out of the dusty earth of Fars. He received tributes from subjects converging on Iran from the furthest reaches of the world, different races living together in tolerance and peace under the embracing wings of Ahuramazda, the Zoroastrian god.

Then we were conquered. First by Alexander the Great who burnt the palaces of Persepolis, carrying away their treasures on 20,000 mules and 5,000 camels, the mighty Persian Empire and all the splendours of the Achaemenid kings turned to ashes.

Then it was the Arabs, whose conquest we have never recovered from. They came out of the desert, the crescent moon of Islam scything across the country, converting the populace as well as absorbing the land into another empire, this time one united by belief and the sweet sound of the call to prayer. Although the Arabs tried to erase all traces of Persian culture, burning our books and changing the alphabet, we Iranians resisted Arab cultural dominion. And yet we fell deeply in love with Islam, with its peace and charity, and this faith in the unseen gave new life to the arts and crafts at which Iranians already excelled. The poet Ferdowsi gave thirty years of his life to fashioning the *Shahnameh*, a mythical history of Iran's past, our *Illiad*, *Odyssey* and *Aeneid* all rolled into one, a work of such devotion to Iran that it rescued our heritage and language from the Arab onslaught. Despite the Arab insistence on devotion only to Islam, Iranians continued to celebrate Nowruz on the moment of the vernal equinox, the ancient Zoroastrian celebration – the basis of Easter and other less ancient religious festivals – legitimised in Islamic society by the judicious placement of the Qur'ān on the New Year table.

Iran had survived the Macedonian upstart Alexander the Great, and even assimilated Islam, but it didn't stand a chance against the genocidal force of the rampaging armies of Genghis Khan. The Mongol hordes plunged in from the north-east, conquering Samarkand and killing and raping innocents as they went, allowing nothing to stand in their way. Genghis Khan poured molten silver into the eyes and ears of his enemies and the plateau was flooded by the blood of the thousands that died. For two hundred years, the brutalised people of Iran lived in a state of terror so acute the stench of fear seeped into our genes. Even the land did not remain the same after the Mongols, who thought nothing of diverting rivers and wiping waterways from the map to subjugate enemy cities.

More Mongol warlords followed with Tamerlane's brutal reign, but Iranians held on to their ways – great art and architecture had come into being under the earlier Seljuq rule and continued to florish under the descendents of Tamerlane. Persians have a habit of thriving when times are tough, somehow finding a way around the obstacles, infiltrating the dominant culture of the invader, transforming it to glory. In the first thousand years of our life as a country, Iranians learnt best of all how to survive. Our elaborate manners are designed to protect our private selves and this trait, born of so many invasions, has made Iranians adaptable above all else. Wherever we are scattered in the world, we integrate.

It passed below us, mountains and valleys, deserts and seas all written, it seemed to me, with the stories of my ances-tors, the whole country crisscrossed with our adventures, losses, passions and laughter. Up in the north-west province of Azerbaijan began my mother's strand of my family's story.

Ali was from a family who for generations farmed land outside Baku in the Azerbaijan region that historically belonged to Iran but, like a hyperactive pawn, changed hands between Russia and Iran repeatedly through the nineteenth century. Ali, after an argument with his brothers, took his family and quit Baku, moving down to the revolutionary hotbed of Tabriz in Iran in 1909. In those heady days of the Constitutional Revolution, Tabriz was a magnet for all sorts of Caucasian revolutionar-ies, and a man who considered himself Iranian may well have chosen to follow his ideals and help his countrymen in their struggle for freedom, going to Tabriz to join the *mojaheds*.

Ali's son Abbas was not yet ten when he experienced the hunger and loneliness of those times, a city under siege, food becoming ever scarcer and the constant fear of attack by loyalist troops both outside and inside the town. Abbas would always bear inside him the hardship of that time and he developed a lifelong obsession with an overflowing *sofra* and multitudes to sit around it. Abbas Abbasian, as he was to become, was taken across the country to Esfahan where the family settled in the Armenian quarter of Jolfa but he was barely in his teens when he quit Esfahan's turquoise domes and headed south to Abadan where he, with his quick wit and ability to work hard, prospered and made such a fortune that he was considered a suitable match for my grandmother Fatemeh Bibi, a khan's only daughter.

I knew my grandfather Abbas for just the first year of my life, and since my other grandfather had passed away long before my birth, I was brought up in a large family headed by a matriarch. Tiny and beautiful as a jewel, Maman-*joon*

held fast the family in her small hands. Maman-*joon*'s minis-
cule frame loomed large in my memory and I knew that she
would be there when, after our time in Tehran, we finally
alighted in Shiraz.

The other strand of my family were my father's people
who hail from the mountainous province of Kurdistan, the
portion of a non-existent country that falls in Iran, and who
made their home in Tehran. Legend has it that King Solomon banished five hundred mischievous *djinns* from his
kingdom, flung by his wrath into the zigzag terrain of the
Zagros mountains, a land so remote that the powerful king
could forget all about the troublemakers. The crafty *djinns*,
finding themselves lonely in the mountains, flew across into
Europe where they chose five hundred beautiful virgins, with
skin pale as alabaster and hair like flax, and transported them
back to their new home where their union begat the Kurds,
a people famed for their ferocity, their pale eyes and their
hospitality; a race given to dancing and loving and fighting,
as strong and stubborn as their beloved mountains. Legends
and myths continue to cling to the slopes of the jagged peaks
that form this land, and the Kurds wear their mythical status
like a comfortable coat, always ready to slip on when the
political climate demands.

My Kurdish family are nearly as prodigious as my Persian
family but, compared to the noisy Abbasians, they are made of
much quieter stuff. The glittering exceptions to this rule are
my Kurdish cousins, the women who were like aunts to me as
I was growing up: Mehry and Guity. They were my mother's
age but always also somehow felt like friends and contemporaries – this was their great gift. Guity always produced
delicious food and loved a snowball fight more than even
the hot sweet tea she was addicted to. And beautiful Mehry
used to take me out to drink *café glacé* after school and has
been there for me through all the worst points of my life.

She had come back to London – where she had completed her PhD – in our first few months there when we were all numb with the shock of exile, and she had turned up again some years later, materialised like an angel when I was bed-bound recovering from third-degree burns, missing sitting for university finals with my peers. I was twenty-one then and still in the throes of denying Iran, but she somehow managed to slip through the wall of Anglicisation I had built around me to fill me with her familiar, wry love. Seeing her sitting perched on the edge of my sickbed brandishing a pair of sharp tweezers, I had allowed her to pluck my eyebrows – though I had refused my mother access to them for years. Her legacies are with me to this day: a taste for good coffee and long sweeping eyebrows.

I knew they were down below, waiting for us and, all too soon, the lights of Tehran were blinking up at me. I shuffled behind my mother and stood on the steps leading down from the aeroplane. That's when it hit me; the night air, autumnal, carrying a suggestion of reddened leaves, the rushing of mountain springs and the snows to come. I had forgotten. I wasn't prepared for the smells of the town where I had grown up – Tehran. I burst into tears.

3

Tehran

M Y FEARS DISAPPEARED when the immigration official examined and then stamped my virgin Iranian passport without even looking up; he only addressed me when he said, 'Welcome back to Iran, *Khanoum* Mohammadi.'

In the baggage hall, I took in the scene as my mother busied herself with trolleys and porters. The hall was busy, clamouring with chatter and movement. Watching over everything, mounted high up on a wall, were pictures of President Rafsanjani and the Supreme Leader, Ayatollah Khamenei. In the centre, the picture that dominated all others, the image that still dominated the country, the blank stare of the dead revolutionary leader, Imam Khomeini.

I looked through the glass wall and there they were, amongst the groups of excited families bearing bouquets of flowers: Mehry and Guity, so inescapably themselves that I was momentarily stopped in my tracks. Older certainly, the years having etched deeper furrows on Guity's face than on Mehry's beauty, but their eyes lit up like excited children's when they saw us. We crossed the line and I fell into their arms, dwarfing them – it was the first time I had hugged Guity as a grown woman and she was so tiny that I could have put her in my pocket.

We drove to their flat and, after the customary tea was drunk, I retreated to bed, my stumbling Farsi exhausted, my heart wrung out. There I found my pillow scattered with jasmine flowers – Mehry and Guity had never forgotten how much I loved them.

The next morning the sunlight burnt through my eyelids, forcing my eyes open. I dressed and headed for the kitchen, where everyone was gathered waiting to make a fuss, give me tea, push on me flat bread sprinkled with sesame seeds and spread with white cheese, a jar of my childhood favour- ite – sour cherry jam – on the table. And best of all, I noticed as I took my seat at the table, there were the mountains. The Alborz framed in the window. Quite suddenly my heart soared. Of course I had remembered the mountains but I had forgotten their looming presence, so close, so vivid. We were in the north of the city, butting up to the mountains, and they were right outside the window, as they had seemed in my childhood home in Darrus, a part of Tehran that was then as far north as the city spread. In those days, opposite our rambling villa was a blank of wasteland, no houses or development yet, just orchards and, soaring up behind them, always capped by snow, the Alborz.

That was before the city exploded to its present size, before the population of Tehran grew to 14 million souls, before the Iranian love affair with the car made it necessary to embroi- der Tehran with a spaghetti of motorways, to join up its furthest reaches with miles of tarmac. Tehran contains almost one fifth of Iran's total population and all those people with their thoughts and dreams and ambitions need somewhere to live, so the only surprise in seeing the soaring skyscrapers punching Tehran's skyline was the unexpected modernity of it.

I had believed the Western media's image of Iran as a land that had been taken back to the thirteenth century. But I soon found out that, while the Islamic Republic reverted to the Islamic calendar (on my first visit back in 1996 it was 1375 in Iran) and adopted Islamic law after the revolution, in reality Iran was a thoroughly modern country.

The Iranians' delight in all things new includes a passion for building the highest towers in the region and Iran's most distinguished architects had begun a race for the most high-rise, glossy, mixed-use skyscraper the city had seen, and residential buildings started to join in, with apartment blocks becoming the norm. Wonderful old Persian houses were deemed spatially too inefficient, and the old houses set behind walls circling large rambling gardens of fruit trees and shallow pools have become a rarity in Tehran. Even villas built by the New Iranians like my father, men who had made their money in the booming sixties and seventies in industries such as oil, were being knocked down to make room for soaring blocks containing multiple lives, while the new rich, the mullahs and their friends, have constructed ever more palatial villas further north. You have to venture further up the Alborz's fanning skirt nowadays to be in the higher reaches of the city. Tehran continues to grow, snaking up the mountain, the flats and houses and palaces creeping upwards. The height of the mountain will contain Tehran one of these days, but who knows how soon Tehranis will find a way to build and live and breathe at 3,000 metres.

I spent those first days in Tehran not quite a tourist, not quite a local; neither British nor properly Iranian, but lost somewhere in the gap between the two, an empty space which was more dislocating than I had anticipated.

Nothing was easy those days. I was a foreigner, though nonetheless Iranian enough to be mortified by my own lack of appropriate manners and language. But the stream of visitors who came to see me didn't care how bad my Farsi was or how clueless I was about everything. They wept over me, they turned to my mother and kissed her hands, saying, 'You took away a girl and you have brought us back a beautiful woman. *Dastet dard nakone.*' All this love was at once comforting and overwhelming – I had accustomed myself to life alone, my answer to exile being an overdependence on the independence that I could not have here in Iran. Suddenly I was joined to my mother by an invisible umbilical cord, the presence of which made me deeply uncomfortable. I chafed but I had no choice but to submit.

The rules of behaviour in this new Islamic Republic were so confusing to me that I learnt to hang back and be quiet and let others take the lead. I was trying to understand my own culture. It mortified me.

At the airport, one of my male cousins, Firooz, had accompanied Mehry and Guity, and, although my heart had skipped to see him, I hadn't dared to kiss him until we got back to the flat. That was another thing to remember in the Islamic Republic – you must not touch men in public.

Actually, in the years to come, I was to discover this to be as relative as many other laws. There would be times when one of my uncles would take my hand as we walked down the street and not let it go. There would be times when they would clasp me in their arms at the airport, soaking my face in their tears. But whatever the rules governing these digressions from the law, I never fully understood them and so I pulled my scarf tightly over my hair, kept my face free of make-up, my coat loose and shoes flat – and I stood motionless in front of every man in my family, from teenager up, until their actions guided me.

I was swept off to palaces and museums. The city I had grown up in had become a confusion of crisscrossing motorways – everything had changed. Everywhere, looming on the sides of buildings and on giant billboards by the highways, were lurid representations of Imam Khomeini. When I was growing up, in Mohammad Reza Shah's time, photographs, usually of him decked out in military uniform, hung at the top of every classroom I attended. After the revolution, the shah's picture was replaced by Ayatollah Khomeini's impassive stare and images of the 'martyrs' of the war with Iraq. Painted poster-style with beautifully calligraphed snatches of poetry or revolutionary slogans, the men were portrayed surrounded by doves or garlanded with roses, the Iranian love of nature transforming even these dubious works into a continuation of the delicate sensibility of Iranian art. This was a new phenomenon, the lavish poster art that covered the side of buildings, often accompanied by verses of poetry or sutras from the Qur'ān, and it was hard to escape the presence of the Islamic Republic and its values at every turn.

Thick smog hung over the city, the pollution choking my lungs. On the rare occasions that the smog would clear, the sight of Damavand on the horizon would transport me back to the city of my childhood. I loved walking down Tehran's main thoroughfare, the wide and long Vali Asr – the new name for Pahlavi Boulevard – with its wide *joobs* gushing water and the plane trees stretched out overhead. Pahlavi was not the only street that had been renamed. The revolution and subsequent regime change had renamed many streets, squares and monuments, anything referring to the monarchy had been replaced by 'Imam' and many roads bore the names of the war's most famous martyrs. Just to confuse matters further, some streets and areas were referred to by both their post and pre-revolutionary names. Navigating Tehran became, as so many things seemed to me on that first trip back, an exercise in confusion.

The most powerful part of that trip, the simplest thing of all, was the love that I rediscovered for my extended family. It went beyond houses or gardens, confusing laws or latent guilt, beyond even the deserts and mountains that I had imagined linked me to the past. The love of my family anchored me and I realised that, for me, Iran will always be about the people whom I love.

In Tehran there was my uncle's family, and in the wild mountainous land of Kurdistan the rest of my father's family, the women still wearing their multi-coloured long Kurdish dresses, like spangly birds of paradise. Kind, quiet people, characterised by wry humour and their teasing manner, the side of the family that produced our most brilliant academic achievers. My mother's huge family is spread across the country now, some still in our native Khuzestan, in the hot and humid climes of Abadan and Ahvaz, while in Shiraz a selection of aunts, uncles and cousins from my mother's side awaited me. So, after a week in Tehran and a whirlwind of the half-familiar faces of my father's side of the family, my mother and I headed to Shiraz to be absorbed into the ample bosom that is the Abbasian family, my beloved *Khaleh* Mina among them, my mother's sister and closest friend – and my favourite aunt.

4

Shiraz and the Abbasians

THE CITY OF poets and nightingales, Shiraz is famed for its gardens, the smell of orange blossom in the spring and the overwhelming sentimentality of its people's souls. It lies towards the south of the country, in the province of Fars, the cradle of the Persian civilization. An hour or so out of town, deep in the scrub, lie the remains of Persepolis, and nearby stand the remains of the tented city of the shah's extravagant celebration of Iran's 2,500 year anniversary, a testament to the folly of this self-aggrandising man. Among the nightingales and the gardens of Shiraz lives *Khaleh* Mina, one of my mother's older sisters. *Khaleh* Mina is like a second mother to me; she was always there with her patience when my mother's hot temper got the better of her, and with her raucous laugh when my mother's frowns would open for no one else. I hadn't seen her for nearly twenty years but the brightness of her love was such that all my attempts to forget her had been useless.

And then there was my grandmother, Fatemeh Bibi Hayat Davoudy, or Maman-*joon* as we affectionately called her. As I sat on the plane and remembered her, a tiny sparrow of a woman, some inches short of five foot with jet-black hair, smooth white skin and green eyes, I had no doubt that she would still be a great beauty at the age of seventy-eight. What I had neglected to anticipate was how moved I would be to see her standing at the head of the family group that gathered at Shiraz to greet us. Doubled over and clinging to her as she

hugged me, her tiny white arms encircled by gold, my face
contorted with emotion as she reached up and patted my
back, murmuring, 'Hush my child, it's OK, my child, it's OK,
my girl,' just as she had when I had howled for my mother
when she went away.

Fatemeh Bibi Hayat Davoudy was born into a family of
khans from the south just before Europe heard the first shot
of the First World War ring out and just a few years after
Iran saw the coronation of Ahmad Shah Qajar, an ambiva-
lent teenager prone to fat who would be the last shah of the
Qajar dynasty. Her family were landowners whose properties
bordered the Persian Gulf, the sea where legend tells us King
Solomon's pearl ring dropped off his finger to be swallowed
by the waves. Their lands stretched west along the coast from
the port of Bushehr, a region traditionally known as Hayat
Davoudy, which, along with the fronds of palm plantations,
included several ports as well as the small island of Kharg, an
innocuous piece of land dropped like an afterthought into
the Persian Gulf.

Fatemeh Bibi had been a longed-for daughter, a late
addition to a family of three rambunctious boys. Her father,
Mirza Esmael Khan Hayat Davoudy, had yearned for a baby
girl. He had named her Bibi Bozorg and had loved her for
the alabaster tones of her skin, the emerald green of her eyes
and the raven black of her hair. But the indulgent khan's
happiness was short-lived and soon he was at the mosque
begging on his knees for God to spare his daughter from the
fever that threatened to carry her away. My grandmother's
fate seemed sealed until, as she often told me, there was a
magical midnight visit to the baby's sickroom by *Hazrat*
Fatemeh, the blessed daughter of the Prophet, and Bibi
Bozorg's health was restored in exchange for the sight in
her mother's green eyes. And so my grandmother's name
was changed from Bibi Bozorg to Fatemeh Bibi to honour

the saint, and her mother endured a period of blindness that lasted some months.

Fatemeh Bibi grew up in a rambling house set behind mud brick walls, outside which the port town bustled with a stream of goods and people. These southern ports have played host to passers-by for generations and once Vasco de Gama opened up the sea route from western Europe to India in 1497 European travellers sailed through too, bequeathing to the likes of my family their green eyes and fair skin.

Maman-*joon* entered the world when Iran was first clamouring for freedom and democracy. The Constitutional Revolution of 1905 to 1911 had left Iran with a constitution and a *majlis* (parliament), the first country in the region to implement such nascent democratic processes – but the corrupt Qajar shahs were manipulated by Imperial Russia and wave-ruling Britannia who, behind the scenes, played the Great Game – the contest for dominion over the near East and central Asia – and Iran was a colony in all but name.

The shahs of the Qajar dynasty were weak and they carved up and sold off the country, giving concessions for railroads, for banks, for printing Iran's first paper money, for fishing for caviar, for drilling for oil. Oil was struck in 1908, and the Anglo-Persian Oil Company was formed. In 1914, a certain Winston Churchill, Britain's First Lord of the Admiralty, persuaded the British government to buy a majority share in the Company; Iranian oil had become crucial to them in 1912 when the Royal Navy converted all its ships from coal- to oil-fired engines. With Great Britain taking 84 per cent of the profits of Iranian oil, by the time Europe was rumbling towards war, profits from the nascent oil industry were already clinking in British coffers.

When the Great War broke out, Iran announced her neutrality, but this did not deter Russia from occupying the north of the country, while the British added the oil fields of Khuzestan to their patch. The land was riven by fighting and famine – the Great War spared no one in its brutality, least of all a backward Eastern nation such as Iran that was so strategically situated. By the time the war was over, the country was in chaos. Tribal revolts and economic failure assailed the weak and unpopular shah. The populace, having survived the battle of the Great Powers in their land, were now starving to death or falling to typhus and the influenza epidemic.

The war had brought nothing but devastation for Iran; her border provinces lost a quarter of their population to the fighting of foreign powers. After the Bolshevik revolution of 1917, Russia had quit the war and Britain was left as the sole Great Power in Iran. In desperation, Iranians resorted to that most Iranian of desires: the wish for a saviour. Whether expressed as belief in Imam Zaman, the Mahdi who will come to save the righteous at the end of days, or in support for a foreign power, we Iranians are apt to always look outside ourselves for both salvation and blame.

The country needed someone to take it in hand, a strong man, someone dynamic. That man was Reza Khan, a soldier born to a humble family in Mazandaran, in a small mountain village in the moist, green northern province of Iran. Reza joined the Cossack Brigade at the age of fifteen, with no formal education, unable to read or write, but his ambition and commanding presence saw him rise swiftly through the ranks. He attracted the attention of the British who saw in his raw form their next ideal puppet and they supported him as he marched on Tehran to execute a bloodless coup so efficient that in the morning no one realised there had been a revolution in the night. Within a few months, Reza

Khan had been appointed Minister for War with responsibility for the whole army. He cut an impressive, if rather grizzled figure, was a formidable disciplinarian, stood ramrod straight and was adored by his soldiers. Reza Khan had arrived and he was determined to modernise the country, whatever the British thought.

Maman-*joon* once told me that when she was a child and still living in Bushehr, Reza Khan had stopped at the port town on his way to Khuzestan to quash a tribal rebellion, and her father, Mirza Esmael Khan, had been a member of his welcoming party. Afterwards, her father had described the great man with such animation, exaggerating so enthusiastically for his daughter's benefit, that Fatemeh Bibi could never be persuaded that Reza Khan was anything but a ghoul – a giant with frizzy hair standing on end, an onion for a nose and manners so uncouth that he was capable only of shouting. That was the first time she had become aware of him, perhaps the only time she had given him thought, but his influence was to shape her life. His rush to modernise the country and his impatient bulldozing of traditions sent out ripples that reached even Fatemeh Bibi's walled-in world.

In February of 1924, a new *majlis*, under Reza Shah's mastery, passed a series of reforms that imposed a two-year national service, and abolished honorary titles, obliging all citizens to obtain birth certificates and register a family name, as well as announcing extra taxes that would finance the Trans-Iranian Railway. Reza Khan's reforms did not stop there; the old lunar calendar was replaced with a solar one which, though still dating from the Prophets Hejira to Medina, replaced the Muslim names of the month with names of Zoroastrian gods drawn from ancient Persian beliefs.

The new centrally organised government of Reza Khan needed civil servants to administer the imperial domains now that tribal leaders and feudal landlords no longer held such sway. Lands were being taken in lieu of taxes and resources finally feeding back to Tehran, and Reza Khan himself was proving no stranger to cushioning himself against the fickleness of Persian fortune with a nest feathered by lands and factories of his own. Reza Khan, casting an envious eye over the achievements of Atatürk next door in Turkey, toyed with the idea of making Iran a republic. But, finding the public and the *ulama* unreceptive, he abandoned the idea and, with the British whispering support in his ear, he instead plumped for ousting the Qajar shah and taking the throne himself.

Reza Shah was crowned Shahanshah – king of kings – in Tehran on 26 April 1926. The illiterate army officer with no surname chose the name Pahlavi for his dynasty, one heavy with heroic overtones. He ordered a new crown to be made and his coronation robe was of white, pink and black pearls sewn together. The new shah sat on the Peacock Throne, built of uncut jewels: diamonds, rubies, pearls and turquoises. Emeralds hung as tassels over the arms of the throne, 200 carats each. The different ethnicities of Iran were represented in processions of tribesmen that marched through Tehran, their heads held high. The foreign dignitaries attended parties every night in the new king's honour, the night skies of Tehran illuminated with fireworks. A preternaturally solemn boy of eight attended the coronation attired in miniature military uniform – Reza Shah's son Mohammad Reza Pahlavi was formally pronounced the Crown Prince of Iran and paid much conspicuous respect, even though it was rumoured that his father thought him soft.

Reza Khan had become the Shah of Iran. The country had less than a thousand schools and only eight miles of railway. There was much work to be done.

★   ★   ★

After Reza Shah was crowned, Maman-*joon*'s life abruptly changed. My great grandfather and his brother gave up their hereditary lands to the crown and oversaw the transportation of their households to Khorramshahr in Khuzestan. The khans of Hayat Davoudy gave up their ancestral rights for positions in the new bureaucracy that Reza Shah's centralisation of power called for. His victory in quelling the post-war tribal rebellions and bringing troublesome provinces such as Khuzestan to heel required a different way of running things, pulling together the threads that knitted Iran and with them spinning a new nation state.

Fatemeh Bibi was transplanted to the unpromising soil of Khuzestan. Once there she flourished, settled happily and always called it home. Known as the birthplace of the nation, millennia back, a people known as Persians settled here even before making it to Fars, laying the foundations for all the splendid pre-Islamic dynasties: the Achaemenids, the Parthians, the Sasanids.

Maman-*joon* had to wait until the ripe age of eighteen before she was wed. Her contemporaries were promised in marriage by the age of nine, but Maman-*joon*'s father doted on her so much that he never wanted her to marry. 'I will keep her by my side until all her teeth fall out,' he used to say. After rejecting suitor after suitor, he had been persuaded by his wife not to let their daughter 'remain in this unnatural state any longer'. Fatemeh Bibi herself was keen to get married and start her life, and all the jokes of being pickled whenever she attended a wedding were beginning to grate on her soft temper. Eventually her father had chosen a merchant named Abbas Abbasian, a serious-looking man, with a lean frame and dramatically strong features, hooded eyes, high cheekbones and a hawkish nose that had taken some growing into. As a skinny boy his nose had dominated not just his face but his whole body, but as a man in his early thirties that strong hawkish proboscis that is even now being borne on prettier faces than his in places as far-flung as North America and western Australia by the children of his children, had come into its own.

The man who finally married the cherished Fatemeh Bibi had grown up with none of her privilege. Abbas had no formal education, but he was a sharp boy, quick to absorb information and particularly brilliant at turning chance his way. After experiencing famine in Tabriz during the Constitutional Revolution, Abbas's family had moved to Esfahan where Abbas had grown up in the mostly Armenian neighbourhood of Jolfa. Before the Great War began, he had already exhausted the slim pickings in Esfahan for work and, at the age of fifteen, he decided that he should seek his fortune abroad. When the stories from Khuzestan caught his ear, Abbas was ready to quit his family and try his luck in the new world being built by the British in Abadan. He took his cousin Akbar aside and started pouring into his head the stories he had heard, of the booming new job market in Khuzestan. Yes, he had heard Khuzestan was unbearably hot and that in winter a wind blew that pierced your very soul, but what of that? They could make money!

Abbas and Akbar pooled their savings, packed their bags, said goodbye to their families and left behind the dusty streets of Jolfa washed by their mothers' tears and the glorious turquoise tiles of the Safavid city for the long and arduous trip across the country and its biggest desert, their destination an unknown dream set somewhere in Abbas' imagination.

Abbas and Fatemeh Bibi had become husband and wife in a simple *aghd* in November 1932. She often told me that she had instantly, instinctively known that this was her man for life, come what may. She had sat cross-legged on the floor, her head covered, and next to her had settled this tall thin man she had never met, this stranger she was to spend her life with. A white veil was stretched above their heads, held up by female members of her family, while a cousin rubbed together two plump cones of sugar, raining granules of sweetness on the veil, a symbol of the taste of their life together.

The first time she saw her future husband was in the mirror set in front of them where they sat on the ground side by side. '*Naneh*,' she confided to me years later, 'I wasn't supposed to look – it's not seemly. But I couldn't resist it. I was so happy to be married at last.' He was thirty-five and Fatemeh Bibi was eighteen but she felt the ripeness of her age more acutely than his.

Abbas Abbasian had made his fortune in the early boom of the oil industry and was settled in Abadan in a large house and made a living from selling ice. In the heat of Khuzestan and with Abadan's large British population so inordinately fond of their G&Ts, ice was a precious commodity and Abbas was doing well. The skinny youth had used all his native wit to find work and build a nest egg since arriving in Abadan. Working on the miles and miles of oil pipelines which had to be laid to transport the liquid money spouting out of various wells in Khuzestan to the refinery in Abadan, he had picked up enough English to be able to charm his masters. Soon he was the favourite odd-jobman for the British running the various oil projects – as well as laying pipelines, roads and jetties had to be built too; the great industry of oil needed modern facilities to turn that black rain into gold coins.

Never one to miss an opportunity, Abbas had diversified his work whenever he could. He worked and he sold on whatever he came across, including bits of opium that he himself did not want and gradually, he found he was buying and selling opium at ever increasing profits. Opium was a favourite – and legal – pastime for the masses that now

thronged Abadan, from the old aristocratic men who loved
to lounge at home with friends and forget the aches in their
bones by sucking on beautifully made pipes, to the poor
Arab workers who slept dozens to a room and made little
money from their backbreaking work, to the refined British
bosses who amused themselves 'playing Persian' by stretching
out on luxurious silk carpets and *takiehs* with a pipe at their
mouths. Abbas, long an opium eater himself, soon doubled
his income with his opium dealing and, as the years wore on,
he prospered.

I have a photo of my grandfather from this period, a black
and white picture that was shot in a photographer's studio
with an elaborate backdrop, my grandfather and his cousin
standing alongside another man whose name has been lost.
He stares into the camera with a suspicious glare, his long
frock coat, slim trousers and Pahlavi cap set off by the small
moustache that sat above his lip like a button. His hair is jet
black and he is skinny, his eyes slightly slanted, his cheekbones nearly as prominent as his nose and he looks serious
and wary, mistrustful of the camera, of the photographer, of
the world in general.

My grandfather lost his suspicious look when his first baby
was delivered in 1934. The serious little boy was named
Ali for Abbas' father but he was always called Shapour – an
ancient Persian name that Fatemeh Bibi loved. Within two
years she had given birth to her next child, and on she went
like that for two decades until she finally stopped after twelve
children. From the age of nineteen until she was in her
mid-forties, Fatemeh Bibi was pregnant or nursing. Looking back at pictures of this time in her life, it is impossible to
tell whether she is pregnant or has just given birth. At some
point, her body just gave up regaining its form after each
pregnancy and assumed a barrel-like shape that somehow
took nothing away from her beauty.

On one of our outings together when I first went back, Maman-*joon* saw me fiddling awkwardly with my head-scarf and launched into a story that I first thought was designed to distract me. She told me that one of the gifts her father gave her on Shapour's birth was a cloche hat of the type worn by the Hollywood sirens. This was the time of Reza Shah's dress reforms, I realised, when the new Shah had displayed an obsession with sartorial control of his people, and, seemingly every year, there was a new edict on what Iranians had to wear. It started with the men, who suffered years of confusion – first it was the Pahlavi cap (which the devout wore turned backwards, nearly a century before American teenagers adopted the habit, so they could touch their foreheads to the ground in prayer), the *chapeau* and finally the fedora – but before long Reza Shah, in his drive for modernisation, was determined not just to homogenise Iran's diverse ethnic population, but also to emancipate women.

In 1935, on his only state visit to another country, Reza Shah popped next door to Turkey, where he'd greatly admired the reforming ways of Kemal Atatürk. In 1936 the edict was passed down that Iran's women must now appear in public only unveiled, something that filled the devout Muslim women of Iran with shame. Maman-*joon* recalled the stories that had circulated at the time, of the women who left Abadan in droves and settled a few miles away over the border in Basra so they could avoid shaming themselves in the eyes of God. '*Naneh*,' she rasped at me, 'I remember helping our neighbours come over our walls to go to the baths – they were at the end of our street you know – because they wouldn't leave the house uncovered.' Her neighbour had told her how she had seen with her own eyes an old woman fall down dead in the street when a soldier had pulled off her *chador*.

Maman-*joon* herself, like most women her age, had settled
on the compromise that was eventually reached – they
could wear a headscarf (allowed as long as it was made of
silk from the shah's own factory in Chalus), and her light
chador was wrapped around her body as she went about her
chores, ready to be thrown over her head should she choose.
Women could choose to be covered or uncovered, at least in
terms of the law. Tradition, religion and pressure from family
and society narrowed the real choice, but the eventual result
of Reza Shah's enforced uncovering of women was that they
could choose whether they wanted to don a *chador* or not.
My grandmother told me that while she had understood that
modernisation was needed, she could never understand what
this had to do with whether she wore a *chador* or a hat.

She might not have understood Reza Shah's ways, but
Maman-*joon* always adored his son, Mohammad Reza Pahlavi. She had fallen for Mohammad Reza in 1939 when the
crown prince and his new wife, Princess Fawzia of Egypt,
had passed through Ahvaz on their way back from their
wedding in Cairo, the royal party alighting at a port on the
Persian Gulf down the coast and proceeding to Ahvaz where
they boarded the royal train for Tehran. Fatemeh Bibi, heavily pregnant with her third child, had got a good look at
the royal party in their full-length gowns, fur capes and long
gloves, with their perfectly coiffed hair and little hats with
delicate veils, the serious-looking crown prince in his army
uniform, peaked cap on black Brylcreemed hair, his back
ramrod straight and demeanour trying to project confidence.
Fatemeh Bibi fell in love with the Hollywood looks of the
women and the glamour that Mohammad Reza Pahlavi
managed to project, even as he looked slightly unsure of
himself.

The day after the crown prince's marriage in Cairo,
Hitler conquered Czechoslovakia. Reza Shah, who loved

to ride on trains, had invited the Germans to build his beloved Trans-Iranian Railway in a bid to reduce Iran's dependency on Britain, and his links with the Nazis worried the Allies.

Reza Shah saw much to admire in the fascists; many of the buildings that were erected in Tehran in the building boom of the thirties bore a sharp resemblance to Albert Speer's. He banned the Iranian Communist Party and managed to worry the Allies so much that, in a secret deal with the Soviet Union, Great Britain removed Reza Shah from power in 1941. Britain invaded the south of Iran where their oil interests lay while the USSR partitioned the north of the country – and again Iran, officially standing neutral in another war, was invaded by foreign powers under the guise of protection of liberty, freedom and democracy. The Strong Man with the grizzled nose and domineering presence was forced by the foreign powers whose influence he had so tried to diffuse to abdicate in favour of his son.

Reza Shah had shown that he meant business by bringing Iranian women out of *purdah* – no matter that in many cases it was done forcibly – and announcing a formal name change from Persia to Iran. The orientalist dream is over, he seemed to say to the world, you too can get to know us as we are, the original Aryan nation. You can call us all Iranians and, multitudinous though we are, we will present one face to the world – we will now look just like you.

Reza Shah fled to South Africa where he died within three years, and his son, who too stood tall and erect garbed in his military uniform and expensive Swiss education, shared his father's nose but none of his forceful personality, took over at home. Mohammad Reza Shah cut from the first an acceptable figure to Western powers – he was the model New Iranian, educated abroad, dressed in suits and speaking several languages with ease. There was nothing uncomfortable or uncouth about him as there had been with Reza Shah; he was young, serious and ready to be guided.

My grandmother, like the rest of the nation, did not mourn Reza Shah – by the time of his abdication he had been extremely unpopular, forcing the people to embrace customs and ways they were little used to and liked less. Reza Shah had shown no particular desire for the love of his subjects – his project was to modernise Iran, to make her independent and great, and he did not care to sweeten the bitter taste of the pills he forced his subjects to swallow.

By contrast Mohammad Reza Shah from the first courted his subjects. He took the throne traumatised by the abrupt removal of the Strong Man and the shame of the crumbling of Reza Shah's army in the face of the Allies' invasion – this institution that had symbolised the power of the monarchy. Stripped of many of his powers he took instead to heart the adulation of the people who thronged to see him on his provincial tours and who seemed to find him easy to love.

Fatemeh Bibi had arrived in the world a few months before the Great War and by just before the start of the Second World War she had given birth to her fourth child and third daughter, Mina. My grandmother, for all the calm of her disposition, could not stand the explosions that shook the walls of her house and left her shaking like a leaf and she was convinced that fortune would not smile on Mina. 'Her step was unlucky,' Maman-*joon* muttered darkly from time to time when they had bickered.

Soon after Mina's birth and the outbreak of the Second Word War, Abbas removed his family from Abadan and moved for a few years to Esfahan where he had a sister. Iran was once more occupied by foreign soldiers, the populace chafed under foreign control and soon Iranians were openly resisting the Allied occupation. Farmland was again laid to waste under the boots of *farangi* soldiers and hunger and poverty was spreading among the populace. Abbas had been asked to spy on the British for the resistance, but he had refused. A man of principle, he declared that after spending a lifetime breaking bread with these people, he would not spy on them now, and he chose to quit Abadan rather than go against his conscience. Maman-*joon* sighed when she told me this story and added, 'Your grandfather was a stubborn man, when he had a principle nothing would change his mind.' I thought about how difficult it must have been for her, newly delivered of a baby, to move her whole family and household to a strange town in the middle of war and occupation. In those days, before internal flights or fast trains, a journey from Abadan took days overland, through dangerous deserts and military lines. She must have wished he could overcome his principles, but although I never knew my grandfather Abbas, I knew well the iron will of his that he had bequeathed to his daughter Sedi, my mother. 'But *Naneh*,' Maman-*joon* continued, 'whatever he was, your grandfather was always a man for living.'

Esfahan, the Safavid jewel, a dream of Persian crafts-manship at its best, lies to the north of Shiraz. She rose to greatness when Shah Abbas I moved the capital to Esfahan and commenced a great building programme, and some of the most ebullient buildings man has ever produced were constructed there from 1598 onwards. The gardens and palaces that bloomed all over Safavid Esfahan turned it into an oriental dream, carried back to Europe in stories relayed by foreign ambassadors to the Safavid court. Shah Abbas may have felt his position so threatened that he gouged out the eyes of two of his own sons and put another to death, but all over Iran the splendid, rich motifs of Persian art flowered, on the famous silk and wool carpets, on printed fabrics, on wrought metalwork, on miniature paintings of lovers drinking wine and on the jigsaw of tiles that decorates mosques and palaces.

The new energy apparent in Safavid Iran was Shiism. This dynasty forced the conversion of Iran to Shia Islam, the faith of the underdog, the branch of Islam whose followers believe that Ali was the rightful heir to the Prophet Mohammad and who went on to fight with the caliphate until a schism was created that forever separated Shia Islam from Sunni. The Safavid conversion could be brutal but nonetheless the Safavid shahs not only arrayed Iran in some of its most splendid attire, but they made her the only Islamic nation that follows Shiism.

The family stayed in Esfahan and my mother was born there in 1943. Her name, according to Maman-*joon*, was given by a passing dervish who Abbas brought home for dinner. He told her that she would bring luck on their house and that she should give her a good Muslim name. Maman-*joon* had acquiesced and my mother was therefore called Sedigheh.

In 1945, when Sedigheh Abbasian was two years old, the family moved back to Abadan. Word had reached them that with the war drawing to a close, Abbas' troubles were over and he was now welcome to return. Fatemeh Bibi smiled in secret satisfaction; she had taken it upon herself to petition the young shah and, having written her petition with great care, Fatemeh Bibi had taken the opportunity of a visit by the shah's Egyptian wife to a local school to push her way through the throng and, holding aloft her letter with one hand while the other clutched the flower-sprigged *chador* she always wore outdoors, she had approached the princess' motorcar.

Maman-*joon* told me that she had somehow shoved her way to the front of the crowd and called out to the princess, entreating her. Eventually a hand had emerged from deep within the luxurious interior of the car and had extended from the open window towards her. Fatemeh Bibi had stepped forward, pushing her letter in font of her. She told me the hand was beautiful, delicate, white with long painted fingernails and laden with jewels. She watched the fingers close around her letter and draw back inside the car. She never told Abbas, but she was convinced that their return to Abadan was the result of a direct intervention from the shah's wife herself.

5

'I wish to go to Iran, to see my much-praised father'

AFTER MY FIRST trip back to Iran, I returned with some precious insights, bits and pieces of information that I been given by various relatives, on both side of the family, that had illuminated my father's background, and told me something new of those dark revolutionary days in which my father's life was threatened.

My father is a quiet man. He has always been quiet, as my garrulous mother will testify. He is also shy, a trait that belies the position he held at work in the oil company. I see pictures of him from the 1960s and 1970s, official black and white photos taken at important events, and I notice that although he looks relaxed and confident in his well-cut suits, meeting some dignitary or other, often one of his hands is clenched tight. This reserved man never spoke about himself and when I became curious about his side of my family, I had to put together many of the pieces from what relatives told me when I went back to Iran.

I knew that my father had been well-loved by our extended family in Iran, that the Abbasians cherished him as much as his own brother, sister and nieces and nephews, and that Bagher's coming into the Abbasian family had changed all their fortunes. The respect and love with which he was spoken of inspired me to find out more. Bagher himself had never been back to Iran and was living near me in London. I saw him every week, but I realised that to find the story of my father, to answer the questions I had, I would have to search in Iran, to find him refracted through those he loved, echoes of him still in the mountains of Kurdistan, the deserts of Khuzestan, the streets of Tehran and in the hearts of his friends and family. Bagher may have left Iran but I found him still there in so many ways that my longing for Iran became also a longing to know him. In the words of Ferdowsi: 'I wish to go to Iran, to see my much-praised father.'

My father's family's roots lie deep in Kurdistan. His grand-father was a merchant who had, on completing the *hajj* to Mecca, endowed a mosque in Sanandaj. My father's parents were both widowed, my grandmother Kowkab was raising two children from her first husband – a handsome tailor – who had died young. I once saw a faded photograph of the tailor, and even over the ages he struck me as remarkably handsome with his twinkling eyes and luxurious moustache. He had been the first in Sanandaj to make the new European style clothes and rumour had it that his death had been a plot by a disapproving *ulama* – or perhaps he was the victim of a husband who could no longer stand the twinkle in his eye. Kowkab was left widowed and before long, she consented to taking Shokrollah's hand in marriage.

My grandparents were living in a village called Ghaslan, some seventy kilometres away from Sanandaj, a simple village typical of the area, beautifully located in a plain fed by several streams banked by bamboo, cypress and fruit trees. Bagher's father, Shokrollah, was the land agent of one of Kurdistan's ruling families, the Asef, and had a broad honest streak, an incorruptibility and sense of fairness that he was to pass on to his only son.

When, on a cold November night in 1925, Bagher was born, the entire village celebrated the birth of the land agent's son. Shokrollah was, as the landowner's representative, the head of the village. He was so well loved that, when the year

before the order had come that family names had to be registered, and Shokrollah had chosen the surname Mohammadi,
the whole village had registered the same name to show him
respect – feudal ways were ingrained in the people. Bagher, a
bright-eyed boy with curly black hair, was born in the village
of Mohammadis and he entered a world where people died
in the same class in which they were born. There was no
middle class and no upward mobility and Shokrollah assumed
that his son would see out his days in Kurdistan. But life had
other plans for Bagher.

Born at the same time as the new dynasty that was reshaping
the ancient country into a new nation, Bagher Mohammadi
was destined to be the one of the New Iranians who would
help remake their country in the new century. Had he come
into the world just a few years earlier, perhaps he could have
shirked his destiny; he would have fallen on the other side of
the line which divided the old Iran from the new Iran that
Reza Shah's ascension to the throne marked. But Bagher's
birth was sandwiched right between the *majlis* vote in the
autumn of 1925, and Reza Shah's coronation in the spring
of 1926.

The Strong Man had officially taken Iran back for the Iranians – in 1928 he denounced all treaties and agreements which
gave special privileges to foreigners and the general consen-
sus was that he was more or less independent of the foreign
control. Filling the boots of a great dictator, Reza Shah was
determined that the Pahlavi dynasty should be legitimate.
He forcibly settled the nomadic tribes and his land reforms
attempted to create modernity at the expense of the poor
and peasant classes, now joined in rank by nomads whose
enforced settlement turned them into impoverished farmers
grazing their cattle on arid land. Trusted political advisors
regularly fell from grace and opposition figures and intellectuals were killed or imprisoned while money was poured

liberally into achieving the dream of the Trans-Iranian Rail-way, conceived to join the ports of the south with the shores of the Caspian in the north. By 1939, the railway project was completed and most of Iran's towns and cities had elec-tric light, power plants and some decent roads where asphalt hardened over the dust, stones and mud that the populace had worn out its shoes on before.

The public health and hospitals were under the cloak of government too and so the growing civil service soon became the employment goal of young, educated men. Tehran's dominion over all aspects of this emerging nation state allowed the Strong Man to keep all the threads of the coun-try directly in his own hands and, in the meantime, become the biggest landowner in Iran. The elementary public school system was set up throughout the country and though less than 1 per cent of the population attended secondary school, Reza Shah had started the great steamroll of education that would finally truly change Iran. Feeling that he had to fight like with like in his quest to make a modern Iran that could be as good as its Western masters, Reza Shah instituted grants for Iran's brightest students to send them abroad to study, to come back with the best *farangi* education with which they could serve their country and so the first state-sponsored students left for Europe in 1928. Some years later, in 1934, Tehran University was established. Women were free to attend the university too – which they freely did.

Bagher's education had started at the age of five when his father taught him to read with a copy of Sa'adi's *The Rose Garden*, one of the masterpieces of medieval Persian poetry. At school Bagher, already in love with words, fell deeply in love with numbers too, with their order and logic, their lack of emotions and surprises. When his father removed him from their rural idyll to live in Sanandaj, the quiet boy said nothing. When Shokrollah abruptly and inexplicably divorced his wife, Kowkab, one day before the New Year festival of Nowruz, taking her to the clerical head of the town, Hojat-al Eslam, to pronounce them divorced while her clothes were still damp from the spring cleaning she was busy with, the ten-year-old boy bit his tongue and said nothing. When he had to learn to live with Shokrollah's new wife Akhtar-*khanoum*, Bagher said nothing, putting silent effort instead into loving the woman who turned out to be kind and warm-hearted. But when Shokrollah suggested that Bagher had had enough education and should be taken from school, Bagher's mettle showed itself. For the first time in his young life, he defied his father, and the shocked Shokrollah, not used to being answered back to, packed him off to Hojat-al Eslam to see the error of his ways. But even God's representative on earth could not prevail upon Bagher's to leave school and Shokrollah never tried to interfere in his son's education again.

Bagher's love of reading even made him fearless in the face of the wrath of Sa'adat-*khanoum*, his older half-brother Ebrahim's new wife. When Bagher was fourteen, Ebrahim remarried – he had been left widowed as a young man with a baby daughter. Sa'adat-*khanoum* was a teacher, one of the first female professionals out of Reza Shah's training college, and a thoroughly modern woman, a new breed. Independent and well educated, she happily stepped out in her shapely two-piece suits, lips stained with dark lipstick, traditionally wrought Kurdish jewellery always hanging from her. Her thick black hair was worn in short bangs that framed a strong square face, her skin glowed and her smile carried a lust for life that floored the shy, sensitive Ebrahim. She exuded confidence and right up until the end of his life, my *Amoo* Ebrahim could not keep his eyes off her.

Sa'adat-*khanoum* spread her protective wings over Ebrahim's life and firmly tucked Bagher under them too as if he was her own little brother. She battled with him for reading at the *sofra*, confiscating one book only to find it replaced by another pulled swiftly out of his pocket. This dance continued for years, Bagher eventually taking three books with him to each meal.

Bagher's life was shaped by Reza Shah's reforms as surely as Fatemeh Bibi's. The education reforms had introduced a central syllabus that was followed in all secondary schools and Bagher's final exams – which would give him a diploma – were set and marked by the Ministry of Education. Throughout Iran there was an educational standard and boys like my father, who previously would have continued his father's profession, were emerging with a degree of instruction, knowledge and curiosity about the world that was unprecedented.

One day, after taking his final school exams, Bagher happened to see a group of his friends who were lazing by the river in the heat of the summer of 1943. Someone had a newspaper from Tehran; the first few years of the new shah's rule had seen newspapers flourish – there were forty-seven in Tehran alone – and though they generally took a couple of weeks to reach remote provinces such as Kurdistan, they were read by everyone. This particular newspaper carried a notice from the Anglo-Iranian Oil Company inviting students to apply for entrance exams to the Abadan Technical Institute where they would be trained to work for the Company, drawing a salary while studying. Bagher immediately wrote off an application.

The Abadan Technical Institute had been established in 1942 to train students in chemical, electrical and mechanical engineering. With the oil industry growing so fast, the Institute had been set up along the same lines as British technical institutes, to search Iran for her top students and to educate them to become as good as their British counterparts working in the AIOC. The Anglo-Iranian Oil Company was filled with British workers – they took most of the positions of power and Iran had only very few men in top management roles. Unskilled labour was provided by ethnic Arabs who were the only ones capable of working the long hours in the cruel temperatures of Khuzestan.

Bagher's application to take the entrance exams was accepted by the Institute and he was requested to travel straight away – he was in danger of missing the exams. In a matter of days, the thin, quiet boy with his black curly hair found himself on the train heading to Khuzestan. He had broken the news to his father, unable to contain his own glee, and Shokrollah had quietly given his blessing. My father recalled his father as being as enthusiastic as himself in planning the journey, but elderly relatives in Kurdistan told me that when Bagher had left that day, Shokrollah had been desperate, running down the street and beating his head, crying that his only son was gone.

Bagher first travelled 150 kilometres south to Kermanshah where he was taken by oil tanker east across the country to Arak in central Iran, and from there he boarded one of Reza Shah's beloved trains to go south to Ahvaz, the capital of Khuzestan and only 120 kilometres from Abadan, where his journey would end. It was a convoluted route but necessary given the limitations of transportation and the war. It was an epic expedition for the boy who had never left Kurdistan.

Reza Shah's prized railway may have been built by the Germans but now it was the property of the Allies and Bagher squeezed on to a train teeming with British soldiers returning to their posts in the south. My father once told me that he would never forget that journey, the rumbling through the night then waking to a dawn so delicate it stained the scrub-tufted desert outside a soft shade of rose. He had pulled down the window to take a breath of air, and promptly drew his head back in as if slapped in the face. What greeted him outside the window did not seem like air at all to someone who had grown up in fresh mountain breezes. Moist and heavy with dust, it was so hot it burned his throat. Bagher had arrived in Khuzestan.

Abadan was a dusty, fly-blown town cut through by the deep waters of the river; its progress and rapid development into such an important city having outstripped the writing of geography books so no mention could be found in any reference books to its existence. Located on a triangle of land lurking in the delta of the Tigris and the Euphrates, some 45 kilometres from pearl-stitched waters of the Persian Gulf, Abadan sits on its own island, bounded on its west by the Shatt al-Arab and on the east by the Bahmanshir, an outlet of the river Karun. Having arrived in Abadan too late to take the entrance exams, the Institute waived the rules and Bagher started his studies, finding fascination in the mechanical engineering workshops. In 1944, the Institute had sent its first group of students to Birmingham University and Bagher had his sights now on bigger opportunities. Bagher was picked as one of ten further students to be sent to Birmingham, and in the summer of 1945, having paid a quick visit to Kurdistan to take leave of his father, he boarded a boat heading across the Shatt al Arab to Basra where they celebrated the surrender of Japan and the end of the Second World War. On they went from Basra to Baghdad, from Baghdad to Palestine, from Haifa to Cairo. There were endless delays as decommissioned soldiers tried to find their way home, exhausted and exhilarated, but Bagher didn't mind. Like his grandfather before him, who made the arduous journey across mountains and deserts in a *caravanserai* to visit Mecca the century before, Bagher traversed strange new lands on his own pilgrimage, his quest for education. With each new

city, each new country, his horizons grew ever wider until
they came to encompass even the drizzly shores of England
where, on landing at a blustery Liverpool, Bagher found that
his carefully learnt English did not resemble at all what the
natives seemed to speak.

Birmingham in the aftermath of the war was a dreary place
of ration books, overlooked by a sky from which all light and
colour had been sucked. But Bagher and his colleagues, sala-
ried by the AIOC and dressed in smart suits, their black hair
Brylcreemed slick, cut exotic figures through the university
and the town and there was no end to their popularity with
the local girls and the women who studied with them at the
university.

Somehow my father thrived in this foggy land and it was
the love of Britain formed in those post-war days that took us
back there so many years later. From his first day in Birmingham, when he had been struck by how quiet the streets were
compared to the cacophony of Iran, my father had loved
British efficiency, the way the traffic moved in calm, quiet
lines, the reserved fortitude of the people stoically standing in
queues. Bagher remained in the UK for more than five years,
spending holidays working in various placements arranged
by the Company and visiting every corner of the green,
misty country that he could. From the Yorkshire Dales to
a Butlin's Holiday Camp in Skegness, there was no place
that was not attractive to this young Kurd; along the way
he picked up a love of Western classical music to add to his
proficiency in traditional Kurdish dancing, and a British wife
to take back to Iran.

He met Audrey at university, a tall and blonde Brum-
mie who impressed Bagher by her self-confidence and her
intellect. British women like Audrey were an inspiration
to Bagher. He recognised the same confident strength that
characterised the Kurdish women he knew, but the Brit-

ish women were able to stride forward alongside the men
without too much fuss. The importance my father placed
on a university education – and a British one at that – can
almost certainly be attributed to the influence of Audrey and
women like her.

As well as falling in love in England, my father also initi-
ated Iranian students' societies and was presented to the
young shah when he paid a visit to Britain. He even broadcast a message back to Iran via the BBC's Persian Service
each Iranian New Year, knowing that in Sanandaj Shokrollah would collect all their family, friends and acquaintances
around the transistor radio to hear his voice crackle over the
airwaves.

My father left the UK for Iran in January of 1951, a qualified mechanical engineer complete with a British wife, ready
to go back home and take his place in the newest strata of
Iranian society – the middle class. Bagher, with his acquired
love of the West, and passion for his homeland, was just the
sort of New Iranian that Reza Shah had had in mind when
he had taken his limping, feudal country in hand the same
year that Bagher was born. In the space of twenty-five years,
it seemed that the seeds that the Strong Man had planted
were already bearing fruit, their roots planted firmly in Iran
while their branches spread across to the Western world.
What none of the New Iranians travelling back on the plane
with Bagher that January in 1951 knew was that the very
soil out of which they had grown was to prove very shallow
indeed.

6

The Family House in Abadan

THE HOUSE IN Abadan was a large corner house that occupied most of the two blocks it conjoined, its outer walls surrounded with shops which Abbas rented out. There were just three bedrooms and a large living room arranged around a central courtyard garden, a shallow pool set in the centre. In the garden there was a mulberry tree whose berries we ate greedily in the summer and whose spreading branches afforded us shade in the hot days, and there were pots of red geraniums all around the pool. The loo was the traditional sort, a tiled hole in the ground kept compulsively clean by Maman-*joon*'s servants, and outside, tucked into the corner of the yard by the stairs leading up to the roof, there was a large stone shower room where we children crowded in with our aunts to be scrubbed down by *kisehs*, silk mitts crocheted by Maman-*joon* and rubbed generously with a chalky white stone called *sephidab* which left our skin tingling and glowing clean, the heat and the dust of Abadan sloughed off. The pace of life in Maman-*joon*'s house was gentle and indulgent, lots of naps and playing; my mother relaxed among her family, and it was my favourite place to be.

When my mother was growing up in that house, the boys shared one room, the girls another and Fatemeh Bibi and Abbas had the final bedroom; in traditional families, the concept of personal space and privacy was as alien then as it is now. Their beds were a stack of mattresses that were kept in a corner and taken out at night as needed, and the Abbasian children learnt to live together in such a merry cacophony that, although as young adults they sometimes longed for peace and quiet and to be left alone, they were always happiest when part of a symphony of loud chatter. In the summer months when the heat and humidity threatened to overwhelm them, they moved up to the roof and in the spring and autumn they would often sleep out in the courtyard.

After the Second World War, Abadan was swarming with foreigners, and it was booming. Maman-*joon* told me that when they had moved back to Abadan after the war, she and Abbas had been shocked at how the population of the town had grown in a matter of a few years. In its social interactions there was a revolution taking place. There were parties where men and women mixed freely, the women wearing Western clothes and displaying a great deal too much flesh for a Muslim man's comfort, and there were sports clubs, yacht clubs, tennis clubs springing up all over for employees of the Company. Although most of the Company's top brass were *farangis*, some Iranians were now in positions of power too and these slick, urbane Iranian men seemed just as dangerous to my grandfather as their foreign counterparts. Abbas was old-fashioned and Fatemeh Bibi, for all her easy ways, was traditional in her habits, so the Abbasian children were brought up with strict discipline and a strong sense of right and wrong, and, even more crucially, of what was proper.

Iranian society is based on values of honour and respect, and being seen to do the right thing is almost as important as actually doing it. While Islam preaches piety and charity, great store too is set by being honourable, and the honour of the family rests mostly in the hands of its women, dependent largely on their behaviour and propriety, their modesty and chastity. My grandparents instilled into their daughters

in particular the values of correct behaviour, of the grace
of always being appropriate, the charm of being elegant
in manner and proper in action. Coupled with the Hayat
Davoudy ease of being, sense of humour and beauty, the
Abbasian girls – although they never went out unchaperoned
– cut quite a dash through town.

Two years after Shapour was born, Fatemeh Bibi had
given birth to her first daughter in 1937. Parivash was pretty
as her mother but with Abbas' brown eyes; her school-
ing had been limited to the *maktab* where she had learnt
to read and write and recite the Qur'ân. A determinedly
jolly little girl, Parivash grew up to be a sweet, devout
woman who laughed easily, especially at the absurdity of
life, a trait that served her well through an adult life which
has been dogged by persistent heart problems. Her heart,
for all that it was already cracked, still managed to flow
with love and laughter and to this day my *Khaleh* Parivash,
who cannot walk up the stairs of her house without getting
puffed out and whose arthritis won't let her kneel at her
prayer mat, has such a talent for hilarity that she is irresistible company.

Parivash, being the eldest daughter, was the first to get
married in 1953. Jahanzadeh – no one, not even his wife,
ever called him by anything but his surname – asked for
Parivash's hand from her father and, once accepted, he called
round regularly to sit with and try to get to know the shy girl
who would be his future wife. Parivash, even then a giggler,
was mortified at first when this stranger sat in their house
and everyone left the room. The first time that Jahanzadeh
attempted to talk to her, *Khaleh* Parivash told me that she
was so bewildered that, on the pretext of getting some more
tea, she raced out of the room to laugh hysterically. Fatemeh Bibi had ticked her off and sent her back in saying,
'Talk to the man! You are going to have a lifetime with him,

better start getting to know him now.' Fatemeh Bibi had no patience with her daughter's protests; it was already radically modern of her and Abbas to allow their daughter the opportunity to get to know her future husband a little before being confronted by him at the *sofra aghd*.

All those years later, after a lifetime together, four children and open-heart surgery, my aunt told me that she was at first horrified by Jahanzadeh, and then she threw back her head and laughed at the idea. She was seventeen and happy at home with her family turning her talents as a seamstress to good use. But slowly she became accustomed to his presence and she even started to like their weekly outings to the cinema. Her father refused to let her go out with her fiancé unless they took all her siblings with them and Jahanzadeh dutifully took his future wife and her siblings and even some cousins to the cinema every Friday, the long line of scrapping Abbasian children – often in double figures – snaking round the building while he attempted to keep some semblance of control over the younger boys who were so naughty they would shoot straight up walls as soon as your back was turned.

After Parivash's wedding she went to live with her husband's family in Shiraz. Then beautiful and devout *Khaleh* Mahvash with her mellifluous voice had been next, happily married to her cousin Jamshid, a tall, gentle man with curling, waxed hair and the same dusky grey-blue eyes that he bequeathed his children. He was the son of Fatemeh Bibi's brother and somehow the combined force of the Hayat Davoudy genes made their children exceptional in both beauty and brains. Mahvash and Jamshid had loved each other and their marriage, although arranged, was full of joy, and their children were born each prettier and cleverer than the other.

Fatemeh Bibi liked the idea of keeping marriage in the family and she had fixed another such match for her next daughter, the unlucky Mina. My *khaleh* Mina was then, as she was to remain, a nurturing creature, bubbling over with creative energy which she poured into the household chores, into cooking and caring for her siblings as if she was their second mother. Mina, like her mother, loved to sit and chat and laugh. She delighted in listening to music and although she was not allowed to dance – none of the Abbasian girls were, it was considered unseemly – her elegant hands were so expressive that each twirl of her long fingers seemed to contain all the rhythm that was not permitted to beat through her hips.

Close in age and similar in outlook, Sedigheh adored Mina, choosing her as her best friend, and when it was her older sister's turn to be matched for marriage, she felt almost as bad as Mina did in accepting the match. Promised to a man twice her age, the only son of a distant relative, at sixteen Mina was interested in nothing so much as finishing high school and adjusting her beehive. But her father deemed school unnecessary and Fatemeh Bibi was deaf to the girl's pleas – she saw that Mina's great gift lay in the abundance of her love and she thought it better for her to be settled and start her family than to finish school. After all, what use would she have for all that education in her life? She was a woman and her life would be devoted to the care of others – her husband and the children she would have. Mina's tears and obvious distaste for the match were ignored, and her marital status suddenly became the primary concern of all the older women of the family.

My mother told me that she watched her sister water unwashed herbs with her tears as they all sat in the courtyard and cleaned bunches of parsley, mint and coriander. She watched her try to reason with their mother, grandmother and aunts – '*Akhe* Maman-*jan*,' Mina would sob through her tears, 'I don't want to get married now, I want to finish school, stay here . . .' But to no avail. Her husband had been chosen: Abdolhossein Busheiry, one of Fatemeh Bibi's own kinsmen. He was a kindly, scholarly man with Brylcreemed hair and a pencil moustache, as short as my grandmother and nearer her age than Mina's.

Mina couldn't cross her mother but she was horrified by the thought of marrying a man more than twice her own age. It was her most passionate wish to have her own family; her elder sisters had already started. No reason why not, my grandmother pointed out. Just because the man is mature, that's no obstacle to love, she said; it hadn't stopped her and Abbas. Mina's silent tears fell into the basket of parsley in front of her; my mother told me she watched each drop fall, feeling sad for her sister, and so had ventured that Busheiry was rather handsome in his own way, rather like Clark Gable with that slim moustache. Mina smiled weakly and in the years to come it became one of their favourite jokes. Her stubbornness had added to Fatemeh Bibi's insistence, Maman-*joon* claiming that her bad back and ill health were the result of worrying about Mina's defiance. Many years later, after her lifetime with Busheiry was over and she finally had her independence, she scoffed at her mother's methods as she told me the story. 'Have you ever heard of such a thing?' she declared as she pottered in her little apartment in Shiraz. 'As if my marital status had anything to do with her health!' She laughed then, the smallest pinch of bitterness creeping into her voice. 'But you know, back then we believed such things. We obeyed our elders – we didn't know any better. I didn't know that my mother wouldn't die of shame if I defied her – and I didn't dare take the chance.'

It was impossible for Mina to defy them anyway – she was a respectable girl and she simply had no other choice, and no way of supporting herself should she flout their wishes and be cast out of the family. Even in Abadan in the late fifties, even with all Fatemeh Bibi's progressive ideas and her daughters' tight jumpers and kitten heels, it was unthinkable for Mina to risk being ousted from her family's bosom and ultimately the fear of the consequences of such disobedience overrode all else. She capitulated.

Mina was married to Busheiry – she called him by his surname for the rest of their lives together – at seventeen in a strapless dress, looking in her wedding pictures like a fifties society debutante in lace, long gloves and a tiara. She had, in the end, given in with good grace, her temperament as soft as her mother's if not quite as carefree, certainly not given to rebellion. As was to be her habit all through her life, she had not fought her destiny but instead had surrendered to it and made the best of her bad lot.

My mother and Mina, so alike in many ways, were different in one crucial respect. The fourth daughter of the family and the fifth child, Sedi bore Abbas' strong nose, but also his even stronger will. Just as the nose had dominated Abbas' face as a boy and had taken growing into, Sedi's childlike face was also presided over by her nose. She had a thick fringe, jet-black hair whose heaviness made it hard to set in the bangs she tried to wear; she always followed the Western fashions she saw in the *farangi* magazines all over town. She was thin and graceful even as a teenager and she was very bright.

Although only six years younger than Parivash, the world was changing so quickly around them that Sedi had somehow managed to imbibe ideas that none of her sisters had dared to think of. My mother wanted to finish school, to go to university, to become a lawyer. She wanted to make a living, be independent, and fall in love. Somehow these ideas had settled so deep inside her that when Abbas wanted her to quit school at fourteen, Sedi had, to the shock of all, simply refused to obey. The night that she had faced down her father, suddenly unafraid to insist on what she so dearly wanted, she had discovered mettle in her soul, a strength and confidence in herself that began to blossom. Though as proper as all of her sisters, Sedigheh's temperament burnt as hot and bright as her father's, and the iron in her grandfather Ali's spirit was suddenly apparent also in hers. Where Mina had conceded defeat when tears and fond appeals had not moved Abbas, Sedi not only stood firm in front of her father – never once forgetting to call him by the courteous title of '*agha*' and looking down at all times out of respect – but she also recruited the headmaster to her cause who called round personally to reason with Abbas and even offer to waive the fees for the last two years of school.

Perhaps my grandfather agreed simply because he was getting old and didn't have the energy for an argument with the obstinate girl, but maybe it was also because her mother joined her cause too. The fickle Fatemeh Bibi had decided that Sedi should indeed complete her education – although just a few years before she had refused the unfortunate Mina the same privilege. Sedigheh was allowed to finish school and became the first Abbasian girl to graduate from high school, though her father would not countenance the girl's leaving home to attend the university in Tehran as she wanted. Sedi found instead another purpose in the Technical Institute's bilingual Pitman secretarial course.

Sedi had picked up English quickly and the accuracy of her typing and quality of her work made up for the bois-terous nature which their British teacher, Miss Gentry, so miserably failed to contain. '*Please* Sedi, do be quiet!' had been Miss Gentry's constant refrain in the year she had been in her class, but Sedi was rarely quiet. Garrulous and enthu-siastic, Sedi loved to laugh and sing at any given opportunity – being noisy and sociable is coded into the Abbasian genes and Sedi was no exception. But she was unique to the family, blazing a trail through her family that bridged the gap opening up between the traditional lives the Abbasians still lived, and the new life destiny had marked her for – as the elegant wife of a New Iranian.

After my mother, until the last of the Abbasian children, *Khaleh* Yassi, was born in 1956 thirteen years later, all of Abbas and Fatemeh Bibi's children were boys. Two years after Sedi, Hossein entered the world, a handsome baby from the first, and now the heartthrob of all the Abbasian boys with looks worthy of a matinee idol. After Hossein there was Pardis, so like Abbas in looks with the prominent Abbasian nose and skinny form that he was nicknamed *mahi kharoo* – fish bones – by the others. Pardis was always a special friend of my mother's, they were so close in age, looks and temperament, and they had a wicked sense of humour in common too. Then came Mostafa in whom Abbas saw no resemblance to himself at all and in his irascible old age, Abbas' punishing iron rod found the innocent Mostafa's back more often than it did the real perpetrators of whichever horror he was being punished for, usually the twins Ahmad and Reza who came next in the family, or the youngest son and the leader of all nefarious plots and mischievous undertakings, Mohammad, known as Mamaly. Last of all was Yassaman who, with her willowy figure and unusual height seemed proof of evolution in action.

These aunts and uncles, *khalehs* and *daieys*, are the characters whose presence coloured my early life and on that first trip back, the overpowering joy of rediscovering my family blew open my shutdown heart. In Shiraz – where the majority now lived, having fled Khuzestan during the Iraqi invasion – we gathered every night, and those who were not in Shiraz managed to take a few days to come and see us.

Surrounded by such love, here within the throngs of aunts, uncles and cousins I found finally some of the context I had been looking for. Bits of myself surfaced in unexpected places – the way an uncle crossed his legs, the way Maman-*joon* sat on the floor, the long fingers of *Khaleh* Mina's dancing hands, the way all my *khalehs* laughed covering their mouths as if trying to keep in the hilarity bubbling out of them. Sometimes I would catch them, my mother and my aunts, all lined up in a row, their legs crossed the same way, their heads held up, bearing the same proud expression, all variations on a theme. My Abbasian aunts and uncles had all grown older and morphed into each other.

We gathered together and threw down a *sofra* that ran from one end of the room to the other to accommodate us all. On any given night, our numbers would total at least thirty, sometimes more, and in the middle of all this activity sat Fatemeh Bibi, small and sparrow-like, grown skinny in old age, no longer with a round, fecund belly and plump, white arms. She dyed her hair jet black and her green eyes still shone out of her once-beautiful face, but her voice, once so rich and deep, had grown husky after an operation on her larynx to cure a lifetime of puffing on the *ghalyoun*. She sat cross-legged on the floor and watched these family scenes with relish, this small woman who was the originator of all those flitting around her, from my oldest aunt already in her sixties to the babies being carried by her grand-children; the matriarch of our clan. She joked and laughed with us, clapping her hands along to the music to encourage us to dance, the louder the noise of our fun the better for her, and she insisted on playing hostess, regardless of whose house we were in. She stroked my hair and I caught her looking at me with delight, her large eyes drinking me in as she told me that she never felt complete with any of her brood missing.

Yet no matter how many of us gathered and how delighted Maman-*joon* was by our presence, we were missing some crucial characters. In the years that had passed since the family gatherings of my childhood, through revolution and war and the ongoing strictures of the Islamic Republic, we had lost some family members along the way, and our *sofra* could never be complete again.

7

New Beginnings

IN THE MODERN history of my country, one man looms large: Mossadegh, the prime minister who nationalised Iran's oil industry, the first leader in the Middle East to claim sovereignty over the country's resources, the first to begin to loosen the quasi-colonial rule of the region by the West. Dr Mossadegh is still revered by Iranians and his removal from power by the CIA and MI6 is remembered bitterly more than half a century later. But the man who has shaped modern Iran as surely as Reza Shah or his son, the man who still symbolises Iran's unfulfilled desires for sovereignty and democracy, is not officially remembered anywhere in Iran itself. There is no memorial to him, no streets named after him and no murals of his long, bald head gracing the side of Tehran's tall buildings. In a country so given to honouring those it holds dear, Dr Mossadegh's image is conspicuously missing.

On returning to Iran from Britain, Bagher had been invited to the *majlis* to hear the oil nationalisation bill being debated by a relative and had heard Dr Mossadegh deliver the bill which proposed to turn the oil industry and its profits over to Iran, the country claiming sovereignty over her own resources. Mossadegh was already an old man, his balding head ringed by a halo of white hair, a prominent nose jutting out of paper-thin skin. He argued that Iran had no chance of being politically independent of foreign powers while Britain continued its economic exploitation of Iran and he sought to put an end to 150 years of British meddling in Iran's affairs.

Ever since Winston Churchill had ensured Britain's dominant share in the Anglo-Iranian Oil Company, Iran had
received just 16 per cent of the profits of her own oil. In 1950
alone, Britain's profits for the year were more than what it
had paid to Iran in the whole of the previous half-century –
and Iranian resentment was running at an all-time high. 'The
moral aspect of oil nationalisation is more important than its
economic aspect,' Mossadegh had insisted, and Bagher had
been so rapt by the powerfully emotive speech that he had
missed his train to Abadan.

In Abadan something similar to an apartheid barred ordinary Iranian workers from occupying high management
positions and from entering Braim, the area the British had
built to house their own people, an enclave of sprawling
suburban villas set behind barriers, with its own shops, sports
clubs, and cinemas. Iranian workers were given their own
housing estates and the large number of skilled Indian workers that the British had also brought with them lived in their
own quarters near the refinery, known as Sikh Lane. Abadan
was booming but it was also effectively segregated.

When finally, late in 1951, the bill was pushed through
and ratified, the British who ran the AIOC in Abadan were
barred from their offices. Bagher was one of three men
appointed to keep the power station supplying the refinery
working when the British departed. A responsibility to his
country was born in my father at that moment and, although
he had been friendly with the British, had gone to wave off
British colleagues as they were evacuated for Basra and even
agreed to take in one of his friends' dogs, he was nevertheless
gripped by the sense that now Iranians had a chance to prove
themselves, and it was crucial they shouldn't fail.

The British refused to recognise the bill and Mossadegh
argued Iran's case in The Hague and at the United Nations,
mocked by the British media who called him 'Mossyface'

and ignored by the US, who found his eccentric personality – with his habit of openly weeping as sentiment overtook him – odd but interesting. Not interesting enough to risk their own stake in the region, however – America was a new world power and hardly wanted its own regional oil partners to start declaring sovereignty over their oil. The British piled on sanctions, restricted trade, put pressure on anyone wanting to buy oil from the newly formed NIOC (National Iranian Oil Company) and even intercepted a shipment of crude oil, but the Iranians grew to love their prime minister even more, seeing in him the saviour we are apt as a nation to look for. The shah's father had been unpopular but he had at least been strong. The new shah was young and ineffectual and growing resentful of his prime minister and he left the country when an attempt to arrest Mossadegh resulted in the prime minister dismissing the messenger without bothering to leave his house.

Mohammad Reza Shah did not have the look of the father that the nation longed for. Mossadegh, however, with his raw emotion and propensity to appear on his balcony in pyjamas, was exactly the sort of father that Iran wanted – a peculiarly Persian creature whose refinement and sophistication sat easily alongside his love for his country and desire to serve. Dr Mossadegh was more than a match for the shah but in the end he could not win against the might of the British Empire and the tough guy tactics of the Americans.

The CIA and MI6 hatched a plot to overthrow Mossadegh and bring back the shah. An American agent named Kermit Roosevelt was armed with quantities of bank notes and gold and rounded up a paid mob calling for the return of the shah and the resignation of Mossadegh. With four out of five newspapers in Tehran controlled by the CIA, soon the prime minister had no choice but to step down. The shah came back to Iran with a renewed sense

of destiny. Meanwhile, in Qom, a little-known cleric
who had been paid to denounce Mossadegh found himself
with a taste for power. The cleric was called Ruhollah
Khomeini and by the time the shah sent him into exile in
1964, he was already known by the title the world would
come to learn years later: Ayatollah Khomeini.

Just as with the Constitutional Revolution, a democrati-
cally elected Iranian leader striving for Iranian democracy and
sovereignty was toppled by foreign powers who preferred a
malleable shah to serve their interests instead. Iran was too
rich in natural resources, too important geographically, to
be allowed to run herself. The Iranian people, who had
lately loved this urbane, eccentric father of theirs, were so
easily blown by the prevailing wind that they stood back
and watched his home be ransacked, his followers rounded
up and beaten, his foreign minister stabbed and executed by
firing squad, while the old man was put on trial as a traitor in
a military court.

The wave of nationalisations that followed in the region
can be attributed to Mossadegh's legacy – the Suez Crisis of
1956 is just one such instance. But he was to remain in the
mass memory of Iran as the ideal father the nation was never
allowed to have.

After the departure of the British, the houses of Braim were
allocated to Iranian managers. Bagher and his wife Audrey
moved into a large house and employed a cook, Karim, who
was expert at cooking English food but had to be taught by
Bagher how to sift and steam Iranian rice and how to mix
the herbs, meat and vegetables that made up his favourite
khoreshts. The Company looked after its employees with the
same sort of care and dedication that landlords had traditionally given to the workers on the land, international flights
were now landing at Abadan airport and the town which had

so recently just been an island in a marsh was thriving.

The British had built Braim for themselves and the mani-cured lawns and ordered gardens recalled a suburbia with a paler sky many thousands of miles away. They stopped short of the mock-Tudor facades and double or triple storeys standard in Surbiton – these houses were mostly bungalows and though the population of Abadan thought that this was exactly like England, an Englishman, confronted by date palms soaring into the firmaments in the garden and walls of tumbling bougainvillea against a humid blue sky, would certainly not have agreed.

They were nothing like traditional Abadani houses, with their desire to hide the family's lives away behind tall walls. Instead the new houses turned this traditional model inside out. What these houses in Braim had imported from the West was the openness, the yard and garden in the front of the house so that anyone strolling casually by had an unim-peded view of the garden and the front door and even into the windows of the house itself. Once they were occupied by the New Iranians, these houses seemed to promise that those who dwelt in them were living different lives, living by different values, inhabiting open, transparent spaces in which everything was out on show. Thousands of years of culture and personal impulse were swept unceremoniously away by these houses and the New Iranians that occupied them, those men and, more importantly, their women, who were not afraid to show their faces – literally – to the world. Less than thirty years after their grandmothers had refused to leave their homes uncovered or died from the shame when forci-bly unveiled in the street, this generation, this enclave of New Iranian women had not only uncovered themselves – their hair, their arms, their legs, as they strutted around in the latest fashion from the catwalks of Paris, Milan and London – but their houses and by extension their lives too.

It was a shock many of the traditional people – who usually served them as housekeepers, cooks, cleaners, maids – never got over. The cultural chasm that started to yawn open between the old, traditional classes and the modern middle class proved – in the years to come – not only unbridgeable, but in part the instigator of the horrors of the revolution.

The shah had spent the rest of the fifties consolidating his own power. Mossadegh's downfall had led to an oil deal in which Iran's oil profits where to be shared 50/50 with a new oil consortium of which British Petroleum owned 40 per cent, the rest being divided up between American and European companies. While this was hardly the vision that Mossadegh had had for the NIOC, it did signify the end of British dominion in Iran. The American era had now officially begun.

After returning to Iran, spurred on by his new puppet masters and his own fear of the Red Menace, the Shah increased his military spending, encouraged along the way by America. The new world may have been nominally at peace, but the Cold War had begun in earnest and the importance of Iran's position as a Western-friendly regime holding back communism's spread into the rest of the Middle East and to Europe was played up by the shah. The shah established SAVAK – its operatives trained by the CIA and Mossad – to gather intelligence on everything as he became increasingly autocratic and paranoid. SAVAK's spectral existence began to cast a shadow that extended over all aspects of Iranian life, and the Iranian mind, long sensitive to conspiracies and plots, soon had all its nightmarish paranoia fed by the activities of the organisation. In the years to come, as the shah's dictatorial tendencies grew ever stronger, the Iranian people felt it unsafe to speak frankly even in their own homes while they were in company.

The shah's secret service was so feared and had so penetrated the Iranian consciousness that even as a small child growing up in the seventies, I was aware of certain associations around that word, SAVAK. The word stank of fear, of silence and wariness, of conversations cloaked in allegory. The poetry of the Persian language and the indirectness of the culture suited such subterfuge – after all the Iranian mind has been shaped for centuries around intrigue, mistrust and insecurity.

After thousands of years of being conquered and subjugated to the whims of invaders and their own despotic kings, the Iranian mind was already ripe for the sort of insecurity that the presence of SAVAK in potentially every aspect of society engendered. Indeed, Iranian manners and codes of courtesy were already well made for the sort of dissembling that now once again became a national art.

Nonetheless, my father prospered. Pictures from the late fifties taken on Shokrollah and Akhtar-*khanoum*'s only month-long visit to Abadan show them standing among the roses in the garden at Braim, their faces lifted to Bagher's camera, their backs straight, pride etched deep in their faces. Akhtar-*khanoum* wore a delighted expression, decked out in the long, flowing Kurdish robes of Sanandaj, her hair pulled back under the headscarf she always wore, and Shokrollah as an old man looked jolly, his head bald, his eyes round, wearing a suit just like the one that the unfortunate tailor Esmael had made for him in Sanandaj back in the twenties. Not only had a lifetime passed, but a whole world too, and Shokrollah looked like a relic from another age, standing in his old-fashioned suit in Bagher's modern Iranian garden.

The newly confident shah entered the sixties with a pretty new wife – having dispatched two others along the way it was hoped that Farah Diba would finally give him a son and heir – and renewed belief in his own divine purpose. Maman-*joon*, whose crush on the shah had never waned, prayed fervently for him to finally be given an heir which, to her joy, he soon was with the birth of his first son later that year.

But the shah feared discontent. The coming of age of those who had been politicised and educated through Reza Shah's reforms had resulted in civil unrest and so, in order to stop a revolution from below, he decided to implement one from above, incorporating socialist language which was designed to please all those whose travels abroad had introduced them to the student politics of the West. He instigated the White Revolution in 1963 – a system of land reforms that were meant to set free those virtually enslaved on the land working for the few families that held the wealth of Iran. At the turn of the century just 150 families held all the power and influence in Iran, and 20,000 villages were owned by a mere 27 families; Mehdi Batmanghelij, one of the richest landlords in the country, boasted that his holdings were as large as Switzerland.

Among the six points of the White Revolution one gave women the vote. The *ulama* were incensed by the whole package and Ayatollah Khomeini was now making waves denouncing land reform as un-Islamic and unconstitutional and objecting most vociferously to the idea of women being given the vote. Ayatollah Khomeini's outspokenness, so rare in the society haunted by SAVAK, won him supporters and got him placed under house arrest for six months.

In his rampant opposition to women getting the vote, Khomeini represented those patriarchal Iranians who did not wish their women to leave the home, who feared their wives would longer have the time to cook and clean for them or present them with a delicious dinner and soothe their brows at the end of the day. Iranian men have always been fiercely jealous of their women, wanting to enjoy their delights privately, wanting their figures only uncovered for their eyes, their hair only to shine for them. Iranian men adore their women and want more than anything to keep them dependent and subjugated – out of an intensity of love, an exaggerated sense of protectiveness. They know how incredible their women are and this mix of love, devotion and fear makes them determined to keep their women under their control, only for themselves.

My mother has always seemed to me to be the epitome of a grown-up woman, a lady. In love with fashion, she had an ever changing range of hairstyles and colours but she was always stylish, whatever the trend. She wore heels without exception, and so she walked slowly; in Iran we drove everywhere so it was only once we were in London using public transport to get around that I noticed how slowly she walked. She walked tall, head held high, her heels clicking and I, who always hurtled as a girl and strode as a young woman, imagined that I too, once I became a grown-up woman, would have to slow my walk down to this stately progress. My mother is not tall, I reached and overtook her height when I was fourteen, but she has presence. She still exudes glamour and self-possession, her figure slim and her hair unfailingly styled, an instant icon in her later years to the gay boys she worked with in London. I am unlike her in style, having always been altogether too sloppy and tomboyish to achieve true elegance, but nonetheless my mother remains the model of feminine self-possession that I aspire to grow into.

Sedi's transformation from the skinny teenager with the prominent nose to the self-possessed lady came when she started work. My mother loved her job and she took her role seriously. Had she been born to a less traditional father, she might have fulfilled her dreams of university and an illustrious career, but as it was she cherished the brief moment she had as a working woman in Abadan. After graduating from the Technical Institute, she started working at the Company as a secretary and her efficiency soon saw her promoted to work for one of the directors. She told me she had been so excited to start work, she had even had her eyebrows shaped before her first day. In those days, tradition dictated that a girl remain untouched until her wedding day, when she would then submit herself to the hours of threading and plucking that marked her entry into the world of women. Portraits of Qajar women at court showed that, even a hundred years ago, Iranians were obsessed with their eyebrows and that the shape of a woman's eyebrows had long been subject to the vagaries of fashion. During that era, it was the height of beauty to train the brows to loop over the eyes and meet in the middle. But in 1964 Abadan it was Gina Lollobrigida and Sophia Loren's eyebrows that were being copied. The beauty of the eyes could not be properly beheld without the eyebrows being cleverly shaped – this was always the case in Iran and, like other Middle Eastern women blessed with quantities of hair, Iranian women had long been preoccupied with finding the best way of getting rid of it.

All Sedi's older sisters had been married at much younger ages than she was now; Sedigheh was pushing twenty-two and, in her mother's day, she would have been teased as being pickled. Fatemeh Bibi's own marriage at the age of eighteen had been seen as radical, but now here was Sedi, setting off to have her face done, not for a husband but for a job.

On the day in 1964 that Bagher Mohammadi walked into a colleague's office to be greeted politely by a new secretary called Sedigheh Abbasian, he had been mulling over his plans to divorce Audrey. She had been living in Abadan with him for more than a decade then, but they had failed to have children and the couple had agreed to part. This was all my father would ever say on his marriage to Audrey and so this is all I have ever known of it, their fifteen years together reduced to those few bare words.

My father once told me that after meeting Sedigheh that day, he found himself increasingly making excuses to visit this colleague. Sedi sat at her desk, her thick hair arranged on top of her head in a little beehive, black kohl on her eyes as was the fashion, and he told me that he noticed the generosity of her lips and the timbre of her voice. My mother had finally grown into her nose, the piled-up hair certainly helped, but it was her high, chiselled cheekbones that really framed her face and contextualised that nose so that now it seemed regal and proud.

She grew more appealing with each visit, her brown eyes alive with intelligence and her form all elegant efficiency, and before long, Bagher took a chance with her that surprised even himself. One day he wandered in with a rose in his hand, a fragrant damask rose known in Iran as the Mohammadi flower, and he casually placed it on her desk as he passed by with a nod. At first Sedi sat and just looked at the flower. She didn't know what to do with it – what could it mean? – and she acted on her first instinct: she grabbed it and throw it into the bin, pretending it had never been there. When Bagher came out, he left the office with no word to her and she didn't know if he had noticed the flower was not on her desk.

Bagher certainly had noticed and at first he was taken aback – in England he had gone out with English girls whose ways were altogether more direct and less complicated than Persian ones. But on brief reflection it was of course what he would expect from a well-raised Persian girl, so he grew unabashed, and a few days later, he repeated the gesture. Sedi threw the flower away again, but she smiled a little to herself this time, and it had become kind of a game between them, him dropping a Mohammadi flower on her desk several times a week, and her disposing of it without saying anything. One day, when he came out of her boss' office, he saw instead on her desk a tiny vase and in it the small pink rose he had delivered that morning. He stopped to take it in, then he smiled at her. Nothing was said, but she looked right up at him and smiled back, and with that began their courtship.

Recalling this to me after a turbulent lifetime together, my mother still grows a little dreamy. Bagher was handsome and mature, his black hair slicked back and a moustache framing his mouth. There was a whiff of a Kurdish accent as he spoke to her, the Raybans permanently fixed on his nose or carried in his hand marked his out as an inhabitant of Abadan – they were famed for compulsively wearing Raybans. Bagher gave her the perfect courtship, one in keeping with her romantic ideas, and my mother was charmed. When eventually he suggested that she accompany him to a dance at the yacht club, Sedi was ready to say yes, despite the subterfuge it would involve.

My *khaleh* Mina told me that on the days she saw Bagher, they would race up to the roof where they could be sure of a little privacy and she would confide in her older sister that she was falling in love. She felt Bagher would be her protector, her rock to cling to in hard times, a man who had seen the world and who would always be able to look after her. Sedigheh had found her fairy-tale prince, the man she wanted to be with, and she was already firmly stuck into her own particular version of the fairy tale, the one in which she married for love and lived happily ever after. Quite where Sedi had got hold of these ideas is a mystery – she was used to seeing her sisters marry men picked by their parents and it was not so long since she had watched Mina be forced to marry Busheiry against her will – but these modern ideas of romantic love leading to marriage refused to be budged.

Sedi set about making a new dress in the latest style for

the dance and told her parents that she had to attend a work event that night and would be home early. Sometimes, when my mother I argue and she tries to make me feel guilty for being a disobedient daughter, trying to bend me to her will, I remind her that she herself hardly listened to or obeyed her parents. This shatters the myth she tries to present of herself as a paragon of filial virtue and obligation, and it makes her cross. But there is no denying the fact that my mother's father hadn't liked my mother's trips out in the evenings at all, and that in careless moments she had told me of his opposition to her romance with Bagher. He did not like his daughters to leave the house unchaperoned, and though a decade had passed since he had forced Jahanzadeh to take the whole brood out on his dates with Parivash, he would have preferred to do the same with Sedi. It was Fatemeh Bibi who prevailed on her husband again, reminding him that the times had changed, that Sedi already went unaccompanied to work every day and that in this new world, it was impossible for Abbas to expect his daughter to live her life in the same way she had done at her age. When Abbas grumbled and his frown set in obstinate lines, Fatemeh Bibi also reminded him that Sedigheh was a good girl, a good old-fashioned girl who gave her father her wages every week – out of which he gave her a small personal allowance for clothes and other such fripperies that he didn't understand – and that she could be trusted.

The well-loved and -trusted Sedi managed to get what she wanted and for the next year, she dated Bagher as if she was an independent Western girl, going to dinner at the Hotel Abadan, dancing at the Yacht Club and strolling together in the cool evening breezes of the velvety Abadan nights. But wherever she went, she was always home at the appointed hour. Bagher told her of his life, of the golden mountains of Kurdistan and the cold rivers he had learnt to swim in, of his journey to the other side of the world and what he had seen and learnt in Britain. He also told her right from the start about Audrey and of his plans to divorce, and Sedi, oblivious to the potential controversy of her actions – after all, she herself knew that she was not acting in any improper way, just sharing meals and conversations with this man in his sharp suits – was swept along by his intelligence, experience, glamour and good looks.

Both Bagher and Sedigheh, although their actions would have been seen as highly improper by Abbas, were in fact rooted enough in the traditional culture of Iran to know that their relationship needed official sanction, that they could not continue to date in secret, that Sedi if was found out she would lose her good reputation – the worst fate that could befall an unmarried woman in a country where a girl's behaviour, especially when it came to her chastity, directly affected the honour of her whole family. Perhaps this was why the likes of Ayatollah Khomeini were so keen to keep Iran's women under wraps and at home, where they could be safely monitored and not allowed to risk acting on their own desires, where they could be controlled to safeguard the honour of the family. Indeed, although Sedi was not compromising her chastity by going out with Bagher, they both knew that they could not go on like this for too long.

Sedi fell deliriously in love with Bagher and the day soon came when Bagher declared his intentions and a delighted Sedi gave him permission to call on her father. She ran to Mina and the two of them danced excitedly around Mina's pristine sitting room, Mina finally able to set free the rhythm in her hips in the privacy of her own home in celebration of her sister's luck in love. Sedi was getting her heart's desire. And Bagher was what her heart wanted, of this she was sure. Sedi had always been gifted a strong sixth sense and she knew this was the man of her life. This is how my mother always told me the story of her meeting and marrying my father, idealised and nostalgic, her own version of the fairy tale in which she continues still to believe.

8

Bending on the Branch

A FTER THE REVOLUTION, when the name of Ayatollah Khomeini became suddenly so familiar to me, my
parents told me how, in the year they were engaged, his name
had first come to prominence. That year the shah had given
in to American demands that all their personnel who were in
Iran – who numbered in the thousands – should be immune
from prosecution in Iranian courts for any crimes committed on Iranian soil. Very soon after, America gave Iran a $200
million loan with which it could buy arms – from the US.

Ayatollah Khomeini had denounced the shah vociferously
from Qom, saying that the monarch had sold Iran's independence, recalling the bad old days of capitulations. Indeed,
he pointed out that if an American ran over an Iranian, he
would be safe from prosecution while an Iranian enjoyed
no such privilege in his own country. Khomeini stoked the
resentment of the people with fiery rhetoric; the shah had
reduced the Iranian people to a level lower than that of an
American dog, he said, and many people were inclined to
agree with him all the way.

This outspokenness led to Khomeini's exile – the
shah could countenance no such opposition. He was
now ruling without any real pretence of submission to
the will of the *majlis*, which he entirely controlled, and
with SAVAK roaming the country eager to weed out any
dissent, Khomeini's forthright views and subsequent exile
to Iraq transformed him from a little-known provincial

priest to a national political leader. And he rose to the role, announcing with what seems now almost preternatural foresight: 'My soldiers are at the moment either in cradles or playing in the streets.' With that he declared his place as their potential political leader.

The wedding took place in my father's house in Braim in Abadan. The large bungalow where Bagher lived sat squat in the middle of a garden that continued round the back – the diametric opposite of the Iranian house where the house surrounded the garden, the inner courtyard, the family's own bit of paradise protected from jealous eyes. Along the front of the house was a wide porch at one end of which a sat a long, metal, swinging bench – a feature of my childhood, we liked nothing better than to sit on the *taab* and gently swing back and forth in the shade of the porch or, more to my taste, in the warm Khuzestani nights.

The wedding was a small family affair. Both Shokrollah and Kowkab had died by the time my parents met but the rest of Bagher's family had come to attend, his sister from Kurdistan and his brother Ebrahim, my *amoo*, with his family from Tehran. *Amoo* Ebrahim adored Bagher and felt somehow responsible for the boy who had lost the comforting presence of his mother so early on in his life. The redoubtable Sa'adat-*khanoum* had sized up my mother and found nothing wanting and, although she kept pictures of Audrey in her family photo albums long after Bagher had cut her out of his, my mother's respectful behaviour, her deferment to Sa'adat-*khanoum*'s superior judgement in everything would win the older woman over, and Sa'adat-*khanoum* took to bringing Sedi traditional costumes every time she visited Kurdistan, encouraging Sedi to wear Kurdish dress at special celebrations, the highest compliment.

By contrast to her careful relationship with Sa'adat-

khanoum, Sedi's developing friendship with her daughters, Guity and Mehry, could not have been warmer had they been sisters.

Sedi was in a wedding dress, one of her own choosing. She and Mina had poured over the *farangi* magazines and *Burda* to find a design and pattern they liked. It was 1966 and everything was being worn short. Sedi was a modern girl and she wanted a modern dress and, after much deliberation with Mina she had found a pattern in *Burda* that she though would fulfil both her father's rejoinder that she should not forget her modesty ('*Va!*' Mina exclaimed. 'As if you would do that, Sedi-*joon*; we are the daughters of Hayat Davoudy after all!') as well as her own thirst for fashion. Her dress was duly made by the dressmaker, a white lace hourglass number that followed her curves without clinging too much, the skirt ending just short of her knees, the long, tight sleeves unlined so the lace drew delicate patterns down her slim arms. Her black hair, bobbed to her chin with thick bangs, was piled up at the back behind a tiara of white flowers that held the net train cascading behind her, the neck scooped to show her beautiful clavicle but not so low as to reveal any cleavage.

Bagher's tailored suit was a distinguished dark grey. He wore a silk tie patterned with polka dots and a matching silk handkerchief peeked out precisely an inch from the top left-hand pocket. Bagher exuded confidence and happiness, his thin moustache trimmed, his black hair slicked back, his cuffs protruding from his jacket sleeves by just the right amount. He was civility and generosity itself, my mother told me, the very model of modernity in his new-style house with his dog and his beloved cook, Karim. Any worries Fatemeh Bibi and Abbas had had about this alien breed of New Iranian dissolved in the old-fashioned Iranian courtesy he extended to them all, and the presence of his brother and sister who had come with their spouses and broods, the women wear-

ing their striking Kurdish outfits topped off by hats made of
solid gold coins, looking to the Abadani Abbasians in their
kitten heels and zoot suits like unimaginably exotic creatures with their coins, sparkles and nets, strapping height and
proud bearing. They were perfectly mannered, reserved in
the most courteous way like Bagher himself and kind and
witty and sweet, their devotion to Bagher was as evident
as the sequins sewn by hand on to their long shimmering
dresses. Bagher had now officially arrived into the Abbasian
family and his arrival would transform the fortunes of the
Abbasian children.

The first Abbasian that Bagher brought into the Company
fold was Shapour. My eldest *daiey*, Ali Shapour had married
Ashraf and settled down to a modest life that Fatemeh Bibi
never really thought befitting of her first-born. Abbas had
approved the match and Shapour had been besotted, so there
was no going against it, but Fatemeh Bibi could not help
but feel that he had married beneath him. 'My son, as fine
as a bunch of roses, marrying a woman like that!' she had
exclaimed in quiet moments; in later years, her daughters
took up the cry too.

As a young girl, I loved nothing more than to visit *Daiey*
Shapour and *Zan-daiey* Ashraf's small house on the outskirts
of Abadan, a world away from Braim's manicured lawns. *Zan-
daiey* Ashraf was always kind and while I loved her I feared
her too. Ashraf-*khanoum* was a formidable woman and she
loved her Shapour fiercely, daring anyone to find fault in
the quality of care she lavished on him. But her tongue was
sharper than even Abbasian ones and no-one liked to chal-
lenge her to her face.

By contrast, *Daiey* Shapour was the sweetest out of all my
softhearted and loving uncles. He was gentle and kind, and
there beat within him one of life's noblest hearts. He and his
family lived in Abadan in a small house whose back yard opened

into a dusty alleyway where we always ended up playing with
Daiey Shapour's five children. I remember well his three eldest
boys as they were just a few years older than me and, being a
tomboy, I preferred to leave toys behind indoors and instead
run in the dust with the boys on their escapades. Of the three
boys it was Ebby who was my particular friend; a scruffy boy
with a crew cut whose nose ran constantly and whose legs were
always covered in the dirt of the streets. Ebby's encrusted nose
and bandy legs notwithstanding, we had the most fun together,
chasing each other for hours. I usually came off the worst and
my mother was constantly scolding me for tearing my pretty
dresses and grazing my knees.

One night, after an especially hard fall in the stony street
when I was playing with Ebby, my *daiey* showed me how he
could make the tail lights of his old 2CV blink like a beating heart. *Daiey* Shapour crouched by the car, and I perched
on his knee as, with great patience, he cut out some shapes
and, dismantling the lights one by one, arranged the shapes
within the lights. He then reassembled them, switched on
the engine and tapped his foot up and down on the brake so
that, to my delight and wide-eyed wonder, the lights turned
into red beating hearts. 'You see *Daiey-joon*,' he said, folding
me in one of his big hugs, his springy hair tickling my cheek,
'that's how my heart goes when I see you – blink blink –
that's how much I love you, *ghorbonet beram*.'

I was charmed beyond measure, the scraped knees
forgotten, and every time I saw the back of a 2CV disappearing down a road in Abadan from then on, I squinted
to see if it was *Daiey* Shapour's heart blinking for me.
Even in years to come and far away from Abadan, I could
never break that habit of casting a lingering look at the tail
lights of passing 2CVs to see if they were blinking their
love for me.

★   ★   ★

Bagher had started Shapour's career in the Company's vehicles division, but he had made Shapour go to night school and get his high school diploma to qualify for the job. Shapour was quickly promoted to head of department and he never ceased to tell his friends and family of Bagher's generosity and faith in him. He became the first of my uncles to be devoted to my father and soon after the other Abbasian boys started to find employment at the oil company. It was the major employer in Abadan and with Fatemeh Bibi so keen on the security it offered, it was perhaps natural that her sons gravitated towards it. But there is no doubt that Bagher's presence in their lives contributed to the attraction – he was respected, held in awe, in fact, by his brothers-in-law and they took his advice seriously. Any help he offered was gratefully received and Fatemeh Bibi noted that her sons, always so cheeky and high-spirited, became more serious and sombre when Bagher was around. They stopped making dirty jokes and minded their manners diligently. This held true not only when they were in his presence – when he extended a helping hand to them they did their best to prove to him that they deserved it. In short, they sought Bagher's approval in a way they had never craved anyone else's, not even Abbas'.

Daiey Pardis, one of my mother's younger brothers, like his *dadash* Shapour and all my uncles that came after him, possessed the softer side of Abbas' personality along with the mettle in his soul, a character so sentimental that he could never pass a beggar on the street without parting with some cash and wiping a tear from his eye. My *daiey* Pardis simply could not bear the misfortune of others. But unlike Sedi, Pardis never displayed the volcanic temper that made Abbas such a dangerous man to cross, instead he used humour and sentiment to try to diffuse the eruptions of temper that often overtook his siblings. At the time my parents were married, Pardis was working in a menial job in the oil fields but Bagher, after talking with him at length on the evenings he came to visit his favourite sister in her big new house, announced to Sedi that her brother had great potential and that he should be encouraged to better himself. With the older man's support, Pardis landed a job in the Company and worked hard at getting his engineering qualifications at night school. As Bagher championed him and Pardis devoted himself to his ambitions, a bond of love and respect was forged between the two men that would not be broken even when the events of the revolution tested everyone's loyalties.

Abbas was an old man by the time Bagher became part of the family. He was thin, in some lights skeletal, even. He still worked and he still extolled the virtues of a traditional *bazaari* life – where a man could make his fortune by combining skill, hard work, an eye for opportunity and a steely nerve for gambling – but his wife had long won out in her love for the Company and now that someone as high up in the organisation as Bagher was part of the family, there was no arguing with her. Despite her carefree, sometimes even careless, nature, Fatemeh Bibi approved of the security, the sense of consistency and continuity offered by the Company. She often told me that her father, Mirza Esmael Khan, had felt the same way. After all, had not he and his brother given up their own lands to become civil servants in the last shah's burgeoning bureaucracy? Had Fatemeh Bibi, born into the unthinking security of their life as khans of Busheir, when she had opened her eyes to the world to realise that chaos and not security was what reigned, had she not then learnt the value of a regular salary, the dependable expectation that each month one knew exactly what one would earn? Had she not, in her own life with Abbas, lived through the abrupt changes of fortune that life as a *bazaari* could bring? Her children would be safe working for the Company. Not only would

they be secure, they would be sheltered from the unseen
zephyrs she knew would always buffet Iran. Hard to imagine
then, with the shah so powerful, so omnipotent, sitting on
the wealth of the nation, untold riches flowing out of those
wells in Khuzestan, flowing through the great pipes across
the desert to the immense refinery in Abadan, the largest in
the world, hard to think that anything could ever change.

Fatemeh Bibi had lived through too much though, and
she knew that in Iran anything was always possible. '*Faghad
yek chiz ghabele pishbini ast to Iran – ke hichiz ghabel-e pishbini
nist,*' was what her father had always said: only one thing is
predictable in Iran – and this is that nothing is predictable.
Fatemeh Bibi had come to understand the truth of Mirza
Esmael Khan's words as she lived through the years, she told
me, sitting on her small mattress in *Khaleh* Yassi's small flat
in Shiraz on my first visit, when she had more energy to
talk. Then, Maman-*joon* reasoned, the Company provided
the riches of the shah, gave the country its wealth, income
and prestige, made it a player on the world stage, and since
the Company served national interests, it was unthinkable
that those working there would ever be vulnerable to
change.

Fatemeh Bibi should have heeded her own warnings and
known that nothing in Iran was unthinkable, that the gales
that were to come, that were already then gaining strength in
the dissatisfactions of the people and the blustery speeches of
the exiled Khomeini, would make the storms that had come
before look like mere puffs of air and that no one, not even
those serving their country through working at the Company,
would be safe from its enraged squalls.

Little did she know. None of them could have known, my
family, my aunts, uncles, my mother and father, living their
lives in Abadan in the sixties, unable to imagine anything
better, money in their pockets, coffees at the Milk Bar, visits

to the Cinema Rex to see Hindi films while waiting for the latest release to come from Hollywood. The country was stable and no one looked to see how deep that stability ran, whether it was real or an illusion conjured up by a despotic shah with a team of expert prestidigitators. No one knew at what price that illusion was projected or even really understood it for the chimera that it was. And in the midst of all their good fortunes, Bagher stood as solid as an oak tree: distinguished, mature, considered, seemingly un-fellable. And Sedi was by his side, slim and elegant, already bent to the new shape of her splendid life. Luckily for Bagher and for my sister and I, Sedi had grown up around the adage her grandfather had been so fond of muttering throughout his eventful life: 'We Iranians are like the cypress tree. We may bend and bend on the wind but we will never break.'

9

Khaleh Mina, *Maman Doh*

I ALWAYS FOUND IT difficult to explain *Khaleh* Yassi's upbringing to my English friends. I could not quite make them understand how my youngest aunt had been reared by her older sister as well as her mother; to them it spoke of rejection and a transgression of the familiar lines of family. The concept of extended family, something so encompassing and supportive that it spilled over the walls of houses and flowed over front doors, was difficult for people born into generations of small nuclear families to fully understand.

Yassaman was Fatemeh Bibi's youngest child, her last daughter and born when Fatemeh Bibi was already in her forties. Mina had been well into her teens when Yassaman had made her appearance, and she had instantly fallen in love with the long and lanky little girl as if she was her own. Fatemeh Bibi had felt from the beginning that Yassaman belonged to Mina and she was glad of it. By then she was tired of child rearing and happy to let the elder children raise the younger ones for her. Yassaman was only two when Mina had unhappily submitted to marriage with Busheiry, and one of Mina's greatest sorrows, in that time of sadness, was leaving her behind when she moved to Bushehr with her new husband.

After three lonely years in Bushehr, Mina returned to Khuzestan and settled into her house in Khorramshahr, soon slipping into seeing Yassaman every day when she visited her mother. She started to bring Yassaman back to stay with her for the odd night and, as she saw Busheiry as delighted with the little girl as she was, the visits grew longer and more of Yassaman's things found themselves to Mina's house. Since Mina visited her mother in Abadan daily there was no such thing as an actual move for Yassaman from Fatemeh Bibi's house in Abadan to Mina's house in Khorramshahr – the family merely extended itself over the miles in between the towns, over the river and its suspension bridge, one house becoming merely an extension of the other. Whether Mina's jasmine-filled yard or Fatemeh Bibi's geranium-potted courtyard, Yassaman's home was in the cocoon of love that her family spun around her and one day, when the little girl was visiting Mina, she simply never left. It had already become a habit of the younger boys to make the round trip at dinner time between the Abbasian house in Abadan and the Busheiry house in Khorramshahr to see who was cooking the more tempting meal – and it was not unknown for them to eat dinner at both houses. The convoy of Abbasian children wore smooth a path between the two towns and the two *sofras* and Fatemeh Bibi beamed her approval, telling the children to remember that when she was gone, they would always have another mother in Mina.

By now it was becoming clear that the large-hearted Mina was not going to have a child of her own. The emptiness had echoed with pain until she, as was her nature, stopped fighting her fate and opened the space up instead to be filled by us – her nieces and nephews. When her brothers and sisters started having their own children, there would invariably be at least one child in each family who would naturally fall in love with Mina. This was a purely spontaneous happening and it did not matter whether it was one of Parivah's children – born and

brought up in Shiraz far from Mina, or Mahvash's children, born and brought up in Burujerd far from Mina, or
one of Mamaly's children, born and brought up in Texas
far from Mina – but there was always at least one who, on
meeting her kind gaze with its own unfocussed baby stare,
would tumble into the heart of this woman whose love
was as vast as the Hayat Davoudy date orchards had once
been. And no matter what happened, we would always
belong to her.

In my family – the Mohammadi family – that baby was me,
and my *khaleh* Mina is still known to me as my mother number
two. Her voice, crackling over the international phone line,
bubbling with love, and the anarchy of her raucous humour
fills me with joy – being around her swells me with self-
confidence.

When my parents got married, Mina was living in Khorramshahr and soon afterwards, my mother introduced her
to the Store. Mina was instantly smitten; the Store was to
become a lifelong love. It was the Company's grocery shop
in which employees could buy subsidised goods – the prices
were not only cheaper than in the bazaar, but the quality was
reliable and, more importantly, the Store carried shelves of
farangi goods that were not available elsewhere. In the early
days of the Company, the Store had been one of the many
ways in which the British had tried to make themselves feel
at home, now that nationalism had seen off the apartheid
of those days, Iranian workers loved nothing better than to
buy these rare *farangi* goods and were not above showing off
to their non-Company friends by turning, before their wide
eyes, a small heap of dry brown granules into coffee just by
adding hot water. Hot water that came out of a kettle that
was filled with cold water, plugged into the wall and came
to a noisy gurgling climax within seconds, and not from the

samovar bubbling quietly on the gas hob where it had been
simmering all day.

Mina loved the Store almost beyond reason – it represented the two things she was most devoted to beyond her
family and little Yassi: modernity and household goods
– and she questioned Sedi closely about everything that
came from there. She adored her Nescafé, especially when
whitened not with milk, which had to be boiled to be
drunk safely, but with another powder, finer and white
this time, called Coffee-mate, which dissolved into the
coffee and not only turned it that particular shade of camel
brown that Mina loved so much, but also gave it a creamy,
artificial taste that she felt to be the height of sophistication. Topped by two heaped teaspoons of sugar, her long,
thin cigarette teased out of the packet stuffed in its leather
cover, poised and ready to be lit, the first drag timed to
coincide with the first long draught of coffee, Mina was to
repeat this ritual daily for the rest of her life, even when
she was no longer in Khuzestan, even when the Store had
long ceased to exist and she had to eke out the giant pots
of Nescafé and Coffee-mate that I would bring her on my
visits from London a lifetime later.

By then, with Mina living in Shiraz and as consumerism had made modernity and sophistication an egalitarian
right for all in the Islamic Republic of Iran, all these
brands were available in ordinary shops all over the place.
But Mina, devoted to her memories of the Store, insisted
that the stuff in Iran, made in the Gulf Arab countries
or Southeast Asia and imported from Dubai, Kuwait or
Malaysia, was simply not the same, not as good, as the ones
that I brought her from the UK, even though they bore
the same labels. She always had two versions in her kitchen
cupboards – the local Nescafé and Coffee-mate with its
supposedly inferior provenance and, hidden at the back,

far away from other, prying eyes, my gifts from London, saved for special occasions, particularly important guests or when the quality of the gossip to be shared demanded nothing less than the best.

The day Busheiry's accounting work finally gave him access to the Store was one of Mina's happiest. She floated around with a wire basket on her arm, running her long fingers over the revered goods, tapping the glass containers with her pointed and painted nails, her stilettos clicking on the floor, her basket (*Imagine! Not woven from straw but actually made from metal, by a machine* – she thought she might faint with joy) growing heavier on her arm, hurting her elbow now, but she didn't care. The powdered eggs, the thing called custard (she had no idea what it was but she added a packet anyway), tea bags – but wait, *tea bags*? No, that would never do. They might be able to do clever things with coffee that left no residue in the cup as traditional *ghahve tork* did, but she knew that there was nothing the *farangis* could possibly teach her people about tea making. Her nose turned up almost imperceptibly as she passed the rows of colourful boxes full of tea bags and clicked her way to the till.

That night, she had treated Busheiry as if he was indeed Clark Gable. Along with access to education – which she loved with an unreserved heart – this was the greatest thing he had ever given her, and she felt something close to love for him as she prepared his powdered eggs and regaled him with tales of the different products she had bought and the plans she had for them. Mina, mistress of her own house back in Khuzestan where she could visit her family daily and dote on little Yassaman, was happy and content. She felt that from now on, life could only get better.

She had decided, with her husband's blessing, to go to night school and study for her high school diploma. Busheiry was a kind man and, unlike her father, he had no objection

to Mina educating herself. In this sense, Mina found a sort
of freedom in her unpromising marriage. Studying the high
school diploma at night school was, apparently, all the rage.
Over our habitual coffee and cigarettes in her kitchen in
Shiraz, she told me the story: how carefully she had dressed
in a natty suit with pointed kitten heels – a respectable length
of heel – her hair shiny as a conker in a careful beehive, for
enrolment day, how excited and nervous she was and then
how happy to see so many other women her age there, from
similarly good backgrounds. It was here that she had met
Haydeh, her lifelong friend. She had been instantly taken
by the regal-looking girl with jet-black hair and a proud,
eagle nose. Haydeh was as proper, upright and correct as
Mina in everything she did, while constantly assessing the
world thorough hawk-like eyes. She was married to a career
soldier and was from the north of Iran, the area bordering
the Caspian Sea, with its tropical climate and rice paddies,
heavy rainfall and a resultantly dense, green landscape unim-
aginable here in the parched, dusty south. Haydeh too had
been forced out of school as a girl and, though she was
newly married, her husband – who was in the military – had
agreed to her attending night school to lessen her loneliness on his frequent absences. Haydeh and Mina found each
other in their entirely formal fashion, not knowing then that
they would become such friends that Mina would refer to
Haydeh's mother as Maman Doh – Mother Number Two
– and that they would share a lifetime of coffees and cigarettes, all the while never failing to address each other as
'*Khanoum* Vaziri' and '*Khanoum* Busheiry', even when revolution changed their fortunes and war tore up their houses
and made them refugees in their own country. Forty years
after first meeting, when I rediscovered my *khaleh* Mina in
Shiraz, they were living close by each other in the suburbs,
speaking on the phone for several hours on the days when

something prevented them from sitting in one or the other's kitchen drinking Nescafé and chatting, their cigarettes held regally aloft, wreathed in blue smoke.

Perched as they had been on the very cusp of the country's heaving shift into modernity, many girls of Mina's generation had suffered the same fate as her – traditional fathers saw education as useful for girls only in so far as it would teach them to read and write and follow the teachings of the Qur'ān. What else did they need to be educated for, these fathers asked when challenged (which they rarely were by obedient daughters bred to hold these men in the highest esteem, little kings of their little castles, never to be questioned or crossed, only to be obeyed) – an over-educated girl was a recipe for lifelong unhappiness and shame for the whole family. No man would wish to marry a woman who knew more than him, had been educated to a higher standard than him, and if a girl went all the way through high school and got her diploma, then chances were she would remain on her father's hands for the rest of her life, giving him another mouth to feed when in fact she should be the one providing for him in his old age. No, it was not natural and gave these girls notions that were *ajib-gharib* – strange ideas of working and earning money and something called independence. Some women had even been known to go to university and there they were, striding all over Abadan like a bunch of men, uncovered and shameless, looking everyone in the eye, working at the Company in positions that were equal to men's – some even higher – and living in little boxes called apartments on their own.

The conservative fathers of Abadan had shuddered. It was horrific and against the natural order of things. No, a woman should know enough so she could stop her husband from becoming bored with her, and if it gave her the wherewithal to balance the household accounts, all the better. Frankly, these fathers already considered themselves entirely modern for even being prepared to let their daughters learn to read and write and this indeed was a leap in itself. Reza Shah's laws had demanded everyone be educated to a certain standard, and his son, the current shah, continued legislation in this field; the Literacy Corps he had created as part of the White Revolution to go into the countryside and teach the workers on the land how to read and write had indeed given many ordinary Iranians access to schools and, although attitudes were hard to shift, particularly among the country people and peasant classes, within the new middle class literacy and education were now the norm.

With Khomeini – his most outspoken critic – now safely exiled in Najaf, the shah felt confident in his own rule and buoyed up by America and other Western powers who truly believed that the shah was busy creating an island of stability in the troubled region, a front of Western-friendly ideology to hold off the Red Menace. The shah bestowed on himself the title of Aryamehr on the occasion of his silver jubilee in 1965 and decided to publicise his greatness and legitimacy further by holding a coronation ceremony in which he also had Farah, his third and final wife, and mother of his children, crowned alongside him. Although the coronation was supposed to celebrate the unbroken tradition of Iran's kings, designed to recall with each gesture the Achaemenid kings' ancient Persia, the Pahlavi crown with which the shah crowned himself supposedly a replica of the traditional Sassanian crown, in fact, the coronation ceremony was a mixture of invented Persian tradition and British practices. A Foreign Office minister had been dispatched to the UK charged with discovering how a coronation ceremony was to be carried out and as for the rest, historians noted that there seemed to be a lot of Napoleonic traditions there, including the crowning of Farah as empress by his side. Farah's coronation was touted as a sign of the progressiveness of the shah's regime – Farah was a symbol of the emancipation of women that the shah imagined he had completed by giving them the vote in 1963.

Such pomp and ceremony had not been seen since Reza Shah's coronation, and with mass media now in existence, the riches of the Pahlavi dynasty could be broadcast not only into every village in the country but to the whole world. My grandmother and Sa'adat-*khanoum* tuned in on their television sets – my grandmother's had been a gift from my father – to see the shah draped in ermine and bedecked in priceless jewels, he and his Empress Farah the very model of modern monarchy, their glamour dazzling the elders of my family. The world too was impressed – here was a progressive king who combined over two thousand years of continual monarchy with a particularly modern sort of allure, ruling over a nation full of quaint costumes and diverse ethnicities that were nonetheless united in progressing into the modern world in a way that looked very familiar to Western eyes.

Iranians were dazzled by the shah and his family's magnetism, although the many poor and illiterate, who were feeling increasingly disenfranchised and marginalised by the new world that the shah was creating in his own image in Iran, grumbled at the inequality even while they admired the monarch and lapped up magazine photos presenting a glittering image of the imperial family. The shah's personality cult was now truly underway, and more statues of his royal person were erected around the country. Now that his coronation had been beamed into homes across the nation via the wonder of television, the image of the shah was set to become as familiar to his subjects as the reflection of their own faces in the mirror. What all the pageantry and opulence served to obscure – even from the shah himself – was that the modern society the shah had created in his own image, the new middle class and in particular the sector of New Iranians who were now living lives that were glossed with a Western patina, were in fact not integrating with an increasingly alienated and marginalised majority.

Unseen by families like mine, cushioned from the grim realities of political autocracy and economic deprivation, the vast majority of traditional Iranians – those peasants and workers who were now uprooted from their traditional livelihoods on the land – were looking with increasing resentment at not only the shah and the unspeakably rich elite that surrounded him, but also at the comfortable lives of corporate New Iranians such as my father. Khomeini's speeches – taped in Najaf and smuggled into the country to be disseminated through the mosques, the only places safe from SAVAK's sharply attuned ears – fanned the flames of discontent, but it would be yet another decade before this trickle of discontent would become a tsunami of disgust and dissatisfaction powerful enough to sweep away not only the shah himself but even families like mine who, for all their innocence, came to symbolise everything that the populace found uncomfortable about the shah's vision of progress.

June is a sweltering month in Abadan with infernally hot, humid days giving way to sticky, oppressive nights. It was at this most stifling time of year that my sister decided to enter the world. A few days after midsummer in 1968, the heavily pregnant Sedi was admitted to the Company's hospital in Abadan and, while Bagher paced the corridors nervously and Mina held her hand, Sedi pushed out her first-born in a matter of hours. The little girl was tiny and perfect and named Narmin – my soft one – because her arrival softened her parents' hearts. Bagher was overjoyed, Sedi was proud and the whole of Abadan sent flowers. There were so many bouquets and gifts that the hospital not only ran out of vases but also space. Sedi's room soon overflowed and before long the corridors were lined by bunches of magnolia, tuberose, gladioli and roses. The multitudes of Abbasians and Kurds that filled Sedi's room from dawn till dusk jostled for space with a kaleidoscope of blooms, bursts of colours and wafts of fragrance that made Sedi's head spin as she nursed her tiny new baby.

Narmin was beloved immediately, not only by her parents but also by the vast web of family of which she was now the newest member. Fatemeh Bibi cradled the little girl – who was destined to take after her grandmother in her petiteness – and soothed her with her vast experience of babies. Shapour, Parivash and Mahvash all had large families of their own eventually collecting between them fourteen children, but Bagher and Sedi, being thoroughly modern Iranians, had already decided that they would limit their family to two children, filled as they were with the latest notions of parenting, as espoused by Dr Spock whose words they had read avidly.

A mere fifteen months later, at the end of the West's summer of love in September 1969, Sedi, with her hair hanging long and straight from a centre parting, was admitted again to the Company hospital to give birth to me, my parents' second and final child. Labour and delivery took a mere four hours – Sedi had inherited Abbas' lack of patience and we, her children, must have sensed our mother's short temper as we raced out of the womb, already unwilling to test her tolerance.

They tell me that I was born with a full head of thick, black hair, long eyelashes and red lips and *Khaleh* Mina spread the news by ringing the whole family and telling them: 'Sedigheh-*khanoum* has given birth to a perfect baby girl, and she had her hair and make-up done before she came out.' Having pored over baby name books to find something that sounded beautiful when said with Narmin – Persian is a poetic language and we Iranians love to make our children's names rhyme – they had come up with Kamin, an unusual name which I am now convinced is unique having, in my travels around the Iranian diaspora, met with a blank even from Persian scholars whose job it is to know the meaning of everything. I understand it as something lyrical that expresses deep longing, and it was whispered in my ear by a *mullah* soon after my birth, along with my Islamic name, thus distinguishing me as a Shia Muslim rather than as a Sunni like my Kurdish father.

My birth completed the little Mohammadi family and again flowers filled the hospital rooms and the two clans that formed my large and boisterous extended family flocked to Abadan to celebrate. My first few days of life were marked by the scent of tuberose and the sound of laughter. I was held and handed from embrace to embrace, filled with the warmth and love of my many aunts, uncle and cousins, as well as my grandparents' kisses, their whispered prayers caught in my curly black hair, their fond wishes for me absorbed somewhere so deep that when, many years later, I spent a lifetime being teased for the thickness of my hair, having my name mispronounced and ridiculed for its rhyming poetry with my sister's name, I never quite lost the feeling that I was not so much an outsider – as I was wont to feel – as a link on a very long chain.

Before I was quite one year old, my father was given a new position in Tehran. For some years, he had been overseeing the building of a house on a plot of land he had bought in Tehran's northern reaches. Not content with occupying the large house the Company had given him in Braim, Bagher was keen to own his own house; having come from a family so tied to the land, the belief was deep in him that true security came with property. Bagher had helped design the house and the villa that he built was modern – this was the age of modernity and progress after all, and our villa was typical of the sort of houses that were going up all around Tehran. A bungalow with sweepingly spacious rooms for entertaining, the villa was set behind walls which hid our lives from curious eyes, harbouring a large garden, our own private paradise where the rose garden was separated from the vegetable patch and the fruit trees bent their fecund boughs around the edge of the double swimming pool that Bagher made sure to include – a smaller, shallower one joined the big pool so that my sister and I – and indeed the other children of the family – would be able to paddle and swim until we were confident enough to graduate to the big pool.

The villa was in an area called Darrus, then on the edge of town, with a clear view north to the sharp peaks of the Alborz mountains, the massif that kept the rain of northern Iran up in the verdant north of the country and the land to the south as desert. The mountains provided a daily show of light and colour which formed the backdrop to my childhood. When we moved in there was nothing in front of the villa, the other side of the street was still a wilderness, *biyaboon*, a mixture of dust and stones that stretched on for miles, most of which ended up embedded in my knees as I learnt to walk and run and defy my mother to play outside the walls of our villa.

I must have felt the change of air as we arrived in Tehran from hot and humid Khuzestan and our air-conditioned house in Braim. Here the winters were cold, and snow – which my sister and I had never seen before – fell in soft flakes throughout the freezing months. Spring was a riot of new life, blossoms and flowers and the rush of melting snow becoming pure spring water, filling channels that ran down the edges of the roads, wide deep *joobs* which were bridged by little metal walkways from the roads to the pavements. The summers were hot but dry, nothing like the moist heat of Khuzestan, and autumn was painted in fiery hues, the air bearing a scent of the icy breezes to come, the first snows appearing on the peaks of the Alborz in October, just as the maple leaves turned the city into a blur of reds and yellows. The distinctness of Tehran's four seasons never failed to thrill and amaze us Khuzestanis formed from the desert breezes. Tehran would be our new home, and in the seven years I lived there, she etched the outline of her majestic mountains indelibly in my heart. Tehran would always feel like home, even after thirty years away.

Settling into life in Tehran came with the same ease as everything seemed to then, in those days when political dissatisfactions with the shah's tyrannical regime were papered over by the economic boom that the high oil prices were bringing even ordinary Iranians. The cost of living had not significantly risen and salaries had increased dramatically and while my own little nuclear family was basking in privilege and material comfort, even my relations in Abadan, who lived much more modestly, were finding their lives sweetened with the ready money jangling in their pockets.

My uncle Ebrahim and his family had lived in Tehran for some years, after his work took him out of Kurdistan and they left their beautiful old-fashioned house in Sanandaj. Now settled in a suburb to the east of the city centre called Tehran Pars, they lived in a two-storey house with large, open rooms, a walled-in yard at the back and large terrace running round the rooms on the top floor. Their children were all grown now – Firooz was working for the Company in Abadan and Guity spent large parts of the year living with him, looking after him, cooking and nurturing him as was her wont. Mehry had shone at high school and was at university in Tehran, beautiful and smart and filled with ideas about something called feminism, which her brothers laughed at. Behrooz too was setting out on a career at the Company and Parviz, the youngest and tallest of them all (although Firooz was so good-looking, with his sharp profile and seductive features that even Parviz in his prime could not really steal the most handsome accolade from him) was in the upper classes of high school.

In the absence of my real grandparents, my sweet *amoo* and his wife Sa'adat-*khanoum*, who had always considered Bagher as her eldest son, were for me and my sister the elders of my Kurdish family, always there with love and indulgence in the way that grandparents were supposed to be.

There were two family events that pulled us back to Abadan soon after we arrived in Tehran. The first was *Daiey* Pardis' wedding, for which my mother undertook to supply from Tehran the finest quality of *termeh* – a traditional paisley cloth woven in Yazd, embroidered with gold thread and all sorts of lavish embellishments – for the wedding *sofra*. Pardis was marrying Shirin, a tiny, doe-eyed girl with a mass of thick, black hair who had an aversion to wearing any sort of make-up. When Maman-*joon* and *Khaleh* Mina had called on Shirin's family just a few streets away to enquire for her hand, Shirin's mother had apologetically told them that her daughter had always insisted on making her own choice about her husband. Thus *Daiey* Pardis and Shirin were allowed to date before she gave her consent, a radically modern state of events in Iran in 1970. *Daiey* Pardis told me that he had dressed up wildly for their dates, buying suits with wide lapels and flared trousers, the first in Abadan to sport the new look the Beatles had adopted. Skinny, with bushy hair springing around his collar and long sideburns, my uncle had been teased mercilessly by his brothers. Now, teasing his wife, he insists still that it was his stylish good looks that she fell for, and she, rolling her eyes but unable to stop herself from giggling, swats him away.

When Shirin was engaged to my uncle, she worked in a bank, and, on hearing of her engagement to Pardis Abbasian, her colleagues warned her with some alarm about those young terrors, Pardis' younger brothers – did she know what she was getting herself into marrying into the Abbasian family? Shirin had laughed then as she is still laughing now and, wearing a long white dress and flowers in her hair (and thick black kohl around her eyes at the insistence of my mother and *Khaleh* Mina), Shirin married Pardis and joined the Abbasian family. Her resilience and wicked sense of humour would help my family to keep laughing even in the days when there seemed to be nothing much to laugh about.

The second event was less joyful. One night a few weeks after we celebrated my first birthday in Tehran, my mother had a dream. In the dream her *dadash* Shapour was telling her to hurry home, that Abbas was waiting for her. She told me that in the morning she was prepared for the phone call from Shapour who told her that *Agah-jan* had suffered a stroke and was dying. 'He is waiting for you, Sedi-*joon*,' he told her, his voice heavy. 'Everyone else is here and he is waiting just for you. Hurry.'

My family was given to visions and dreams. Maman-*joon* had always told us that as a child she saw *djinns*, playful spirits that messed up her clothes, and she was convinced that she heard the call of the Vag Vag birds, as she called them, before something terrible happened. '*Naneh*,' she rasped at me, 'I heard the Vag Vag birds one day in Abadan just after your *khaleh* Mina was born, and that night we were sleeping on the roof when, suddenly, the war started.'

My mother too sometimes had prophetic dreams, although they stopped abruptly after we had moved to England and the events of the revolution had driven a wedge between her and God. My *daiey* Pardis to this day can read the future so accurately from the remains of Turkish coffee grounds that his family periodically pleads with him to give up work and become a full-time fortune-teller. For the Abbasian family, the curtain between this world and that was thin at best, and they accepted the magic of life without seeking too hard for rational explanations.

My mother kicked into action after Shapour's phone call. Before long, we were back in her childhood home in Farahabad in Abadan where my grandfather was lying in a bed made up on the floor – the Abbasian household had never shaken the habit of living on the floor – looking like a bag of bones. My mother joined all her siblings gathered around his bed – they had flocked from all corners of Iran to be there. Abbas did indeed wait for his favourite daughter to arrive before he slipped away, holding Sedigheh's hand, her head bowed over him, her tears falling on his face.

In the days that followed, people poured into Maman-*joon*'s home to pay their respects, to add their voices to the howls of pain and the downpour of tears that racked through the Abbasian house during the seven days of mourning that followed. Abbas' sons-in-law had come to attend the ceremonies from their different corners of Iran, and my Kurdish cousins were there too. Our families were united in grief for this man who had come so far in his life, had created not only this large family but even himself from nothing, from some lost place behind the Caucasus mountains.

Abbas Abbasian had realised his final and greatest ambition – to produce a family so numerous, and be head of a household so generous and welcoming, that often when he returned home at the end of the day there was no room for him at the *sofra*. His wishes had come true, but so he did the curses he was so quick in invoking when his disorderly younger sons tested his patience. Unable to control his temper, quick to shoot off his tongue when the fury overtook him, Abbas would curse his children for fighting so much: 'One day you will all be scattered all over the world, like the seeds of the poppy, so far away from each other that you will finally understand the value of family, finally learn that you should have known the worth of having each other close.' Abbas' unthinking fury was to prove strong for indeed the events of the years to come were to see his descendents scattered wider than even he had predicted.

Fatemeh Bibi mourned her husband in the traditional way – she wept and beat her head and tore at her chest when the loss felt too much to bear. Shia Islam, being a religion built on grief and mourning, sanctions such releasing actions, and my grandmother, aunts and uncles allowed the deep suffering of their loss to be expressed in such operatic lamentations. In calmer moments, Fatemeh Bibi sang the praises of her husband, remembering the time Abbas had made the hazardous overland journey to Iraq with the body of her dead mother to fulfil a promise that he would make sure she was buried next to her own mother in Kerbala. Abbas was a serious man, a man of his word, a man pricked by a strong conscience. My grandmother was, until her dying day, a woman with the lightest of hearts. She loved to laugh and enjoy herself, was still that carefree girl who wasted the mangoes and coconuts of her father's storeroom with no thought to the future, relaxed in the knowledge that there would always be someone else ready to do the worrying, someone else who would knit their brow and let anxiety cast a shadow across their face. Fatemeh Bibi liked the fun side of life, was never one to miss a party; in her eighties, bent double and hardly able to walk, she nonetheless tottered across the world to be at my sister's wedding in London, saying to anyone who would listen: 'As if I would miss my little girl's big day, *be khoda*! She was like my own child, I brought her up myself.'

Abbas had been a man for living, as Maman-*joon* often said, and he had made life sweet indeed for the cherished only daughter of Mirza Esmael Khan.

10

New Iranians

A FTER THE FIRST week of mourning for Abbas was over, after helping her mother, sisters and sisters-in-law prepare the customary foods for the ceremonies marking the week of his death, Sedi scooped us up and returned to Tehran.

Settling into her new life, Sedi was glowing in both Bagher's attention and the respect that her new status afforded her. My mother was a born hostess, charming and attentive with beautiful manners. Hospitality has never been in short measure in Iran – the Islamic belief in the blessing inherent in extending welcome to strangers met, on colliding with the ancient culture of Iran, a well-established system of courtesy and hospitality that already had roots thousands of years old. The combination of these two heritages knit together in such a way in Iran that the practice emerged deeper, richer and more striking that in any other Muslim country. In this way – as in so many others – Iran Persianised Islam and gave it a depth and refinement not present when the religion was born in the barren deserts of Arabia.

Sedi Mohammadi embodied the latest incarnation of the hospitable Iranian wife. She served her dinners on a large dining table rather than on a *sofra* flung across the floor, and her guests sat on straight-backed chairs, rather than cross-legged on the floor reclining on cushions. But nonetheless the choice and variety of dishes on her table, the steaming *khoreshts*, mountains of saffron-stained rice, the 'belly-full' stuffed fishes, yoghurts sprinkled with crushed dried rose petals and mint and a myriad of pickles and salads. Her table was abundant and if it differed from the *sofra* at the Abbasian house, it was only in the style and the presentation. The same spirit that animated the Hayat Davoudy and Abbasian *sofras* moved through the Mohammadi table. As with so much in the New Iranian lifestyle that Sedi was now fully entered into, underneath the Western laminate, they were still Iranian through and through.

My mother loved to sing and she was apt to break into song at any given moment. Sometimes as she was talking, she would stop and sing a snatch of an Iranian tune, complete with expressive intonation, clearly deciding that the music better expressed what she was trying to say. I have often thought that, had my mother had her way, she would have lived her life as in a musical movie, the most important events in her life lived as big song and dance numbers. My father had discovered musical theatre in England and always made sure to take in the latest shows whenever work took him to London, telling me in years to come of how he saw Julie Andrews playing Eliza Doolittle in *My Fair Lady* on the West End stage and how Carol Bruce had sizzled in *Pal Joey* as I excitedly riffled through his record collection to find the original cast recordings of the shows. We watched all the old MGM musicals together, all of us muttering approval of Gene Kelly's moves, Fred Astaire's lightness, Ginger Rogers' twirls. My parents passed on to us their love of singing, music and musicals and I too have wished that life allowed more spontaneous singing and dancing in moments of great emotion.

My mother sang one song so frequently when we were living in Tehran that it is etched into my brain even now. '*Morgh-e Sahar*' – 'Bird of Dawn' – is an old Iranian song dating back to the Constitutional Revolution, speaking of my nation's long yearning for freedom in the customary Persian metaphors and symbols, a song whose popularity penetrates every strata of Iranian society and whose lyrics, speaking of caged nightingales and the cruelty of tyrants, are as relevant to our nation now as during the Constitutional Revolution. I can still recall it today.

Every summer, Fatemeh Bibi would visit for the three months that the schools were closed. My grandmother was then a small white-skinned creature with a barrel-like figure and legs that were beginning to bow out at the knees. Maman-joon may have been small but there was a charisma and *joie de vivre* to her that belied her size. At the airport where we went to greet her, she would walk out into the arrivals hall, her steps tiny but each one possessed of a graceful confidence, leading Yassi and Mamaly, who were both already taller than her, by the hand, to our excited squeals. We always met them ourselves – although there was the Company-provided Lincoln at Sedi's disposal in Tehran, she never let a member of her family be met by anyone else.

My mother drove us to the airport in her Paykan. Although the shiny BMW that was parked in the garage in Darrus belonged to her too, she preferred to use the Iranian car that had been modelled on the British Hillman. The Paykan was reliable, if not especially glamorous, and famous for its tenacity – *Daiey* Shapour had once completed an eight-hour journey in a Paykan held together by the skin of some persimmon fruit.

Khaleh Mina was also a frequent visitor to our villa in Tehran. Once she had graduated from night school, finally the proud possessor of her high school diploma, she would leave Busheiry in Khorramshahr and come for blissful extended visits with us. When I was just nine months old, my mother started travelling the world with my father again, spurred on by Fatemeh Bibi who urged her to wean me and return to being 'the wife of your husband'. Maman-*joon* believed strongly in the importance of the sensual life of a wife and husband – to which her twelve children bore testament – and she thought it unhealthy, if not downright dangerous, for my father to take those long foreign trips, touring the world to negotiate and bargain on behalf of Iran and her oil projects, on his own. While my parents took off for regular trips, my grandmother and *Khaleh* Mina would move into the villa in Darrus to look after me and my sister and I felt I belonged as much to them as I did my parents.

My Kurdish family were equally present in our lives and, led by Sa'adat-*khanoum*'s example, I grew as fond of picnics and hiking in the hills as she was herself. Sa'adat-*khanoum* instilled in us her love of the outdoors and on weekends we would squeeze into two cars, my *amoo*'s family and mine, and we would drive out to the foothills of the Alborz, picking a beautiful spot shaded by trees and gurgling with streams. We would take a long walk, my sister and I running off the path, for which we were normally scolded by my mother, then playing while Guity and Mehry helped our mother spread out the Persian carpets and set out the feast that issued, as if by magic, from the trunks of the cars.

Our picnics were no different to the meals we ate at home – rice would be par-cooked and brought along in a huge pan to be steamed on a portable gas ring, while the men built a fire over which skewers of chicken soaked in lemon juice and saffron would be grilled, the whole served up in large pieces of flat bread, bought fresh from the baker that morning. A samovar would be brought along and while we were eating, tea was made and the pot left to brew. Along with the china plates, we always packed the little pinch-waisted glasses which we drank tea from, and these, with quantities of sugar cubes and little silver teaspoons, would complete the *sofra*.

The only thing I loved more than our picnics was winter, with the water frozen in the *joobs* and the city chilled to its bones. As children our ambition was for the snowfall to be so heavy that schools were closed and when this happened – which to my memory was often – we would excitedly phone our cousins across town and, practically panting with excitement, announce to them: 'It's snowing and they have closed the world. Let's build snowmen!'

Snowy winters never failed to thrill us Khuzestani kids especially when, in *Amoo*'s house, a room was given over to the *korsy*, the traditional answer to the cold. A low table was covered in quilts, a brazier was placed underneath and the heat spread under the table. Large cushions were ranged around the *korsy* and placed against the wall for leaning on. The top of the *korsy* was used as a table, always scattered with delicious nut mixes and bowls of winter fruit. We sat around the *korsy* and tucked our legs underneath, eating meals there and, as little children, getting lost under the table as we played our games, invariably pulled out by an angry adult who would tell us off for going near the hot brazier.

Khaleh Mahvash and her family were frequent visitors in Tehran, and her children learnt to swim alongside us in our children's pool. Of her four kids I was especially fond of Mahnaz, the second daughter who was a few years older than me. I loved her huge smile and generous spirit, she was funny and her grey eyes twinkled with intelligence. Our bond had only deepened one winter when, out playing in the snow-covered garden, she had slipped and fallen into the iced-over pool. I had dashed inside and fetched the adults, and they had fished out a shivering Mahnaz who from then on maintained that I had saved her life.

Although I was shy when I had to put on a pretty dress and be presented to my parents' friends at their many lavish parties, when in the midst of my huge extended family I was a confident and cheeky child, spoilt by all. Even the strict Sa'adat-*khanoum* would pause as I passed to plant a kiss on my cheek, stroking my hair and calling me her 'Kam Kam' and I thrived, nourished by such love.

Sa'adat-*khanoum*, like my Maman-*joon*, adored the shah. She was a woman who had been liberated by Reza Shah's reforms and her version of modernity was always tied in with the Pahlavis, who she found as admirable as Maman-*joon* found them glamorous. She kept scrapbooks devoted to the royal family and these swelled in 1971 when the shah finally held the long-promised celebration commemorating 2,500 years of Iranian monarchy. Vowing to deliver the 'greatest show on earth', the shah neglected to mention which date he was commemorating since this celebration had first been mooted in the fifties. As with so much else in the shah's insistent myth making, the details were vague, but the image was brilliantly drawn, designed to dazzle, to spellbind the public and fill their scrapbooks.

Many years later, when the Pahlavi dynasty had long fled and I was visiting the Islamic Republic for the first time, one of my cousins took me to visit the site of the shah's big party in the desert on our way to Persepolis. The tented city was no longer impressing anyone, empty and flapping in the desert wind, the tents that had once harboured heads of state were now as faded as the dynasty they had been erected to celebrate. The shah's city was in reality fifty luxurious suites that were no less opulent for being constructed of canvas. Inviting sixty-nine heads of state – monarchs were given precedence over presidents – the shah laid on the biggest party the world had seen; it even made the *Guinness Book of Records* as the most lavish official banquet in modern history. The foreign dignitaries lapped up 20,000 litres of wine, magnums of Chateau Lafite flowing like water. Quails' eggs, pheasant and Iranian caviar were on the menu – in this celebration of Iranian monarchy and nationhood, there was a surprising lack of traditional Iranian cuisine on the tables, or Iranian culture on display. To his critics, an impatient shah replied, 'Should I serve heads of state stale bread and radishes instead?' in one fell swoop reducing the way most people lived as not good enough to be served up to his foreign friends.

The ordinary people did not care for the adulation the shah was enjoying abroad. Alienated from the celebrations, they found the sum of $100 million spent on the entertainments distasteful when so many lived in abject poverty and the fiery Ayatollah Khomeini – who had become ever more vocal from his exile in Iraq – vociferously criticised not just the celebrations and the shah himself, but all Iranian monarchs. The parade of the Iranian army at Persepolis was intended as a display of Iran's military might, a subject close to the shah's heart since taking over from his military father and being the recipient of so many millions of dollars in aid and arms from America. The shah's ambitions had extended beyond strengthening his position at home – he wanted to not only be the top power in the region but, within the space of a decade, the world.

At the climax of the celebrations the shah walked ceremoniously to the grave of Cyrus the Great – the man who had founded an empire, had freed the Jews of Babylon from slavery and had encouraged ethnic diversity and tolerance within his empire – at Pasargadae and, lit up dramatically and turned out beautifully in the middle of the desert, he made a rousing speech in which he declared, 'Cyrus, we have gathered here today at your eternal tomb to tell you to sleep in peace for we are awake.'

The shah had truly arrived on the world stage.

The shah was increasingly thumbing his nose at the West and declaring that he would create in Iran a Great Civilisation, a project that he promised would see all of Iran literate and economically and technologically as advanced as the West in a matter of twelve years. The shah embodied the peculiarly Iranian paradox of being both in awe of the West and at the same time considering himself and his own nation and culture to be far superior. This contradictory mixture of shame, inferiority and superiority has blighted the Iranian sense of self ever since our once great nation fell into backwardness and we saw the newly enlightened West take our crown of achievement and accomplishment. The Iranian psyche had never really recovered from its encounters with a stronger and more advanced Western world, and the machinations that had seen Iran used as a pawn throughout the twentieth century did nothing to heal this damage. The shah, like his subjects, craved acceptance by the West while claiming superiority to it, and with the power that controlling the world's oil supply gave him, he increasingly used his influence to lecture the West on its failings, on the corruption of its morals and social systems and to insist on a new world order. *Time* magazine crowned him 'Emperor of Oil' and warned the world that it had better take him seriously. His star could not have shone brighter.

Since the fifties the shah had insisted that political freedom had to follow economic democracy but though Iran had enjoyed a decade of economic growth, by 1974 he was stating, 'I think that the people of Iran respect their shah in the same way that children of Iranian families respect their fathers.' With no more pretence at democracy, the shah showed his true paternalistic colours. Within Iran the very people that the shah wanted support from – the middle class of young educated Iranians such as my Abbasian uncles and Kurdish cousins – were joining two new political movements: *mojahedeen-e khalgh* and *fedayin-e khalgh* in droves. The educated young people were not interested in being children in an infantile relationship with the head of their country, they wanted to be citizens, equals with a stake in their own land. All those who had been convinced that the shah was, by necessity, a 'transitional authoritarian' until the country had stabilised economically, could see clearly now that he was, in fact, simply authoritarian.

, The decade turned and, in spite of the dissatisfaction with the shah and his regime, my family, like so many other middle-class Iranians, was cushioned from the lack of political freedom by the ease of a life that was sweet and financed by the ready petrodollars pouring in. The shah had led the way in the quadrupling of oil prices that had taken place at the end of 1973 so oil prices were higher than ever before and he was feeling very important, having held the West to ransom.

My own nuclear family was without doubt privileged – we now all travelled every year to London, Europe and America with my father, and my sister and I were being brought up in a cosmopolitan manner. Bagher and Sedi had planned their family carefully and my mother and her other New Iranian friends had determined that their children should be brought up in the child-centric manner that was espoused by Western childcare experts, rather than in the traditional Iranian way that they had been – left to fend for themselves in multitudinous families. Narmin and I not only attended a French Catholic school run by nuns in Tehran (the best schools were those run by Westerners – there was an American school and a German school too), but alongside French lessons and suchlike offered at school, we had a busy weekly round of extracurricular activities such as piano lessons and ballet classes – the latter proving particularly irresistible fodder for my younger *daieys'* jokes. The Abbasian men – my mother's brothers – were all, in their different ways, great comedians and they never tired of making fun of our precocious lifestyle, and our ballet lessons were endlessly mocked by *Daiey* Reza – one of the twins and the Abbasian family's most gifted comic – to the delight of the whole family.

Compared to their upbringing, my sister and I were spoilt, but within this child-centred world that my parents created for us, we were still instilled with traditional values – modesty, restraint, service, chastity, respect for our elders and gracious acceptance of our place at the bottom of the family's hierarchical ladder which was headed by our father, the patriarch, residing over our world with my mother, his queen, majestically at his side.

I remember learning to read, write and do maths all year only to promptly forget how to do all the maths sums in the idyllically long summer holidays that seemed to go on forever. I never forgot the reading and writing because, like my father before me, I had fallen deeply in love with words and could not be parted from my books even at the *sofra*, not even by my mother's threats. Our classrooms all had large pictures of the shah mounted on the wall above the black-board, usually a picture of him looking resplendent in his military garb in front of a blue sky with wispy clouds halo-ing his proud head. The shah wanted to be the father of his people and, in making his image so omnipresent, we grew up almost as familiar with his face as with our own father's.

One day Mehry came to collect me from school and, instead of taking me straight home, she drove me to down-town Tehran, where I followed her into the Café Naderi. This was Tehran's oldest European style café where people sat, drinking coffee and talking with passion, their conver-sations wreathed in whirling cigarette smoke. Mehry, fresh from her day's studies at Tehran University where she was now studying for her MSc, ordered herself a French coffee and me a *café glacé* – a tall white coffee heaped with vanilla ice cream. I sat opposite my pretty, intellectual cousin, her hair

cut in bangs as her mother's had been, and felt unutterably
smart and sophisticated, drinking my sweet coffee and talking
like a grown-up. From then on, Mehry and I went weekly
to Café Naderi where she talked to me as if I was an adult
about the day's intellectual adventures, of her professors and
their foibles, the places in the world she wished to see and of
something called feminism. I learnt to love the taste of coffee
– sweetened as it was for my juvenile taste buds – and longed
to be as free and clever as her when I grew up. She was the
only grown-up woman I knew who was independent and
unmarried – although she must have only been in her late
twenties then – and she was an inspiration to me.

In 1976 the shah celebrated fifty years of the Pahlavi dynasty
and my father his fiftieth birthday. The shah imposed a
new calendar on the country, while my father announced
that we would be moving back to Khuzestan. The Imperial calendar was supposed to date from the reign of Cyrus
the Great and suddenly we went from living in the year
1355/1976 to floundering in the twenty-sixth century in
the year 2535 – regardless of the fact that, a mere five years
before, the shah had celebrated the 2,500th anniversary of
Cyrus' reign. While Iranians attempted to get used to this
new state of affairs my little family started to prepare for
our move back south.

    The next year, in time for the new school year, we were
ensconced in our new life in Ahvaz, the capital of Khuzestan, another hot and humid city built on a river, this time
the River Karun. We lived in a neat and artificially green
Company compound as we had in Abadan, in another Type
A house that was almost identical to the house in Braim. We
had a large garden with a green lawn, the flowers of Khuzestan adding bursts of colour and heady perfume, blowsy
opium poppies growing at will on the lawn and the tallest

date palm tree I had ever seen soaring into the hazy blue
sky, its trunk so straight and fine that I was always afraid that
one of the cruel winds of winter would snap it in half. Fuch-
sia and scarlet bougainvillea tumbled down the walls which
separated the back yard from the front of the house. We had
a vegetable patch in the back for growing our own greens
and a chicken run filled with fluffy yellow chicks. The back
door opened from the kitchen into a walled-off yard which
housed the staff quarters and a traditional outside loo – a hole
in the ground set around with tiles and scrubbed clean every-
day – which I often used when I was too busy playing to go
in to use the *farangi* loo.

I soon started to lead the neighbourhood children on
explorations of the street's rooftops, scaling the bougainvil-
lea-clad wall to land on the flat roofs that linked the houses.
At school I amazed the Khuzestani kids with tales of snow
and, when not playing in the yard, I pulled apart the fluffy
blooms of cotton flowers that grew wild in the playground.
I was still an irrepressible tomboy, my knees permanently
scraped, and Sedi's attempts to free my hair of its knots exasperated her so thoroughly that one day she swept me along
to her hairdresser and had my hair cut as short as convention
would allow.

My hair turned out to be the least of my mother's worries
with me. As a small child I would put anything that intrigued
me, from cigarette butts to my mother's favourite metallic
green Biba stick eyeshadow, into my mouth, and on more
than one occasion I had to have my stomach pumped clear.
Later when I could walk and talk, I needled my mother with
endless questions. Sedigheh, not the most patient of women
at the best of times, usually fobbed me off with an impatient exclamation. Luckily for me there were so many other
people in our lives that there was always an aunt or uncle
around who had time to answer me.

One hot and humid day, as we drove along a country track, I saw an Arab peasant standing on the side of the road, next to him a straggle of little dusty lambs. My heart demanded one of the curly creatures and I begged my mother who decided to indulge me for once. We pulled up in our car and drove away with a tiny white lamb, leaving the bemused Ahwazi man behind on the side of the road, where he resumed his journey to market to sell the remainder. My pet lamb came with many conditions: he was to live outside, sleep at night in the outside loo, and be kept clean. I was to ask permission to touch and caress him. I named him Baboo and would sneak out to see him late at night when everyone else slept, running the risk of being caught by my mother as well as facing the scary cockroaches that swarmed around him. He would get up and approach me, his tail wagging frantically and I would give in to his insistent nuzzling and stay to pet him late into the night.

Khaleh Mina's jasmine-scented yard in Khorramshahr was my second home. The first time I went home with *Khaleh* Mina alone, she came to pick me up from school in her beige VW Beetle and the two of us sang at the top of our voices the radio blasting out the latest hit from Googoosh. Googoosh, with her ever-changing hairstyles, melodious pop songs and pretty round face was the icon of my mother's generation; her songs were always on, her petite figure dancing around on television. She was Iran's first true pop star and she still symbolises the golden age for those who flock to see her concerts in America. *Khaleh* Mina was then still young and voluptuous, in her mid-thirties, her hair piled high and her eyes smudged with black. Her house had a courtyard and a flat roof where, in years to come, we would sit at night, my mother, *Khaleh* Yassi, my sister and myself, under a sky inlaid with stars. My sister and I would refuse to go to bed, drifting into a delicious semi-consciousness while the women chatted, gossiped and laughed and laughed. I had my first drag of the hubbly-bubbly pipe up there on that roof, at the age of five.

At my grandmother's house the family would gather in the two weeks of holidays after Nowruz. During those holidays, Maman-*joon* engaged in all-night card games with her sons and sons-in-law, stopping at nothing to win a game, cheating as often as she thought she could get away with. In her later years, when she was living with Yassi and her family and had nothing left to gamble with, Fatemeh Bibi would keep Yassi's children up half the night playing cards and would bet the washing up.

That summer we took our European trip as usual and before returning to Iran, we visited London. I liked London. On the two summers preceding the revolution, we stayed there for a few weeks in our summer holidays. It was a place of pale sunshine, big green parks and fancy restaurants. I fed the pigeons in Trafalgar Square and petted the goats in the children's section of London Zoo. I twice got lost on its busy streets, wandering along Oxford Street in a daydream and failing to keep my mother in sight until, in a panic, I realised she was nowhere to be seen. Eventually I was found and she was angry, even slapped me once, then burst into hot, remorseful tears, clutching me to her in relief.

The tension that was already present in my mother that summer in London in 1978 only got worse over the coming months, as the demonstrations that had started in January and were now turning into street wars gained momentum. I was eight years old and oblivious to my country's turbulent political problems. We were in London where my father had business; Mehry was also in town studying, and she accompanied us everywhere. More of my parents'

friends than ever were also in London – unbeknown to
me part of the great exodus of the revolution that had
already started – and we were busy. One day, Mehry
arrived at the brown flat in Notting Hill where we were
staying and asked my mother to tune in to an Iranian radio
station. The programme reported on the demonstrations
that had taken over Iran's towns and now spread to the
cities. The radio announcer gave details of a demonstration that would be taking place that afternoon in London,
on Kensington High Street in front of the Bank Melli Iran
– the National Bank of Iran. 'Come on, Sedi,' Mehry said,
her eyes alive with excitement. 'Let's go and see what it's
like.' We had duly taken a bus down Kensington Church
Street, my mother decked out in designer gear, Mehry as
always simply dressed in plain, good clothes, and my sister
and I accompanying them.

The demonstration had been large but quiet – there were
a few police around, the ones called bobbies with their tall
black hats, but they had nothing to do. A whole mêlée of
Iranians were gathered and I remember distinctly the black-
clad women in their plain black coats and black headscarves,
their faces shiny and plain, and the skinny students in their
beige flares, all chanting for freedom and equality.

By the time we got back home to Iran just before my
ninth birthday and the start of the new school year at the end
of September, martial law had been imposed and the great
massacre of Jaleh Square– a turning point in the struggle –
had already taken place. Troops had shot into the massive
crowd and the fatalities numbered hundreds – thousands
according to the revolutionaries. Disgust with the regime
infected everyone – not just those young people who formed
the different factions that were coalescing under Ayatollah
Khomeini's leadership. The father of the nation was being
rejected by his children in a way that had never been seen

before in Iran, the Pahlavi imperial sun in threat of being eclipsed by the crescent moon of Islam.

Soon after we had returned to Iran in September 1978, Mehry, having finished her studies in London, also decided to return. She had a wanderlust that inspired her to buy a car and drive it back across Europe and through Turkey to Iran, a leisurely trip that she calculated would take her a few weeks. Guity had joined her for her last few weeks in London but her parents, not enamoured of the idea of their two single daughters driving themselves across continents, forbade them from doing any such thing. Mehry, with her customary charm, would not be moved and so Behrooz, her younger brother, was duly dispatched to London to fetch his errant sisters. Behrooz was a young father and he had no real desire to leave his little family, his six-year-old son and the wife he had met when a car accident had put him in hospital with an ear hanging off his head. Behrooz lost the ear but he found a wife in Firoozeh, the pretty nurse who was solicitous and kind and who laughed at his jokes. She was not Kurdish and though Sa'adat-*khanoum* would have preferred not to welcome another Persian bride into her family, Firoozeh proved herself to be such a sweet girl, such an obedient and respectful daughter-in-law and such a devoted wife to her son that, after living for several years under the same roof, my *zan-amoo* learnt to love Firoozeh as if she had been a Kurd after all.

Behrooz, mindful of his parents' concerns, went to London where, not only did he not succeed in changing Mehry's mind, but was instead persuaded to join his sisters on the drive back. Their arrival in Iran a few weeks later, full of tales of the beauty of the Alps and the shimmering Italian lakes, was such a relief that my *amoo* and *zan-amoo* forgave them their defiance for the sake of being able to clasp them safely to their breasts.

Martial law was already in force in Tehran and my gentle *amoo* and his formidable wife were happier having their brood close to them, although their blood ran cold every time Mehry, independent and headstrong in her smiling way, went out to the protests. Her friends and colleagues at the University of Tehran had kept her abreast of events while she was in London and, like so many educated women, Mehry was buzzing with excitement, her vision for a new and free Iran seemingly becoming a possibility, and she and so many of her female contemporaries joined the protests that women's rights were presumed to be part of the revolutionary story. She longed to travel and see the world, but she planned to first remake her country before resuming her globetrotting. After all, the world was not going anywhere and there would be plenty of time for roaming after Iran was refashioned.

11

Revolution

JUST AS THE fault lines that ran through the country and converged underneath the wide boulevards of Tehran were apt to shift suddenly, in an instant obliterating villages and settlements, lives and people, mountains and buildings, wiping them out with one heaving sigh from deep within, so the soul of Iran bore the tyranny and bore it until it could bear it no more, and with a pressure built up over years of repression, burst forth in an anger that could no longer be assuaged. Set off by a newspaper article denouncing Khomeini, the terrible wild-eyed fury of the people, so long shoved down and stored up until it had choked them, suddenly found in the simple words of this implacable priest – 'The shah must go' – a release that was so gratifying that once they too opened their mouths to yell what had once been unthinkable they found they could not stop.

The chants became bolder – *Marg bar shah* – Death to the shah – and in the terrible, delicious anger of the protests, the adrenaline accompanying the street battles, the deaths and injuries that followed – the people of Iran found their thirst for venting their fury could not be slaked. With each protest, the troops sent in to control the crowds ended up shooting into the group, violence would follow and there would be fatalities. The dead would be buried and more demonstrations would follow to mark the ritual forty-day period of mourning. Each protest led to more fatalities and more protests, a chain of events that had stitched its way through the fabric of the last few months.

Banks, cinemas, off-licences and other symbols of Western cultural imperialism would be attacked and the soldiers would once again open fire on their own people and more deaths, more funerals, more mourning, more protests and more deaths would follow. This macabre ritual – a sort of gruesome relay game – fed the flames of the people's wrath and spread through the main cities of the country like forest fires, devouring all reason and argument that stood before it, the people already addicted to the heady sense of liberation that came with finally throwing off the yoke of repression. After so many years of being fearful of what they said, where they said it and to whom, the spectre of SAVAK keeping them silent, the protestors were hooked on finally standing in the streets and complaining not just out loud, but at the tops of their voices, in plain terms and slogans that were easy to understand. Their energy united the disparate groups that were now joining together to make each protest bigger, stronger, more difficult to control.

The furies had been unleashed and had taken hold of the soul of the nation. After so many centuries of invasions, battles and conquests, so much blood spilt in the same streets from so many innocent Iranian veins for so many thousands of years, this time it was Iran's own sons and daughters who were wreaking the havoc, running forward to have their blood spilt, preferring death and this new word being bandied about, in reference to the battle at Kerbala of Imam Hossein – martyrdom – to living one moment longer under this regime, this tyranny of the shah, the modern-day Yazid who was oppressing the people and drinking the country's resources in order to bedeck himself and his wife in ermine and furs and strut and pose on the global stage. 'Nothing,' they said, rushing towards death, 'could be worse than this.' They were naïve, they did not know what was to come.

During the holy month of Muharram, Khomeini, already so proficient at using language that the simplest souls could understand, called on Iran to show its opposition to this new Yazid and so, in the processional marches of Ashura, it seemed the whole of Iran came out on to the streets. Two million people converged on Tehran's wide boulevards, the ritual self-flagellation and religious songs joined by revolutionary slogans and chanting. The ayatollah called on Iranians to show their resistance to the decadent monarchy by taking refuge in Islam and, as well as the two days of protests – as the marches of Ashura had become – and their attendant violence and casualties, the populace protested peacefully by praying in public. Suddenly from every rooftop at the hours of the day appointed for prayers, scores of the faithful would bend and straighten and beseech God in unison, an unearthly dance ensemble choreographed from afar by the exiled leader. At night, the streets would echo with two words as the people, again directed by Khomeini – stood on their rooftops and chanted, over and over again, *Allah-o akbar* – God is great. The words echoed through the city under cover of night which shielded them from SAVAK's eyes, and this eerie new sound added to the hum of normal city noises, this beseeching of God, this offering up of prayers for change.

Khomeini was the answer to the prayers of the oppressed, who were already calling him Imam. In a world that was rapidly changing into something the traditional majority of Iran did not recognise, with everything shifting and changing shape, Khomeini's particular brand of nationalism offered what the shah's new world did not: certainty. And the certainty was built on a return to Iran's traditional culture, of which Shiism was a vital part. The shah's brutal oppression of political opposition had left the country with no other viable leaders and Khomeini's long years in exile had kept him untainted by the changes that had swept through the country so quickly. After Saddam Hussein, at the shah's request, removed Khomeini from Iraq (the shah rejected the Iraqi government's offer to have the turbulent priest assassinated), he settled in a suburb of Paris from where, although now many thousands of miles further away from Iran, mass media coverage meant that his message was more available to people in both Iran and the rest of the world than it could have been at home.

The various factions who were clamouring for change – the Marxist groups, the socialist groups, the students, elites and intellectuals – united under Khomeini, seeing in his uniquely austere charisma and ability to communicate with the ordinary people an expedient leader who would, once the *harj-o-marj* – the peculiarly Iranian brand of chaos – was over, quietly step aside and allow those best qualified for the job of running the country to take over. The Western media flocked to Khomeini's headquarters, desperate to understand this new phenomenon. Khomeini, an old man, humble in his robes and turban with an authority in both Islamic jurisprudence and, allegedly, Western philosophy, gave interviews that assured a nervous world that he had no intention of ruling Iran, that the Islamic system of government he proposed would be one based on social justice and freedom of expression, where everyone would be equal.

Far from being a throwback to medieval Islam, Khomeini's ideas were, in fact, radically modern, adapted from young radical Islamic thinkers such as Ali Shariati, who had been frequently arrested and jailed by the shah until he died in 1977. Shariati, educated in Paris like so many young Iranian intellectuals, had synthesised ideas of Marxism – of class war and revolution – with resurgent ideas of Islam and had in the process revitalised Jalal Al-e Ahmad's ideas of *gharbzadegi* – Westoxification. Shariati harmonised his ideas into strains that resonated with Shiism and advocated that Muslims, instead of just waiting for the return of the Twelfth Imam, should instead work to bring about his return – by fighting for social justice – 'Red Shiism'. After Shariati's death in Southampton where he was exiled from Iran – and which his supporters maintained was the work of SAVAK in spite of the British coroner's verdict of a heart attack – Khomeini came to represent the marriage of modern and traditional that Iran was looking for, a modernity that sat more comfortably in this deeply devout society. In his unyielding figure Khomeini managed to embody the two themes that had haunted Iran for nearly a century – tradition (he was a man of God) and modernity (in the Marxist Islam of his followers). With the vitriolic sermons and the uncompromising exterior, Khomeini led the dispossessed and the traditional sections of society, the *bazaaris* with all their money and influence and the passionate young intellectuals with their burning ideas of freedom and equality.

To most of his followers, political philosophy and theory were not what Khomeini was about. He had appeared to lead them out of oppression, of poverty, of exploitation, and, dispatching with reason altogether, they chose instead to believe that he was the manifestation of an eigth-century Shiite prophecy: 'A man will come out of Qom and he will summon the believers to the right path. There will rally to him pieces of iron, not to be shaken by violent winds, unsparing and relying on God.'

For them Khomeini was this man, this unshakeable man with the uncompromising stare whose coming had been foretold. The people of Iran were furious and they were possessed by righteousness. There was a full moon that winter which, it was promised, would bear the face of the Imam Khomeini. His spin machine promised that the moon would show the face of the implacable priest and the people of Iran, in a sort of heinous love with this dark energy that

flowed through their veins, looked up at the moon that night
and saw – actually were sure they saw – the face of the priest
shining down on them.

The next day, *Daiey* Pardis was at work as usual in Ahvaz
and he told me that all around him he could hear the buzz.
'Did you see it?' went the whispers, whipping around the
office. 'Did you see it? The imam's face in the moon?' And
so convinced were those who believed, their faces shone
with such a strange light of zealotry and demented passion,
that Pardis heard even those who still had hold of their reason
hesitantly admit that yes, yes in fact, they too had seen the
face of the imam, they just hadn't been quite sure at first.

'*Besmelah-o rahmane rahim*,' chanted the faithful, and those
who still had their reason had reason enough to sense the
folly of not joining in. Pardis saw many of his beloved friends
and colleagues mutter the *salavat* under their breaths, afraid
to appear at odds with these burning-eyed devotees. A new
energy had been unleashed in Iran and those who first spotted that it was like nothing they had seen before, started to
worry and assess their own positions. Many of those who
still believed in socialist principles, in the equality of man, in
the rights of the workers and the prerogative of self-deter-
mination and self-rule of Iran without the barely disguised
colonialism of foreign powers, they looked about them at the
white-hot energy of these zealots and, preferring not to cross
them, told themselves that for the sake of the revolution that
now surely must come – could no longer be held back, was
roaring towards them like an unstoppable train – they could
let these fearless 'martyrs-in-the-making' take the initiative,
bring down the shah, change the order of things. Then, they
told themselves, reason would prevail and they would step in
to take over, to make new laws and build a new paradise for
all of Iran along socialist, nationalistic and Marxist principles.
And these Iranians who should have stayed upright, who

should have stood firm in their secular principles, instead like my great-grandfather's fabled cypress tree they too bent to the prevailing wind order not to break, and they let the scruffy youth that made up the armies of Khomeini take the country through revolution to even more horror beyond.

The shah, beleaguered and already suffering from the cancer that would soon take his life, prevaricated. On the one hand, he instituted martial law and his troops continued to kill their own people. On the other hand, he tried to mollify the nation by sacking and arresting anyone within reach who had wielded any political power, landing all society's ills squarely on the shoulders of his own ministers. He brought in a new government that made concessions to the protestors, and enacted Islamic laws that were supposed to please the people. He went on television to acknowledge his mistakes and even tried to install himself at the head of the revolution, assuring his people that, like a good father, he had heard their cry of anguish and wanted nothing more than to salve the people's pain. Always so free and easy with that word, the shah himself was the one who, having prepared the ground by promising the people 'revolution' for so many years, now referred to the protests and confrontations as a revolution before anyone else thought to. And so this mighty movement for social justice was now officially a revolution, a force of such electric energy that it lit up the land.

The shah's attempts to conciliate Iran were rejected. It was too little, too late and his children now had the confidence to spurn this bad father of theirs and let him know that what he offered, after so many years of repression and killing, after so many people tortured and destroyed, was simply too late. The masses had found someone else to look up to, another strong man who would lead them to paradise, a better father who would stand firm no matter how strong the gales blew. The elite peeled away from the shah, abandoned him as easily as he had abandoned them, every-one busy bending to the prevailing wind as the shah was himself; the wind was ushering in the era of Khomeini and even those whose aims seemed at odds with the ayatollah's chose to be carried along. Khomeini's peculiar detachment and his great care in making statements meant that, like the moon itself, his was a reflective radiance. The vastly differ-ing factions that he was now leading could all look into the unmoveable face and have reflected back at them what they wanted to see. The socialists, Marxists, communists, liber-als and intellectuals saw someone who could be discarded once the monarchy was overthrown, a simple priest with no desire for a public role, a man of faith, a mystic who was not interested in the minutiae of government. His followers, the Islamists and simple people, saw a saviour. The liberal West-ern media saw a man devoted to his country, his God and his ideals, someone who was leading a revolution for social justice in curious clothes.

The revolution had turned everything upside down and for a while it seemed as though no one dared to think of anything, had no space to imagine anything other than the great happenings that were changing the very shape of every-one's existence. My *khaleh* Yassi, who by now had started her career at IranAir, had chosen this moment to fall in love with a work colleague. The first time I returned to Iran in 1996, *Khaleh* Yassi sought me out and told me, as if still a teenager, about her husband Seini whom I had just met for the first time, about their meeting and courtship in Abadan. Yassi's was the most modern *khastegari* of the family, her husband a boy she met at work in 1978, fell in love with against the backdrop of the revolution and married in the early days of the war with Iraq when they were first refugees in Shiraz. It was clear *Khaleh*

Yassi still adored her husband, she visibly thrilled at everything he said, bestowed liberal caresses and endearments on him and, believing like everyone in the Abbasian family that food equalled love, she fed him to within an inch of his life.

During the revolution itself, Yassi and Seini were caught up in the unrest too. There had been a fire at the Cinema Rex in Abadan, the doors locked deliberately from the outside and the people trapped in the cinema while the building burnt to the ground. It was such a horrific event that it turned everyone in Abadan into a revolutionary – everyone it seems knew someone who had been inside the cinema. The screams of those trapped inside haunted the town for months, and those who had actually heard them could get no peace from the memory of the bloodcurdling anguish of those people as they burnt alive. Even those who did not hear the screams could smell the aroma of the charred burning flesh which was whipped around Abadan by one of those famous winds that could pierce the soul. It seemed to Abadan as if hell had really come to them on earth. *Khaleh* Yassi described it all to me, explaining how the feverish atmosphere of those days had infected her too.

Although Fatemeh Bibi and Mina refused to let Yassi and Seini go to the protests, they slipped out and joined the 10,000 people who marched through Abadan the day after the blaze, protesting that the fire, far from being the work of revolutionaries (although they regularly attacked cinemas) had been engineered by SAVAK – how else had the doors been locked so no one could escape?

And somehow, in the middle of the *harj-o-marj*, Seini one day called around with his mother, first to Fatemeh Bibi's house and then to *Khaleh* Mina's (because he knew that nothing would happen without Mina's blessing) and asked for Yassaman's hand in marriage. Yassi's two mothers concurred with much delight and congratulations, subsequent meetings were set up to agree terms and the lovebirds were free at last to go out together alone, albeit only in strictly portioned chunks of time.

While Abadan burnt and their friends were killed, while the country lit up with the zeal of change and revolution, Yassi and Seini fell in love.

12

Covering Up

W OMEN HAD FARED well under the shah. Although
Iran was still a deeply patriarchal society and sharia-
governed family relations meaning that a man could have
four wives and a woman needed her husband's permission to
travel outside the country, women in Iran had the same rights
as men when it came to education, employment, the protection of the law and political participation; they could hold
property, vote and work as they wished.

The culture was more advanced than the laws in most
cases, and in practice it was unknown for men to take more
than one wife. In 1975 the Family Protection Law had made
it mandatory for a husband to get written permission from
his original wife if he wanted to get married again, had raised
the marriage age for women to eighteen and given them
crucial equal rights in the divorce courts and when it came
to the custody of children – the most progressive such law
in the Middle East. Now these politicised, educated, working women were also clamouring for change from the shah's
repressive regime, some even donning a headscarf or more
elaborate Islamic *hejab* in order to reject what they saw as the
Western objectification of women. Forty years after Reza
Shah's dress reforms had forced them out from under the
veil, Iran's women were now themselves politicising the
Islamic *hejab*.

Mehry would phone us in Ahvaz to report to us on the
protests in Tehran, telling us of the scores of *chador*-clad women

who were now fronting the marches, protecting the men from the gunshots, of the new chants that could be heard: '*Esteghlal, azadi, jomhooriy-e Eslami*' – Independence, Freedom and an Islamic Republic. She was astonished by those of her peers who had taken to wearing headscarves, their faces suddenly clean of make-up, their shoes flat, those radical feminists who were now making this innocent scrap of fabric a political issue. But she told herself, as so many others did, that this was all for the overthrow of the shah, that what was important was the common goal they shared. Afterwards reason would prevail again, but in this moment, whether in miniskirts and false eyelashes or scrub-faced in *chadors*, the women of Iran banded together to join their voices to the demand for the end of the monarchy and the removal of the shah.

At Khomeini's behest, workers all over the country had been holding strikes and in October the oil workers went on strike for over a month, paralysing the national industry. Bagher, who had been promoted to a director of the oil company in January of that year, saw it as his duty to continue working and management, for all the concessions made and wage increases offered, could not prevail on the revolutionaries.

We had returned from our long European trip to a different world. Although my parents tried to protect us from what was going on, the power cuts caused by the strikes and the rushing back from evening visits to beat the curfew had their effect and the violence that had taken the streets burst into the Company compound when three senior managers were shot on their way to work. Soon the many foreign expats working for the consortium were ordered by their respective countries to leave and these *farangis*, our friends, neighbours and parents of our playmates, left literally overnight for Kuwait, their houses abandoned, still filled with all their possessions.

Every day more of our friends would be missing – spirited away by their parents to Paris, LA, London – and after school, we would find ourselves increasingly restricted to playing indoors or in our own garden, the rooftops and streets we had roamed so freely now out of bounds. Our parents told us nothing but we watched the shah addressing us all on television and, unbeknown to me, my beloved younger uncles and Kurdish cousins were all in the revolutionary movement, either as socialist activists or Kurdish separatists who had also been co-opted by Khomeini's promises of more Kurdish autonomy. My *daiey* Pardis was a member – some even said a leader – of the *Komiteh* that was now policing Ahvaz, the revolutionary committees that had sprung up and were taking power, inspired by the way the French Revolution had organised itself so many centuries before.

On the dark, candlelit nights, I would pore over the latest book I was reading, as compelled by Oscar Wilde and Charlie Brown by torchlight as I was by events outside the compound and the wild scenes I saw on the television every night. After school, the neighbourhood kids would gather on the street corner and exchange whatever information we had managed to glean from the adults, who were trying so hard to shelter us from the storm. We heard from the Company staff who worked for our families, tended our gardens and cleaned our houses, that soon they wouldn't have to come to work at all, that Khomeini had said that there would be oil wells spouting black gold in their back yards. I asked my mother about this, thinking she would answer or laugh but instead she grew tense and hushed me, telling me not to talk in front of the staff about anything. What 'anything' meant I didn't know – the people who worked for us were part of our lives and our Arab guards, the driver and couple who cooked and gardened for us were too much enmeshed in our daily life for me to suddenly freeze them out. And so I started to become quietly divorced from the impetuousness of my gregarious personality, started watching what I said and to whom I said it. It was the end of spontaneity and the start of the watchfulness that was to become second nature to me.

Then one day we came home from school to find all the furniture in the front sitting room pushed to one side away from the windows. We started living in the back of the house, moving the television into the back sitting room. What I didn't realise was that a firebomb had been lobbed at our neighbour's house that day and that was why we had retreated. The New Iranian lifestyle, so confident and open and on display, was being defeated, and we withdrew to the part of the house that was protected, that could not be seen by the eyes of the *hasood*. Iran may have seemed to progress but this was proof that it was still the same old Iran where you needed high walls to protect yourself, your family and your life from the invader who could strike at any moment. We had nothing to be ashamed of, but fear taught us to hide and from then on, I gazed out across the scrub dirt of the desert across the wide British-built road from our house, unknowingly towards Iraq, and shuddered with a pervasive feeling of insecurity, of invasion. Fear became part of the daily fabric of life and my constant companion.

What I also didn't know was that there were ugly rumours carrying my father's name on this wind, rumours that he had been named by the mullah from the pulpit and that his name was now nailed to the door of the mosque. In this new world that was so precipitously coming into being, there was a pattern to the assassinations that were adding newly empty houses to the compound – first the victim's name was announced by the *mullah* in the mosque, then it was pinned to the mosque door, and finally the name would be etched on a gravestone in the cemetery.

Bagher took no notice of what he heard, ignored his driver's grumbling about having to come to work when soon he would be able to collect his wages without having to leave his home. It was only when a colleague, newly returned from Europe, phoned him to say that he had been in Paris and that they needed to speak that he took notice. The next day, sitting in his office in Tehran, Bagher had received this colleague who told him that while in Paris, he had gone to pay his respects at Khomeini's rival court. 'Bagher-*jan*,' he warned, 'your name was being bandied about. Is your passport in order? Do you have an exit visa?' When my father had replied no, this man had ordered his driver to take Bagher's passport and get it stamped. As soon as Bagher had his passport back, he returned to Ahvaz where we watched as, on 16 January 1979, the shah and his family left Iran.

The shah packed up his family and departed, just as he had done in 1953. But it was a very different Iran that he was leaving, one of his making, the place where he had managed so successfully to identify his own person with the institution of the monarchy itself that, once he stepped on to that plane in January 1979, supposedly bound for a holiday, his departure not only spelled the end to the brief Pahlavi dynasty but also over two millennia of monarchical rule. The shah, throughout his reign so paranoid about the threat of 'the red and the black' – socialists/communists and the *ulama* – had, as people are apt to do, made his own nightmares come true as a result of his own actions. Unparalleled jubilation followed his departure – millions of people were on the streets giddy with triumph, and the newspapers summed it up the next day when they printed, in towering letters, the simple headline – *Shah raft* – the shah is gone.

A wave of elation swept the country at this immense victory, this historic moment and even us children, locked up in the compound and not allowed to go to school, felt the change in the air.

Things were breaking up, people were leaving or disappearing overnight, we no longer went to school. My mother cried a lot, we had tense meetings with our friends in the yard and, very occasionally, on the rooftop. At night there were more power cuts and I buried myself in books, willing the comforting words to shut out the chaos that had encroached our haven. I knew that with shah gone we were threatened in some way and we all watched the implacable ayatollah come back to Iran, greeted by at least a million jubilant followers, the airport which had been shut exactly to avoid such an eventuality was kept open on this fateful day by airport technicians who had sworn allegiance to the priest.

The next day on the street corner we kids whispered his name to each other, all trying to imitate him, passing around the *chador* I had stolen from my mother's drawer to don as his religious robes, those words he had spoken that had shocked us all so much – *I feel nothing* – always at the back of our minds. We couldn't comprehend that he felt nothing on returning to Iran. Nothing. For all the slogans of the revolution that we had taken to chanting under our breaths on the rare occasions we managed to escape unseen to the roof to hold our own version of the revolutionary demonstrations, this one word had such power that it obliterated everything. He felt nothing and soon, that was what we would all be left with.

It took only ten days after the priest's return for the army and the shah's troops to swear allegiance to him and all the remaining apparatus of the shah's regime to collapse. On his arrival, Khomeini had appointed his own prime minister and provisional government, simply ignoring the government of the shah and, just like that, he took over. The guerrilla forces of the revolution had overrun the army bases, factories, military academies, armouries and the TV station and we gathered that night to watch the revolutionaries display the torture chambers of SAVAK to the nation. Evin, the most notorious prison in the land, always bursting with the shah's political prisoners, its walls thick with the cries of those tortured and killed by SAVAK's agents, was stormed and its prisoners set free in the same way that the Bastille had been during that other revolution half a world away and two centuries before that had served as such inspiration to this revolution. Everyone was adopting an Islamic look now – clean-shaven faces were, along with ties and suits with collars, seen as symbols of Western decadence – and I watched the unshaven revolutionaries as they led the cameras through cell after cell, showing SAVAK's horrors to the country.

We watched it all play out on our television sets in the back room, and the rest of the world watched too. The Iranian revolution – as even Khomeini was still calling it then, before it took on its Islamic shape – was the first revolution that the world had had beamed into their living rooms, and it left one overwhelming image of my country that would remain for the decades to come – one of terrifying rage.

The celebrations and jubilation soon turned into violence. The *Komitehs* which had started out by organising demos and co-ordinating strikes, had taken over from the disintegrating police and militias and were now running the show in every town and every neighbourhood. Comprised at first largely of revolutionaries of all colours, they increasingly took on an Islamic hue after Khomeini's return.

On a rare trip through town with my mother driving the Paykan, I saw what looked like a cavalcade of these militants, heavily armed and riding spluttering motorbikes, unshaven and dressed in black as at Ashura, holding high the black flag of Shiism as they roared through the street. They made me shudder and sink back against the seat – although accustomed to seeing on television these young men who looked so radically different from the smartly suited, clean-shaven men in my own world, it was still a shock to see them in person. Such hungry power emanated from them and the firearms they brandished so carelessly terrified me. My own family who were involved in the revolution were socialists or Kurdish activists, not religious fundamentalists, but increasingly the more reasonable elements and groups that made up the myriad colours of the revolution were being obscured by these men who followed only black.

It didn't take the *Komitehs* long to become drunk on their own power. Heavily armed with weapons take from all the police and military armouries that had been stormed, they took justice into their own hands and the justice they wielded was arbitrary, random and highly personal in nature. The violence began to spread and even Khomeini repeatedly called for calm in the days following the final capitulation of the shah's regime, the official day of the revolution's success commemorated hence as *dah-e fajr* – the tenth day of the new dawn.

The day after his friend's warning, my father had gone to work as usual, the words ringing in his ears. But he could not believe that he, who had done nothing but serve his country's most important industry faithfully for over thirty years, could seriously be in danger. When he arrived at his office, his secretary warned him that a list had been posted on the door with the names of those who would be barred from work should they bother to show up. Bagher's name was on it.

A few hours later my mother answered the telephone at home to one of Bagher's friends who was asking for his whereabouts. When Sedi replied that he was at work as usual, the friend hesitantly told her that he had heard that two senior managers had been arrested by the Revolutionary Committee and she would do well to locate her husband.

Sedi, already living with such a tight grip of panic about her heart, immediately phoned Bagher's office and, when there was no answer, she called *Daiey* Pardis in tears. He reassured her as best he could and promised to come round as soon as he had some information.

A few hours later, my uncle arrived at our front door, pausing to let Bagher enter the house first, deferring in respect to the older man. What happened to my father in those intervening hours we never found out but *Daiey* Pardis stayed with us from then on, refusing to leave us alone and telling us not to leave the house.

Imprisoned within the walls of our own home, I soon grew bored of playing in my room and went to beg my mother to let me go out and pay a visit to my lamb. But my mother, exasperated with me for interrupting their hushed conversation, swiftly dispatched me back to my room with a sharp telling off. Bored and frustrated, I sulked alone until my uncle came and found me. Always so funny and patient, he explained to me that in the next few days we would all be taking a trip to visit Maman-*joon* in Abadan. I was thrilled, little knowing that the journey we were making was to usher my father to safety in Tehran.

Daiey Pardis, after visiting the *Komiteh*, had advised my parents that it would be safer for my father to leave Ahvaz. '*Agha* Mohammadi,' he said, 'this is a small town and it is a mad time. All sorts of people suddenly have power and there is no rule of law, so any petty jealousies or grudges are reason enough for executions and assassinations. Anyone can denounce you as being against the revolution for their own reasons. It is better to just go to Tehran where this kind of madness won't touch you, and let things die down here. Then you can come back.'

My father agreed, the day's experiences having at last impressed on him the danger he was in. He wrote a letter asking for a month's leave from work and *Daiey* Pardis phoned my *khaleh* Yassi at the IranAir office and asked her to book a ticket to Tehran under his name. She confirmed we had a flight for the next day. I knew nothing of these plans being made in whispers, but I was delighted on this strange day to have my fun *daiey* to play with. And play he did. Pardis devoted himself to keeping us children amused, staying with us that night as he would in the months to come.

Restless and bored, I plagued my parents with questions, my endless curiosity not satisfied with their rote replies. Tired, tense and impatient, they flapped me out of the way, telling me nothing. But the pervasive atmosphere of fear had affected my sister and me too and later that night, we both crawled out of bed to find *Daiey* Pardis lying sleepless in the corridor. 'Why are you sleeping here?' I demanded and *Daiey* was clever enough to give me answers that for once, satisfied me and persuaded me that there was some great game afoot. I tucked myself into one side of him, both scared and excited, while my sister tucked herself into the other side and there, embraced by my skinny young uncle whose heart was more loyal to us than to his revolution, we slept in the parquet-floored corridor with a gun under our pillow.

The next day we were taken to Fatemeh Bibi's house in Abadan where *Khaleh* Mina and Maman-*joon* awaited us. I was always happiest when sitting in my grandmother's court-yard pretending to be one of the women helping with the chores of the day, and I waved off my father, *Daiey* Pardis and mother who was driving her Paykan. I cannot remember where they told us they were doing or whether we actually said goodbye to my father or not, but now I realise that they had as little idea as us kids as to whether he would be able to get to Tehran or not.

At the airport, the scene was one of disorder; members of the newly formed Revolutionary Guard (*Pasdaran*) – Khomeini's politicised police force – had orders to let in only actual passengers. But my uncle's revolutionary credentials and lifetime spent in Abadan saw them through – *Daiey* Pardis knew the *Pasdars*, and had been at school or on marches with most of them – and, with much reminiscing and joking, he persuaded them to let all three of them through to the departure lounge. Pardis phoned *Khaleh* Yassi from there and asked her to change the name on his ticket to my father's name and, with no more scares or hold-ups, my father checked in and left for Tehran. Thirty-six years after he had arrived in Khuzestan, the arid land that had given him a career, a wife, children and a loyal extended family, Bagher looked down at the salt marshes for the last time as he flew away to safety.

13

God's Government

M Y FATHER'S ARRIVAL in Tehran was cushioned by our equally devoted Kurdish family. Firooz was there to meet him at the airport and Kaka Ali, one of his sister's sons, installed a Kurdish couple in the house in Darrus ostensibly as housekeepers. In reality they were *peshmarga* – Kurdish guerrilla fighters – armed and ready to protect my father against anyone who might come looking for him. Ali, always addressed by the Kurdish title 'Kaka', was tall and balding like his father and he bore a fierce love of his land and culture. We saw a lot of him as I was growing up and I adored his wry manner and the way he perched me on his shoulders – he was so tall that I got giddy. And now, Kaka Ali whose nationalism was dovetailing with revolutionary aims, used all his revolutionary credentials to protect his uncle.

My mother, sister and I continued to live in Ahvaz, my parents insisting that we should finish the school year, still sure that everything would blow over, that normality would return and, in the way that the shipwrecked cling to any floating scrap, they held on tight to whatever routine they could salvage for us from the wreckage of those times, adamant that our education should not be interrupted.

Every morning we would wake to the news of more disappearances from our street, more neighbours and friends killed in their beds or hauled off to the Revolutionary Committee in the middle of the night, many never to be heard of again. We children continued to stand on the street and exchange any titbits we had found out and we would piece together the puzzle of who had been killed and who had merely gone. We worried constantly about our friends and vied for the best toys of those who were leaving in a hurry, wondering about such important questions as who would get whose dog to look after, what would happen to the shiny bicycle of another. We thought we were smart and sophisticated, but none of us had a clue that these disappearances, these hasty retreats were going to separate us all for ever. With the innocence of children, we waited for the chaos to be over so we could return to our rooftop games and normal lives.

Daiey Pardis stayed with us and, on weekends when we didn't retreat to Maman-*joon*'s house or go to *Khaleh* Mina's, we were joined by Shirin and their son who was so small and perfectly formed that we never called him anything but Koochooloo – Small One. We tended to stay in Ahvaz, my mother not feeling safe enough to leave the house unattended or drive the long dangerous road to Abadan through the scrub desert. Gunshots had replaced the night-time song of the cicadas and in town, *harj-o-marj* had taken over, with the *Komitehs* and Revolutionary Guards, Courts and Councils taking the law into their own rough hands. High on victory and armed to the teeth, these young people were now intoxicated by their own power, by this new order that had put them somehow at the top, and every disgruntled worker, maid, driver or labourer who had a grudge against their bosses could see vengeance served swiftly and mercilessly by merely whispering the words, 'So and so is against the revolution'.

We went to join my father in Tehran for Nowruz at the end of March and, despite being in the city that I loved and in the house I adored, I felt dislocated and sad. As was the custom, we helped clean the house, laid the beds with new sheets and dressed in our new clothes before gathering around the

New Year table. But this year there was little joy in the ritual celebrations to mark the New Year that I ordinarily so loved. The city, while coming to life with bursts of blossoms and the appearance of red goldfish and fragrant hyacinths for the New Year table outside every shop as usual, was in mayhem. There were demonstrations and protests, this new habit of marching out their dissatisfaction was proving hard for the people to quit and the marches were now accompanied by violent looting and even attacks on private property – public property having long been appropriated by whichever group felt it had the most right or the biggest guns.

A national referendum was held at the end of the month to give people the choice of an Islamic Republic – a choice that consisted of one option: Islamic Republic, yes or no. No one knew what that meant, despite the grand speeches and propaganda issuing from Khomeini's people, and when my parents went to vote they found the polling booth surrounded by heavily armed Revolutionary Guards who told them, as they handed out their ballot papers, 'Brother, Sister,' the new Islamic Marxist way that the revolutionaries addressed people, 'please step this way. You know . . .' with a meaningful pause and a hand resting on their guns '. . . how to vote, of course.'

Voting was not secret and everyone's identity cards were stamped and marked as they went in, and my parents were sure that if they voted no, their dissent would be noted and revisited on them in the middle of the night. So they voted yes for a system they neither understood nor wanted, as did the majority of the country.

The result was announced on 1 April 1979: 98 per cent of the country had voted yes. Khomeini, who, despite going back to Qom in the first few days after his arrival, had already broken his promise not to take charge of the country, had a mandate from the people and Iran became the Islamic

Republic of Iran, the calendar yanked back centuries to the Islamic one and Khomeini declared this as 'the first day of God's government'. He was given the title of imam and became the Supreme Leader of Iran, not just our political head but the master also of our souls and spirits.

Women protested, leftists protested, liberals protested – everywhere people took to the streets to demand their rights. In May a protest in Tehran drew 1.5 million people. But Khomeini's regime was unmoveable. The revolution was now an Islamic one and, seeing the killing that had started, the way his followers were ruthlessly eliminating fellow revolutionaries who were not from the Islamic faction, our Supreme Leader, the representative of God on earth, the head of God's government, looked at the killing and, instead of preaching peace and calm as he had just two months ago on his return, issued instead his decree: 'Blood must be spilt'.

The bloodletting took on hideous proportions as the revolution proceeded to eat itself. The socialists, Marxists, Kurdish separatists, intellectuals and liberals who had not already adapted themselves to the new Islamic regime, who hadn't grown their beards and toned down their clothes, hadn't taken to praying in public and showing their faces at the mosque for Friday prayers, were eliminated.

Those same prison cells that the revolutionaries had displayed to us as symbols of the corruption of the shah were filled once again with political prisoners, with people who were 'against' the revolution. Those same instruments of torture were wielded and ad hoc firing squads dispatched thousands who had been summarily 'tried' and found guilty by random Revolutionary Courts. The worst excesses of the shah's repression were back already, only this time the executioners talked a different line and wore different costumes. The killing, the torture and the terror was much worse, and made worse still by the randomness of it all.

The law was becoming a loose, elastic thing, decided by people who until recently had sat fat in their mosques, men who had no education outside the *maktab* and *madresseh*. The class system did not disappear, it was merely replaced by a different structure, one in which your welfare and progress depended on which influential mullah you knew. As a response to the shah's overly centralised systems of governance and administration, the country was now in the hands of local factions making decisions that differed from street to street. In Iran your wellbeing had always depended absolutely on whoever was above you on the social ladder. Now the ladder had been hacked to pieces and reassembled willy-nilly.

My family now seemed to represent the decadence of the shah's regime in the eyes of the revolutionaries, despite our innocence of any actual crime. We were so used to the rule of law, to working within a logical system, but now we were threatened. Our survival was thanks to our extended family, the respect that all the Abbasian children had for their elder brother-in-law whose good fortune in life had extended to them, left them all with jobs and money for clothes, shoes, school and university. My father had been generous, his hand had always been open, and the Abbasians had taken him to their heart. And now my aunts, uncles and Kurdish cousins used all their connections within this random new order to save us from death.

14

Escape

I T WAS JUNE and school was out. My father's months of exile in Tehran had convinced him that he no longer had a future in the oil industry, that things were not about to return to normal and the danger that had lurked around every corner in Ahvaz was also in Tehran. He made the decision that we should leave the country and, unbeknown to me, both my father in Tehran and my mother in Ahvaz were preparing for our departure.

My sister and I thought that we were all going to join my father in Tehran, so we packed our things too. Our hearts were heavy but we were sure that we would be back in the autumn for the new school year. As we climbed into the Paykan for the drive to Abadan, we had no chance to say goodbye to any of our friends; my mother had told us it was better for no one to know what we were doing. We snuck away from our home with nothing but a quick secret hug with Baboo – by now hardly a lamb any longer. A few hours later we pulled up outside my grandmother's house in Abadan. Maman-*joon* shuffled out into the street to greet us, *Khaleh* Mina on her heels, ready to envelop us in jasmine-scented hugs and kisses.

Khaleh Mina was crying and I couldn't understand why until, a few minutes behind us, *Daiey* Mostafa pulled up in his car, packed to the rooftop with cases and visibly buckling under the weight. My mother ran towards him sobbing, holding him tight, thanking him as she washed his face with her tears. It was then I understood that this was more than a summer trip to Tehran, that *Daiey* Mostafa had followed after us with more of our things at some danger to himself, that the small suitcases we had packed for our summer were merely to fool anyone who might see and be spying on our movements. When I saw my mother overwhelmed by emotion, I knew that we had left Ahvaz for good.

I was beside myself all day. I hadn't said goodbye to my friends, to our house, not to anything and my heart could not accept such a thing. I followed my mother around all day – even *Khaleh* Mina could not hold me still – and I heard her making plans to return to Ahvaz the next day to oversee the sale of our remaining possessions. I pleaded with her to take me with her. 'Please, Maman, please take me,' I begged her, tears falling down my face all the while. 'Please, Maman-*jan*, please take me. I will be good, I promise. I just want to say goodbye to Baboo and the Armenians across the way. I won't tell anyone else I swear on the Qur'ăn.' I bargained, I promised and I swore and finally, when my mother's patience was exhausted, she wearily agreed.

That night, with a joyful heart, I helped *Khaleh* Mina and my other aunts and uncles gathered at Maman-*joon*'s that day to unroll the pile of mattresses in the corner of the room and make up the row of bedding we would all sleep on. Exhausted from the emotions of the day and from playing with my cousins in Fatemeh Bibi's courtyard and rooftop, I fell into a deep sleep. When I woke up the next day, my mother was already gone.

When my mother returned late that night, accompanied by *Daiey* Mostafa and wrung out from the day, I flew at her with accusations and recriminations. I had never felt so angry with her before and had certainly never spoken to her like that. Sedi tried to take me in her arms and soothe me, tried to explain that it had been impossible, but I could

not forgive her. She stroked my hair and pretended to have
done all the things I had wanted to do myself – she told
me she had found a good home for Baboo and had said
my goodbyes to the Armenian boys who had been hanging
around asking where Narmin and I were. She brought me
messages from them but it was no consolation and I cried
for days, inconsolable. The first of many cracks had appeared
in my young heart and when, a few days later, I heard that
Baboo had been slaughtered and had made a very tasty meal,
I though I would die of grief. 'You see,' I spat at my mother,
'I knew your friends would do this, that's why I needed to
give Baboo away myself, to someone who would love him,
not eat him.'

Once we were back in Tehran, my parents had more to
worry about than my heartbreak over my lamb's untimely
end. They were busy packing and arguing about the best
course of action, my father was adamant that my mother
should take my sister and me out of the country immediately, leaving him to put his affairs in order, while my
mother wanted us to stay until we could all leave together.
I don't remember much of those days, lost as I was in a sea
of sorrow, but my father obviously prevailed as, before long,
my mother, sister and I boarded a plane bound for Heathrow. I don't remember saying goodbye to all the people
who gathered in the house in Darrus to see us off, but I
know that I still had no idea of the significance of those
farewells. Had I known we were not coming back there is
no way that I could ever have told any of them the things I
would have wished to say. My parents tried to keep things
as normal as possible for our sakes, for the sake of themselves
and for our family, and we were all as breezy as could be
managed.

★　　★　　★

At the airport, where only travellers were allowed, it was pandemonium. Mehrabad airport was bursting with people, anyone who smelt the slightest whiff of danger was leaving, and taking what they could. I was a veteran of Tehran's airport but no matter how busy I had seen it during the Nowruz holidays, I had never seen anything quite like this. There were mêlées of people thronging from every door, those who had tickets and those who had come hoping to find a place on a plane – any plane – heading out of Iran. It was a hot day and the smell of all those bodies rose up and choked me. I remember the rich smell of fear above all else, hovering over us all.

Armed Revolutionary Guards were everywhere and I was scared enough to keep my mouth shut, terrified they would shoot me for being my father's daughter or that they would take my mother away. We clung tightly to her as we watched people being searched for any money they might be trying to smuggle out of the country. I saw a middle-aged man, smartly dressed in a suit and tie, being abused by the Revolutionary Guard who had discovered a false bottom in his briefcase filled with jewels. The man flung the jewels into the face of the young *Pasdar*. '*Ahmagh-e bisho'oor*' – stupid idiot – he screamed at him, spitting out the words. 'Take them, have them, *noosh-e joon* – bon appetit. You are so stupid that you don't realise that you can take all the money and jewellery you want, but I am taking with me the one thing that this country needs now more than any money. My brain. My educated brain.'

We fled for our lives as did thousands of others. My mother, the upright Sedigheh, led us out of our turbulent country with a strength even she had not known she possessed. I did not know what I was doing as I boarded the plane to leave my beloved country and my treasured family but Sedi did, and every step she took rang out with a pain that her heart had never felt before and never fully recovered from. We left our country and our people and yet, along with our tears, we breathed a sigh of relief.

But for us – and for Iran – the most difficult part was just about to begin.

EXILE

Not in the pursuit of pomp and pageant, to this door we have come
For shelter from ill fortune, here we have come.

Hafez, *From Behind the Caravan*

15

London

O N 3 JUNE 1979, Sedi led my sister and I by the hand from the plane at Heathrow. We had been to London before but this time we were arriving as refugees, not wealthy Middle Eastern holidaymakers. We were all nervous and, waiting at immigration while Sedi answered the British officer's questions in the language I did not yet understand, I was almost sick with anxiety that he might refuse us entry, that we would be sent back to Iran to be killed. To my relief we were given leave to stay for three months but that time, and every time the following year that we had to leave and re-enter the country in order to renew our stay, usually flying to somewhere in Europe for a day, I always shifted about guiltily in front of the immigration officer, feeling as if I was on the run, and would be stopped and found out at any moment. To this day, even when wielding my British passport, a knot of apprehension tightens around my belly as I approach immigration. I have still not completely shaken the refugee who is convinced her safety and security is in the hands of the stamp-brandishing officers, but they no longer glance up from my passport as I pass.

'Not in the pursuit of pomp and pageant, to this door we have come/For shelter from ill fortune, here we have come.' Having lost so much in those days, more than I could comprehend, I learnt this verse of Hafez and it has stayed with me. I remember my mother muttering it a lot then, her copy of Hafez well-thumbed as, like most Iranians, in times of trouble she turned to the medieval poet for wisdom.

It turned out that the small brown flat in Notting Hill Gate where we had stayed the summer before belonged to us and my parents had, it seemed, always planned to send us to England eventually, to finish our education. It had been usual among New Iranians like my parents to send their children to the West for their higher education, and we knew many families whose children only visited Iran in the holidays, on leave from their British boarding schools or American universities. Indeed, my parents had decided to move to Ahvaz because the retirement age was lower and they had bought the flat in London so that by the time we finished high school, my father would be able to retire and we could all move to London together. My mother's heart would not allow for the thought of being parted form us for months at a time and my father was more than ready to spend half the year back in the Britain he so admired, coming back to Iran in the school holidays. 'You see,' my parents explained many times in the year to come, 'we would have been going anyway. We just have to do it a few years earlier than planned.' In fact, we left for England a good ten years before they had intended, and in very different circumstances.

The revolution exploded into our lives, everyone's lives, and changed everyone's plans. Arriving in Notting Hill at the age of nine, not understanding at all what was going on, but feeling uprooted from everything I knew, was bewildering. I had always liked London, and here I was again. But the sense of unease that had started in Iran, the simmering of the revolution, the shattering of our world, was hard to shake off, and would haunt me for decades to come. No matter how well I learnt to speak English and how totally I reshaped myself to fit this new world, I would always feel out of place.

We lived in the little brown flat and took long walks in Kensington Gardens every day. My mother made friends with an upright Englishwoman, Angela Baker, who lived in our building and who happened to be an English teacher. She agreed to teach my sister and me English and we started to visit her flat for lessons. As she attempted to communicate with us, I took in the details of her life, especially fascinated by the little fruit bowl that proudly bore one orange, one apple and one banana. Its paucity never failed to surprise me – where were the piles of grapes, the little sweet cucumbers, the cornucopia of different fruits arranged delicately on top of each other? When at the supermarket with my mother I could see other English people doing the same, buying their fruit wrapped in cellophane in ones and twos, and fruit seemed, in late seventies London to only mean oranges, apples and bananas.

Despite the fact that we were living solitary lives, just the three of us, my mother still shopped in the Iranian way, filled her basket with all the varieties of fruit she could find, buying in kilos rather than ones and twos. Before long, she had found Church Street market in Edgware Road where, among the stalls run by Arabs, we could find the large bundles of herbs, big oval watermelons, stacks of white peaches and even, once in a while, pomegranates, sweet lemons and the small sweet cucumbers that we cut into long slices and sprinkled with salt before eating. She found one Iranian shop at the end of Kensington High Street where there were sacks of lemon-roasted pistachio nuts, large roasted almonds, little figs and all the other dried fruit and nuts that always sat mixed in a bowl on our table. In our culture, the day shaped itself around food – breakfasts of flat bread spread with a crumbly white cheese which I loved to mix with sour cherry jam; in the middle of the day a plateful of at least four different sorts of fruit; lunches and dinners of rice and *khoresht*; nuts before dinner;

fruit again in the mid-afternoon and perhaps a mouthful of our traditional ice cream late at night. And throughout the day, permanently brewing on the samovar, a pot of fragrant black tea, drank constantly and flavoured with little sweets made of honey and rose-water that were sprinkled with nuts or made of chickpea or rice flour into little round treats. All meals were accompanied by basketfuls of mixed herbs which we would eat in between mouthfuls, pink radishes and various yoghurt dishes topped by fine, pink rose petals.

The seasons dictated what we ate – in the winter we would stain our faces and fingers with the jewel-like seeds of the pomegranate, the summers would be spent wrestling fresh walnuts out of their hard, green coats, and by September we would gorge ourselves on fresh pistachios which were peeled out of blushing skins to reveal the rose-coloured nut, still soft and tasting of the valleys. In the heat of the summer crescents of watermelon like the half-moon would cool us down, the skins later used to cool hot, itchy insect bites, and we crunched into tart greengages scattered with salt. We smeared our mouths with three different sorts of mulberries and cut sweet lemons into quarters to suck through our teeth. Our land was one of plenty and everything tasted of sunshine and made us giddy with flavour. We used ingredients in our cooking that did not exist in the north of Europe and had names for tastes that do not exist in English. Green apples, bananas and oranges could not compete with the plentiful produce of Iran and ready salted crisps were a poor substitute for the fresh or roasted nuts we consumed so liberally.

My mother kept our *sofra* as Iranian as she could, given what was available to her. In the days before multiculturalism, the ingredients for our feasts were often impossible to find and there was still an austerity in Britain that made food not only meagre but also tasteless and somehow antiseptic.

We made do and tried not to mind too much, not complain too much to Sedi who was, we could see, doing her best.

In Iran, fighting had broken out among leftists and ethnic separatists who realised that Khomeini's rule was not going to be what they had been promised. In Kurdistan something approaching civil war broke out when, in August, Khomeini declared a *jihad* – a holy war – on all those groups who were at odds with his central government, including the Kurdish groups who had helped him come to power. God's government could countenance no opposition and the Revolutionary Courts had become expert in holding trials which were little more than brief preludes to execution. There was no legal representation or proper legal process – the accused had no rights at all and thousands were sent to their deaths. A round, jovial-looking little *mullah*, Ayatollah Khalkhali, became famous for the sheer numbers of those he sentenced to death, and the apparent relish with which he did so. The Hanging Judge was said, at the height of the suppression of Kurdistan, to have dispatched up to sixty Kurds a day.

Men like Khalkhali, whose loyalty was with Islam rather than with Iran, were now in charge. They wanted to tear down Persepolis and denounced Cyrus the Great as a homosexual; Khalkhali even went so far as to go to Persepolis and, in a fiery speech, try to rally people into destroying the ancient ruins themselves. But the Shirazis in the crowd, sentimental to the last and protective of their region's great history and artefacts, managed to disperse the Hanging Judge's band of thugs by pelting them with stones. All around the country, Iran's greatest achievements in art and architecture were being defaced by Islamic fundamentalists who broke into places such as the exquisite Safavid palaces of Esfahan and defaced the magnificent murals that showed women's faces. Women, who finally could see what was coming, took to the streets in their droves, Mehry among them, chanting, 'Without women's liberation, revolution does not make sense.'

But sense had long left the country and the revolution was now an Islamic one, and it was deadly serious about everything. 'There is no fun in Islam,' declared Khomeini and the Iranian character, that has always encompassed both a profound sense of the devout and a love of more earthly delights, simply bent itself to this latest dictate in order to survive. Praying, which in the shah's time had been a private affair, now became a public act of loyalty to the regime, while partying, which previously had been very much on show, moved strictly behind closed doors. The twin strands of the Persian soul merely reknitted in a different way, they did not snap apart.

Still in Iran, my father watched developments and later told me that he slowly realised that this Iran – in which people could be prevailed on to destroy its glorious pre-Islamic past – had no place for him; it wanted nothing of his experience and expertise, or pride in his nationality, in his country. This Iran which had thrown itself willingly into the fire, had faced the guns of the shah's forces to fight for freedom was now ruled by a man who denounced the term 'democracy' as a Western concept and banned its use in Iran. The country's decades-long struggle for democracy had been hijacked by something altogether darker. It wasn't yet clear quite what – Khomeini's main purpose was still not entirely clear, but the signs were not promising.

My father remained in Tehran, his nieces and nephews around to help, Sa'adat-*khanoum* making sure he was well fed, while he arranged for the sale of the house in Darrus and put his passport in order. Every day more names of people who should report for questioning were announced by the Revolutionary Court, and every day Bagher and his devoted kin would scan the newspapers in dread of seeing his name appear. It did not happen in the three months he was in Tehran but they all knew it was a race against time.

Finally, carrying whatever he could and entrusting the rest to Kaka Ali and the Kurdish couple, Bagher bought the only ticket he could find out of the country – bound for Kuwait. The scenes he saw at Mehrabad airport were, if anything, even more chaotic than the one that had greeted us at the beginning of the summer. But, finally, as the plane lifted off the earth which he so loved, Bagher felt a lightening of the fearful burden he had been carrying for the last year.

A few days later, my father's name appeared on the dreaded list.

In August of 1979, just before Bagher left, more than forty newspapers were shut down, leaving only those who would spread the new Islamist message. A constitution was drawn up although any debate on it was declared 'treacherous', and elections for the *majlis* were disregarded when the representative of the Democratic Party of Kurdistan – so active during the revolution in supporting Khomeini – was stopped from taking his seat in parliament. The peculiar new system that makes up the Islamic Republic's current political structure was born, a mixture of democracy, which saw the people voting for members of parliament and the president who had a range of overseeing committees, and the councils appointed by the Supreme Leader, who controlled the judiciary, the military and had the final say on everything. The constitution declared that the Supreme Leader was accountable only to God and so Khomeini became, to all intents and purposes and despite the legislative machinery underneath him, the new ruler of Iran.

Although 'Death to America' was one of the more popular revolutionary chants, the new Islamic regime had been engaged with the US in making rapprochements until America decided to allow the shah to enter the country for cancer treatment. Anti-Americanism now ran riot, the United States not yet forgiven for overthrowing Mossadegh in 1953 and for interfering so heavy-handedly in Iran's affairs ever since. In November 1979, the US Embassy was overrun by a militant Islamic student group who took everyone working there that day hostage. The long siege that obliterated all Iran–US relations began and Khomeini, who had moved to end an earlier storming of the embassy, this time threw his weight behind the hostage-taking, spotting in his canny way that it could be used to unify the people behind him and eliminate opposition to Islamic rule. The priest proved himself a consummate politician, expert at turning events to his own advantage, increasing his own power all the while. He tightened his grip in other ways too, and the purge of the military and even of schools and universities turned into a Cultural Revolution when, in the spring of 1980, universities were closed down so that books could be rewritten and any staff not on message could be dismissed. Piles of books considered un-Islamic were burnt in conflagrations that recalled the Nazis' act of vandalism and intellectual control in the thirties. Many more books, including innocuous classics by Jane Austen, were banned and 20,000 teachers lost their jobs, prompting another mass exodus of Iran's finest brains to the West.

In London we were visited that first year by *Khaleh* Mina, *Daiey* Pardis and his family and Mehry. Their visits made a semblance of normality for us, for although our surroundings were so different, there were at least the same voices talking in the sitting room, the same delicious smells issuing from the tiny kitchen. Shell-shocked and grief-stricken as we were, my family still managed to laugh its way through, my mother and *Khaleh* Mina tricking Shirin into entering a porn shop in Soho and dissolving into floods of laughter when she looked about her and realised the nature of the merchandise that surrounded her. '*Khoda margam bede!*' – May God strike me dead! – Shirin had exclaimed, wide-eyed, slapping one hand on top of the other, while Sedi and Mina clutched at each other, tears of laughter coursing down their faces. 'Who knew such things existed!'

I remember another day, Angela Baker called round to meet my mother's family and, sniffing the unusual smells drifting from the kitchen she had asked what they were cooking. *Khaleh* Mina and my mother had explained that it was *aash*, a sort of broth and detailed the ingredients, adding that it would be missing the mint which was crucial as they had not been able to find any in the supermarket. At that point, Angela Baker clapped her long-fingered hands in delight and said, 'Oh, I have mint from my garden in the country, do let me bring you some.' With that she disappeared downstairs only to reappear a few minutes later with two sprigs of mint, tied prettily together with a fine red ribbon, which she presented proudly to my dumbstruck mother and aunts. They exchanged the subtlest of glances, accepted the gift with much thanks and managed to contain their mirth until the Englishwoman had gone. I had found them all shaking with laughter later, clutching the beautifully presented mint, unable to believe that anyone could imagine that a broth which filled the vast pan on the cooker could be flavoured by two such small sprigs. Everything in our world was so much bigger, larger, more abundant and, in comparison, England seemed so small, pale and controlled.

But England was also safe and we carved a little routine for ourselves. Narmin and I attended a language school which was filled with other Iranian kids, so we learnt little English outside of Angela Baker's flat, and I tried to fill the place left empty by my lamb's death with a new passion for ponies. We found a riding stable behind Hyde Park Corner where Sedi would take me once a week. While I learnt to walk and trot around the park, she retreated to a park bench where, in a rare moment of solitude, unbeknown to me at the time, she would sit down and cry for the full hour I was gone.

The rhythm of the Iranian year continued to beat through me in England where I learnt that early spring does not necessarily warm the days or bring the blossoms out on the trees. Perhaps the thing that unites Iranians above all else is our passion for our New Year, the festival of Nowruz, meaning New Day. In London we went about our lives alongside the millions of other Londoners, there were no coloured lights festooning the streets, no special decorations for the New Year table or rows of goldfish bowls outside the shops along with makeshift tanks of small, sparkling, red fish as there would be in Iran. Despite the indifference of our surroundings, we nonetheless fussed and planned the New Year table, laid it with symbolic objects, the goldfish representing life, coins representing wealth and a mirror representing light – as it has been for thousands of years. Nowruz ties us to our past and for us in London it was always the one inviolable occasion which could not be missed. Although there were no other family members to celebrate with, to go out and visit and wish happy New Year to – a custom that would take most of the two-week holidays that followed Nowruz in Iran – we still gathered around my mother's lavishly laid table at the exact moment of the vernal equinox, even when that meant getting up in the early hours to dress in our new clothes. We circled the table, my father tuning into an Iranian radio station which would pip the last moments till *tahvil-e sal* – the changing of the year – and we watched the goldfish to see if they did indeed jump at the exact moment of the equinox as legend has it that they did. This we would do every year, the four of us in London; we sat down to the traditional meals and we were jolly and full of New Year cheer although, in reality, it threw into relief our isolation. We are proud of this tradition and we regaled our English friends with its meanings and rites, inviting them round to see the table for the two weeks it was on show, but we never invited anyone to join us for the *tahvil-e sal* itself, keeping it close to us, protected, our little piece of Iran in exile.

My parents kept up appearances, even for us, and we never mentioned or talked about what had happened and whether we would go back. My mother had discovered Abba and their melodious songs; 'Winner takes it all,' she would sing mournfully as she moved about the brown flat, the song providing the soundtrack to this depressing period.

My father's permission to stay in the country excluded him from work and so he was at home most of the time. I had never seen him so much and I was rather intimidated by this brooding, silent figure who had been such a vital and busy man in Iran. Just as it extinguished the Pahlavi sun that shone on the nation of Iran, the revolution took away my father's aura of power and strength, and this man who had been the centre of our world, around whom we all orbited and who I was convinced knew everything, was suddenly helpless. He had been unable to protect us and our lives and sitting here in the brown flat in Notting Hill, I realised that we were not only homeless but also helpless. It was the first time in my life that I had brushed up against such concepts and the feeling of defencelessness dug deep.

Every time we had to leave the country to re-enter, and every time in the coming years after we requested asylum that we had to travel to the Home Office in Croydon for interviews and applications, the whole edifice of normality and security that my parents managed to build up around us in England would be shattered, and our official status – as political refugees – made me permanently anxious. Iran was every day being shrouded in more black, more madness and chaos radiating from it, this new Islamic regime unlike anything the world had seen and so easy to fear and loathe. The US Embassy siege did nothing to help the Western world understand Iran and what it was going through, my country seemed to embody just one emotion towards the rest of the world – hate – and there was no room for analysing why Iran and her people had come to this place, whether the West had anything to answer for in helping it reach this dark destination.

All I knew was that now the world was one in which I might, at any moment, have to run for my life. My greatest fear was, if I had to leave England too – which was strange for sure but at least had given us shelter – where else could I possibly go? After growing up in a large family, being cradled throughout my young life by so many loving arms, the extreme dependency I felt on my parents – suddenly the only two people in this country that we belonged to – was very frightening indeed.

The first thing I learned in England was shame. The second was shyness. I was ashamed of my inability to understand what people were saying to me and shamed by the stare of the cashier when I, as a nine-year-old who was large for my age, bought English books in large print, intended for children half my age. On my second day at the language school, having already learnt that no one had the slightest idea how to say my name, when the teacher taking the class register stumbled on a name beginning with 'K', I assumed he was trying to say Kamin and so I raised my hand helpfully and said it for him. It turned out he was butchering some other poor kid's name. He fixed me with a baleful glare, his cropped red hair clashing with his fast-reddening skin. He refused to let me answer to my own name when he came to it, declaring, 'As you clearly don't know your own name, you shall have to go unregistered today.' I sat in the class, rendered nameless, and shame swallowed me up.

As I left school that day, I wet myself on the street and thought I would die of shame until a Spanish girl offered to take me to her house, which was nearby, and let me change so my parents did not have to know. She was called Patrizia and she was my first friend. But even with her I learnt to be quiet, to hold back, to be shy, because it seemed that when I wasn't, I committed some unknown crime that resulted in my humiliation. I had never before met adults who were as cold and unkind as the ones in the supermarket, bookshop, the school or the local library, where I was constantly being told off for touching the books too much. My personality began to warp and I, who had once been so gregarious and chatty, took to spending long hours at the window of the little brown flat silently watching a Scottie dog who was walked by its owner several times a day.

One night my parents told us that our Armenian neighbours from Ahvaz were in London and we were going to have dinner with them. They expected us to be happy but all the joy had gone out of us, so we merely nodded and went back to watching the television. We met them in a restaurant where all of us kids were on our best behaviour and after dinner we all went back to our flat, our parents expecting us all to run to the room my sister and I shared to play as we had done every day in Ahvaz. But we all silently elected to stay with the adults, looking down at our toes and unable to connect, saying nothing. The evening was tense and sad and became deeply awkward. It was already too late, too much had passed and we had all become too self-conscious and too scared of life to leave our parents' sides for even a few minutes. We children had all retreated into the new shells we had acquired and there was no way to reach out. When they left that night, promising to write and stay in touch from whichever corner of the globe they were bound for, we knew we would never see them again. They were relics of a life that was too painful to remember.

Most of all I learnt to be ashamed of my country, this Iran which everyone I encountered in England was so horrified by. My country was now known only as a place of fury and death, the scenes on television reducing our millennia of history and culture to a bunch of wild-eyed youths burning the American flag, chanting slogans against Israel, holding hostage American diplomats in the embassy. I didn't recognise this place, despite having been there so recently, because my Iran was not one of *mullahs* and fundamentalism, but a place of kindness and love, an abundant paradise of mountains and deserts and turquoise seas and trees from which we would pluck cherries as we hiked in the cool hills. My Iran was not populated by implacable priests and unshaven blood-hungry young men, it was the home of Fatemeh Bibi with her shuffling gait, my *khaleh* Mina with her raucous laugh and ready embrace, of Mehry with her ability to bring to life complicated ideas. It was where I had hoards of cousins and playmates and where the language even of strangers was affectionate and poetic.

I could not relate the two Irans to each other and I had no ability to explain to those shocked and disgusted by the actions of the new Islamic regime that this was not Iran, that there was another Iran lurking unseen behind the slogans and the black flags, the Iran I had grown up in and loved so deeply. I could not explain and I could not reconcile the two Irans in my heart. I turned my face away from my country and wished, yearned, to be from anywhere else, to make my skin white and my hair blonde and to fit in. I wanted desperately to be ordinary but for all of my efforts to integrate, my colouring, my name and my accent as I hesitantly spoke English gave me away every time.

Early in 1980, my mother made a return visit to Iran to try to collect the scattered remains of our belongings and, if truth be known, to curl up in the bosom of her family. Standing strong as she had for all of us in London, Sedi allowed herself to fall apart a little on her return to Iran. In Tehran, she visited Bagher's family, my *amoo*, and the formidable Sa'adat-*khanoum*, flanked as always by Guity and Mehry. Bagher's nieces and nephews flocked around her and they sat, night after night, with the vast Persian carpets we had not been able to take with us and tried to work out what to do with them.

In the end, the carpets and my father's large library of books – in both Farsi and English – stayed at *Amoo*'s house in Tehran Pars where, nearly thirty years later, Mehry and Guity were finally forced to sort through them before the old house was razed to the ground. On one of my visits back to Iran, we found them packing up the old house, preparing to move into the heart of the city and into an apartment, unable to resist the growth of Tehran any longer, having capitulated to the insatiable thirst for erecting tower blocks on the site of old houses and villas. They presented me with a handful of my father's books they thought I might like to keep.

My mother was with me on that trip and they started to talk about that visit she had made in 1980, the first after the revolution, so many years ago. At first they all chimed in, recalling their conferences about the fate of our belongings, but eventually my mother's story took over and Mehry, Guity and I sat and listened quietly as my mother recalled those days, for the first time in my hearing. She told us that after a couple of weeks in Tehran, her heart lurching every time she drove by our old house in Darrus – the place behind the walls with a rose garden and swimming pools in which her daughters had learnt to swim – she kissed Bagher's brother's family goodbye and boarded a flight to Abadan.

Back in Abadan she had retreated to Fatemeh Bibi's house and found that suddenly she didn't much want to get out of bed. Fatemeh Bibi had let her be for a while, allowed the family to come and buzz around her. Mina had come to stay too, leaving Busheiry to his own devices and throwing a mattress on the floor next to Sedi's so they could talk all night, Sedi crying all those tears that had been unshed in London, and then falling asleep in her sister's arms when the tears exhausted her. Pardis and Shirin had brought little Cyrus to cheer her up from Ahvaz on the weekends, and all her other brothers and sisters had fluttered around her like ministering angels. She had found, after some time of this, after those noisy family meals gathered around the *sofra* in Fatemeh Bibi's courtyard (for it was now late spring), that she was beginning to feel better.

Fatemeh Bibi watched this and she let her daughter be, she let her pour out her heart to Mina and Pardis and Shirin and let her hear them tell her of what they had seen in the year that she had been gone, the arrests, the disappearances, the blood being spilt every day in the name of this revolution that was supposed to bring justice to the people. 'Sedi-*joon*, *bavaret nemishe*, you won't believe it,' Shirin confided. 'But now, if you say something your cleaning lady doesn't like, she goes to the *Komiteh* and reports you. And tomorrow they turn up and arrest you for being against the revolution.'

'It's true,' Mina agreed. 'No one now dares say to anyone, *bala cheshmet abroo* – there are eyebrows above your eyes – in case they offend someone and they get reported.'

'And think, Pardis was even the head of the *Komiteh* in Ahvaz at the beginning . . .' Shirin stopped. 'Well, you know, *azizam*. But now everything has broken down. We don't know who's who or what's what any more.'

But for all the horrors she was hearing, Sedi could not believe that anything could be worse than being stuck in London so far away from her family. Loneliness was new to her – even when she had lived in Tehran, there had been Mehry and Guity, my *amoo* and his wife, and Mina, Fatemeh Bibi, Yassaman, all of them, had come to stay for months on end, and she had visited Abadan regularly. There had been no real distance between them, she saw that now. How far she had thought herself from them then, just a few hundred miles away in Tehran! Now, thousands of miles stretched between them and the rapidly devaluing *toman* meant that soon no one would be able to afford to come and see her. And all the time, this unknowable ideology that had taken over the country looked like it may be there to stay for at least a little longer.

But with us, her daughters, away at boarding school, she was bereft in London and she kept talking of staying, of making her home back in Iran. 'The girls can come back in their holidays,' she said brightly, 'and I am sure all this will blow over soon and Bagher will be able to come back.'

She saw Pardis and Shirin exchange glances.

'OK, let's say this isn't over soon,' she assented. 'But surely it won't be long before they realise that Bagher is innocent of whatever it is they think he has done. He has done nothing but serve his country for the last thirty years. He never took a backhander, he wasn't corrupt, he wasn't a politician . . . what could they possibly want with him?'

Pardis took her hands. 'Sedi-*joon*,' he said with infinite gentleness, 'Sedi-*joon*, just after he left, Bagher's name appeared on a list of people who should present themselves to the Revolutionary Court.' He stopped to light a cigarette and dragged deeply on it; Sedi had not known, Bagher had managed to protect her from this piece of information. 'Sedi-*joon*, *azizam*, *jigaram*, do you not know what that means?

Not many people who have had to present themselves to the Revolutionary Court have ever reappeared. And Bagher is not here. Well, that means they will want him even more, he will be an even bigger prize.'

Sedi was deflated. She had no idea what to think. There was no logic, no possible reason, everything in her wanted to cry out – he had done nothing wrong and so he should be safe. But she had seen enough of the revolution, had felt enough of the charged and dangerous atmosphere on the streets on the rare occasions she now went out to know that this Iran was one she did not understand. It was governed by things other than a logic she could comprehend. But still she dithered and drew out her visit on excuses and none of her brothers or her sisters pushed her to decide, glad as they were to have her back among them. And they gathered every night together and they laughed and sang and spent all night confiding in each other. Mina always stayed and sometimes some of the others did too, and they would throw down a row of mattresses and lie together as they had when they were children, and laugh and tease each other into the night.

It was Fatemeh Bibi who decided it. One day, after Sedi had been there a month, she called her daughter to come and help her clean some herbs in the courtyard. The others were out and she had engineered a rare moment with Sedi alone. As they sat cross-legged on the carpet and sorted through the bundles of herbs, throwing out little stones, plucking out the yellowing leaves, chatting about the quality of the produce in the bazaar these days, Fatemeh Bibi quietly regarded her daughter.

'And when do you plan to see your children again, *be salaamati*?' she asked, her green eyes fixed on Sedi's face.

'Maman-*jan*, I don't know. They are at school and, well, they are probably settled and happy . . .' Sedi knew she was lying to herself as a guilty vision of my sister and me in floods of tears at the airport crossed her mind. But she was always good at seeing what she wanted to, and she pushed the image away.

'Sedigheh, listen to me.' Fatemeh Bibi spoke in the low voice that Sedi knew to take seriously. 'Sedigheh, this is *harj-o-marj*. It is not going to get better, it is going to get worse. Trust me, I have seen a lot more of life than you. Your husband is not safe here and your place is with him and your children.'

'But Maman—'

'Listen to me, Sedigheh-*joonam*.' Fatemeh Bibi softened her tone but carried on regardless. 'My daughter, listen to me. This is *harj-o-marj*, and there is going to be a war, at least here in Khuzestan. I can feel it. You are a mother and a wife. Your place is with your family.'

'But you are my family.' Sedi was crying now.

Fatemeh Bibi got up, hands pressing on her knees to raise herself, and crossed over to squat by her daughter, taking her head in her hands.

'They are your family, my girl. You are a wife and a mother and you are their family. And there is going to be a war. This is no place for you. You must go back to England.'

And she sat by her daughter and stroked her hair and let her sob until Sedi's breathing calmed and became softer.

Three days later my mother returned to London. She did not go back to Iran or see her family again for fifteen years.

16

An English Boarding School

ONE AUTUMN DAY in 1980 we drove to a picturesque East Sussex village to start school at Wadhurst College. For my parents it was to be the beginning of the legendary British education they had so keenly anticipated, an education that would make us ready for a new life, as my father's years at Birmingham had transformed him. What none of us knew was that we were no longer rooted enough in our own culture for the change to be anything other than a transfiguration. After all, Khomeini had come along to start changing the soil in which our roots grew even before we left. Hadn't he dug up the earth in which we thrived and condemned the nutrients that fed our beings as unhealthy, corrupt and un-Islamic?

After a two-hour drive from London, we arrived in the village of Wadhurst where my parents dropped off first my sister and then me at our respective boarding houses. My sister entered Wadhurst College at secondary level while I, starting at the bottom of the school, entered Beech Hill, the junior house. Wadhurst College was a Church of England school with a strongly evangelical flavour, a favoured repository of the children of Christian missionaries – the sort of people who at the other end of the century had taken their Christian zeal to the Iranian province of Azerbaijan and set up mission schools, had helped educate Iranians and had even joined the forces of the Constitutional Revolution at the same time that the original Abbasian family had migrated from Baku to join the revolutionary movement.

Arriving at the school, I was shown up to my dormitory. I clung to my mother but the minutes passed in a blur and suddenly I was alone, stunned. My brain was working hard at trying to take in this new world with its schedules for bathing, eating, waking and sleeping; there were even timetables for praying and writing letters to parents – life was neatly segmented so that there was little time that was left free for us to let our minds – and hands – drift in ungodly ways.

Soon we were herded into the dining room, a plain room at the front of the house looking out over rolling lawns. We were all given set places, and that first night I was sitting on the table of Miss Pottinger, the Deputy Head of House, a woman who exemplified the type of teacher to be found living-in at the school; unmarried women of indeterminate age with solidly set hair in a style still favoured by the queen, all committed Christians of the old school, their lives revolving around the Church and the Christian calendar in a way that actually, had I paused to think about it, was quite similar to the rhythm of life in my grandmother's house which pulsated with the beat of Shiite festivals, commemorating the births and deaths of our various imams.

But our religious festivals, whether they were based in mourning or celebration, all came with a flurry of activity and life force. They involved giant pots of thick soups full of beans and herbs bubbling on gas hobs out in the courtyard, the women staying up all night to stir, muttering prayers over the food to fill it with blessings while giggling in asides as they told their dirty jokes, folding into the *aash* their humour and energy, their hopes and devotion to the divine before taking the food to mosques strung bright with coloured lights and busy with human traffic to distribute it to the poor and anyone else who wanted it. In comparison, the religion practised by these women seemed as dry to me as they appeared themselves.

Sitting neatly at the head of the table, her hands folded in her lap, Miss Pottinger quietly bowed her head as grace was said, and I silently copied everything that she did while trying to absorb the peculiar rules of meal times. The food was of a sort I had never experienced before: powdered soup for starters, some kind of reconstituted protein and two veg for mains and usually tinned fruit or packet crumble with congealing custard for dessert. It was a world away from the fresh Iranian meals that I was used to. Instead of handfuls of fresh herbs to accompany the main meal, now there were watery vegetables that had been boiled out of all recognition (perhaps a merciful fate for rubbery tinned carrots and peas), and instead of baskets piled high with fruit, tinned peaches or pineapples would have to suffice. Here at Miss Pottinger's table there was no choice about the food on offer, our only allowed preference was for portion sizes, and the rule was for plates to be cleaned.

All this I learnt that first night and, being naturally eager to please, well-mannered by upbringing and dazed by my situation, I kept my mouth shut and reached the end of that first meal without incident. Later, after our introduction to Beech Hill and its ways, I retired to my dormitory where I got ready for bed, washed my face and teeth in the draughty washroom with its row of sinks and slid into my bottom bunk bed as early as I was allowed. I was the only one without a menagerie of soft toys – in Iran our toys were for playing with during the day and at night we simply went to bed, there were no soft bears or fluffy wool dogs to cosy up to. I didn't really understand this custom and the nearest approximation of it that I could bring to mind was when I used to sneak out of our house in Ahvaz late at night to go and cuddle my Baboo in the yard.

I didn't say anything and, as the other girls flounced around bouncing on each other's beds, I wormed my way into my bed and lay as flat and still as possible and finally let the tears fall silently down my face.

The morning brought no relief to my mortification and every day, from the moment we were woken by a loud bell until the moment I slid back into bed, I was trapped in a sort of nightmare world where nothing made any sense. I was careful not to be the first at anything so I could follow the other girls' leads. I had my first bath that second night – I had never filled a tub with water and lain down in it and to my Iranian sensibility, our culture so conscious of bodily hygiene and fond of elaborate showers, it seemed the filthiest of habits to soak in water you had just washed in. I didn't say this to anyone, I would never have dreamed of being so rude as to point out that something they all so clearly thought was normal was in fact disgusting. But no one extended the same courtesy to me and so many of my Iranian ways and habits were frowned on as transgressions that I soon learnt to abandon them in order to save myself from the teachers' frowns.

The first days passed and somehow I made it to Friday evening. I almost choked with relief when I saw my mother. Back at home in the brown flat, no matter how much I begged my parents not to send me back, they counselled me to be brave and think of the education I would get, of how good my English would become and how well I would fit in. I was silently furious at their decision – helplessness was now becoming the distinguishing feature of life after Iran but I still found it hard to capitulate.

The following Sunday there were no brave faces for me. I sobbed and clung on to my mother and dramatically begged her not to go. She settled me in my dorm and helped me unpack all the new things I had returned with, including a white furry

toy Scottie dog with long white fur and a tartan ribbon around
its neck, chosen by me (from Harrods, of course) in honour of
the dog I had spent the first year of my life in England watching from the window. I threw it on my bed, uninterested,
although my mother scolded me for that. But I was interested
in nothing other than persuading my mother not to leave me
in that house, with its squeaky floorboards and the awful smell
of its inedible cooking, its pale green walls and unsympathetic
spinsters. Despite my entreaties she left, promising to phone
me later that night when she got back to London even though
phone calls were against the rules.

Eventually my overwhelming sadness carried me downstairs where I knocked on the door of the staff sitting room to
beg a bemused Miss Pottinger to let me ring my mother, tears
coursing down my face as I pleaded with her. The answer
was an implacable no, though she tried to be kind about it,
promising me that if my mother rang as promised she would
come upstairs and tell me all about their conversation.

Finally I gave up and dragged my unwilling feet back up
to my dormitory. I was accompanied by Miss Pottinger who
turned to another girl idling by her bed and suggested to her
that I could use some company. I lay disconsolately in my
bed, depressed beyond reason, feeling totally abandoned, and
this girl came and sat on the floor by my bed. With some
instinctual wisdom beyond her ten years, she started to talk
to me, picking up my new Scottie dog and asking his name
and his history, as if he were a real animal. I slowly began to
answer her, and as we talked, I grew calmer. Together we
worked out a story for Scottie and I learnt to cuddle the toy
and treat it as if it was a thing made of flesh with the ability
to love me. I cherished the girl then, for reaching out and
pulling me out of my loneliness and grief. She was called Jane
and she became my best friend.

*   *   *

On Friday afternoons we were allowed to pick a book from the assortment that weighed down the bookcase in the back corner of the classroom and sit quietly and do nothing but read for pleasure. That double period every week was my haven, an hour and twenty minutes in which I was freed from the intense vigilance to nuance and form that preoccupied me. Those Friday afternoons were spent lost instead in books, in words and pictures that demanded nothing of me other than my imagination, unshackled and borderless. Books transcended everything and my love of stories made my imagination the only place that was safe, unchanging and consistent.

Buoyed one day by a reading session, I had taken part in a conversation in class between our form teacher and some of the other girls and had confessed that my birthday was the following week. The next Wednesday, after lunch, one of my classmates, already the lucky recipient of a nickname – Frog – led me up to the dorm ostensibly to ask me something, and then insistently led me back down to the common room a few minutes later. Her peculiar behaviour didn't alert me to what was coming next. As we opened the door, I saw, standing in front of me, a crowd of all the other Beech Hillites. Frog skipped off ahead of me and everyone started to sing *Happy Birthday*.

Standing alone in the middle of this circle formed by all my housemates, I stared, my hand covering my open mouth, slowly turning around to take in the fact that everyone from the house was there and that they really were singing *Happy Birthday* to me. When they finished, they cheered and clapped and I blinked back tears and, for the first time since leaving Iran, I smiled unreservedly.

After choking in the smog of fear, confusion and mortification that had polluted my life for the last year and three months, I suddenly felt able to breathe. Here, at last, was kindness.

That was the moment when I drew a veil over the past and, like a refugee stumbling gratefully over a longed-for border, I set my face towards this new world, determined to fashion myself perfectly to it. From then on I stopped speaking Farsi and refused to speak to my relations when they rang us. I rejected everything about my country and remade myself as an English girl.

17

War is Coming

FATEMEH BIBI HAD known the war would come, this she always told me every time I went back. She told me years later that although her sons and daughters listened feverishly to short-wave radios, tuned into the television, scoured the papers to try to fathom what was happening, she just felt it inside her. It was hard to know what was really going on, they complained, this new regime had taken over the media with extreme proficiency – this was the media age after all – and they were good at slogans, at propaganda, at feverish revolutionary pronouncements dripping in populist rejoinders and socialism wrapped up in a Shia Islamic package. It was therefore nearly impossible to decipher what might actually be happening through this spin, even for those in Iran who had always been good at decoding propaganda of some form or other to get at least a gist of the truth.

But it mattered not what the news said or failed to say, Fatameh Bibi could feel it was coming. She told me that sometimes, at the fish market by the lazy waters of the Shatt, she stood out among the scribes who had their carbon papers and typewriters and plain paper set out neatly on their tables, ready to help those illiterates who needed letters written – despite the shah's reforms, and his father's, most people in Iran still could not read or write. She gazed out over the river, beyond the boats docked and those sailing gently by, some with the triangular sail of the dhow, others powered by engines spewing diesel fumes, spluttering like smokers at

the end of their lives, and her eye raked the other shore.
Iraq. There it was, looking so much the same, innocuous, the
shore covered by lofty date palms, fecund and sun-drenched
just like Khuzestan. Her mother was buried there, as Abbas
had promised.

She would look around at the ethnic Arabs who were part
of Iran but preserved their tribes, their sheikhs, their own
dress and customs – and called Khuzestan Arabestan. She,
and other Fars people like her, had dwelt happily with the
Iranian Arabs for years and while it was true they didn't mix,
there hadn't been any trouble. Would these people, these
women with their tattooed faces and black, sleeved *chadors*,
the men in their *abayas* and headdresses, would they, as it was
rumoured, turn against their Farsi neighbours and join the
Iraqis to fight? Maman-*joon* had heard the rumours and she
wondered if they were really sending out signals in the night
to their Iraqi brethren on the other side of the river, letting
them know when would be a good moment to attack?

'*Naneh*,' she would say, pointing a crooked finger.
'Remember I have never liked war, I was born into one and
and I have lived through enough.' She didn't think she could
face another war. 'You know,' she would usually break off,
'that just before the war was when I got my first great-grandchild!'

Parivash's eldest son, Alireza, Maman-*joon*'s first grand-
child, had recently been married to Shahnaz, a modest young
girl that Parivash and Jahanzadeh had picked for their eldest
son, small and round-faced with a pretty smile, and around
the end of the summer of 1980, she was delivered of a baby
girl. Shahnaz was pious and she called her daughter Maryam,
and Maryam, born on the eve of the war with Iraq and one
year after the revolution, always had a special bond with
Maman-*joon*.

*   *   *

While I was busy trying to severe the ties that bound me to my homeland, Iraqi forces were preparing to invade my country. In escalating skirmishes that started the devastation of Khuzestan, Iraq disputed the border between the two countries – set at a certain water level in the Shatt al-Arab – and the ancient enmity between Arab and Iranian was reignited. Fuelled by a historic disagreement over land, old racial resentment that stretched back to the Arab invasion of Iran in the seventh century and fanned by Western powers who did not want to see a revolutionary Iran spread its Shiite zeal across the Middle East, soon modern armies with modern methods of mass slaughter were rolled in to solve a historic problem that had been made worse by modern nationhood and the map-drawing skills of the superpowers.

On 22 September 1980, four days after my new friends had sprung on me my birthday surprise, Iraqi forces invaded Iran. One month later the Iraqi army reached Abadan, the place of my birth, the town where my parents fell in love and were married, the Paris of Iran with its oil refinery and Fargilisi patois, where my grandfather had created himself and built a house in which he had waited eagerly for Fatemeh Bibi to return after her trips away, the town that transformed my father into a New Iranian and where my aunts and uncles had wooed and been wooed, had fallen in love and strolled by the river – Abadan was besieged by a hostile army.

In Abadan my family had laughed and danced and fought, had celebrated and mourned and wept and made love. Abadan, where my grandfather Abbas was buried and my aunts, uncles, sister and I were born, its children made up of its dust and its humidity, of its flowing river and towering palms. Our Abadan where my father was trained and where he, in a moment quite beyond design, collided with history and found his vocation for life. From Abbas' opium deals to Bagher's oil deals, from the marriage of Fatemeh Bibi to the

unknown Abbas to the union of my parents after a year long
love story, Abadan had been part of us and we had been part
of it now for more than sixty years, the dust and the blood
mixed together to shape us into a family.

On 24 October, Khorramshahr – then Iran's largest port
– also fell to the Iraqis. My great-grandparents' first home
in Khuzestan was in Khorramshahr and it was still home to
many of their descendents, including my precious *Khaleh*
Mina on whose roof I had spent so many blissful summer
nights. Our little corner of the world, the place from which
our roots sprung, was now occupied by Iraqi forces and, for
the next eight years, would be the scene of carnage so savage
that Khorramshahr became known as *khunistan*, the land of
blood. During the two-year Iraqi foray into Khuzestan, 1.5
million people were made refugees in their own country.
Among them were my family.

On that first trip back to Iran, my lasting impression was of how
much the war with Iraq had affected both sides of my family.
It had already been over for eight years by then but I could still
feel its presence everywhere. Everyone I spoke to mentioned it
in conversation – there was no getting away from it.

In Tehran Pars, Mehry's younger brother, the jovial
Behrooz, who had grown round as a laughing buddha,
slapped his prodigious belly and said, 'We all got fat in the
war. They closed the mountains, you know, we couldn't
walk there any more.'

When the fighting reached the cities and Tehran was
suffering daily bombings, all the trekking paths through the
mountains had been closed. My family found their movements restricted not only by the new laws of the regime,
which made going out a 'war of nerves' according to my
cousins, they were enclosed also by the curfews and restric-
tion that 'the war of the cities' brought.

In Shiraz, Maman-*joon* and *Khaleh* Mina told me the story of how they left Khuzestan. It was early in October and the Iraqis had still not reached Abadan but they were on their way. The inhabitants of Abadan were leaving in droves, pouring out of the city like a plague of locusts, commandeering any transport available. Petrol was in short supply and the few planes still flying were so overbooked that even Yassaman with her job at IranAir could not get tickets for her family.

Fatemeh Bibi had grown obstinate into the bargain. She had maintained there was nowhere for them to go. Her mind had roamed over the children she had living in Abadan, Khorramshahr, Ahvaz, and her brothers' children too, all with their own families, their numbers legion, too many to count and certainly too many to move. It was impossible to contemplate and though they all begged her to pack up her house and prepare to leave, Fatemeh Bibi went about her daily routine as best she could and refused to budge.

'*Naneh*, this is my home,' she was just that morning telling Mina who had rung her to reiterate the request. '*Naneh*, where will we go? No, I am staying put, *ghorbonet beram*. Anyway, the Iraqis probably won't make it this far, look how fiercely our boys are fighting them. And then we will have got up and left for what? Just so people can come and steal our things? No.'

But Mina had a bad feeling that day. Something in her was worried, her belly was pickling and, despite her own fear of the Iraqis and the dangerous road to Abadan, she got into the sand-coloured Paykan that had replaced her Beetle a few years before, and drove from Khorramshahr to her mother's house in Abadan.

She found Fatemeh Bibi shuffling round the courtyard. The weather was just becoming clement, it was the time of year that they would start to think about moving their mattresses indoors to sleep. 'Maman!' she demanded shrilly,

'*Alo*! Maman what are you doing? The whole world is running for their lives and you are here, *ghorbonetam*, pickling fruit, *engar na-engar* as if nothing is happening. *Bejomb*, move!'

As they stood and argued in the courtyard – Fatemeh Bibi and Mina always bickered, it was their favourite method of communication – the sound of planes flying overhead buzzed closer. And closer. Before either woman had worked out whether they were the Iraqi planes or the Iranian ones they usually heard, or had time to feel the fear that had haunted them for the last few weeks since Iraq had crossed the border, an almighty bang pierced the air and they were both thrown to the ground, the sound of windows shattering all they heard as they landed, winded, on the courtyard floor. An age seemed to pass in which they both struggled for breath. Then, a high-pitched scream, the sound of sirens and everywhere around them crashed waves of wailing. A bomb! A bomb in Abadan itself! And not just a bomb but one that had clearly hit nearby.

Mina, as consciousness dawned on her, looked over to Fatemeh Bibi from whom, she realised, the scream was coming. She picked herself up and ran to her mother. 'Maman! Maman-*jan*, *khak bar saram*, are you hurt?'

Fatemeh Bibi lay on the ground, screaming and muttering, 'Her step was unlucky then and it is unlucky now.' Mina's presence obviously reminded her of the terrible world war and how it had arrived so soon after the birth of her daughter. But Mina was pulling her up, examining her, clutching her to her breast, crying and wailing too, from relief that her mother seemed to be all right and also from the immense fear that now engulfed her. She chivvied Fatemeh Bibi through the house and into her car. Everywhere was strewn with broken glass from the windows that had blown in. Fatemeh Bibi said nothing as Mina drove them away, careering through the devastation all around them, and spirited her away to her house in Khorramshahr and to safety.

There the two women clung to each other, only letting go to take sips of the hot, sweet tea Busheiry had made them. When they revived a little, Mina grabbed the phone and started to call all her siblings, to check that they were OK and to reassure them that their mother was unhurt. 'Do you need anything from the house, Maman-*jan*?' Mina asked her, the receiver cradled against her ear. 'Mostafa is going to go to your house and bring your things.'

'My photos,' cried Fatemeh Bibi. It was all she could say so Mina instructed her younger brother to grab some of their mother's clothes, find her handbag and her identity papers and bring them over. 'And Mossy-*joon*, bring her photo albums will you – she keeps crying for them. May your hands be blessed.'

Mostafa arrived a few hours later with a bag in which were thrown whatever of his mother's possessions he could grab and under his arm were the stack of her photo albums, her most precious belongings apart from the gold that she wore in her ears and around her wrists.

In the next few days, the women wandered about Mina's spotless house in a daze. Fatemeh Bibi, never given to much reflection, had recovered from the shock, but Mina had instead slumped into a trance. She wandered dazed, uninterested in even getting dressed in the mornings. The shock of war had terrorised her and she had become a shadow of herself. For one more week she wandered lost in herself until one day Yassaman rushed in.

'Mina, *bejomb*, move! Seini has found a bus – a bus, I tell you! – and he has managed to fill it with petrol. I don't know how but . . .' Yassaman paused, a smile crinkling her face. '*Be khoda*, Mina, I don't know how that man does it, he is so amazing . . . Anyway,' shaking herself out of her reverie of love for her fiancé, she went on, 'Mina, *bejomb*. He is on his way now and there is no time to lose. They say the Iraqis are only a few days away, our boys can't hold them off that much longer. Come on! Get Clark Gable. Get packing. Just bring essentials, we will be able to come back for our things later, *inshallah*! They are picking us up in half an hour.'

Mina couldn't care but Busheiry, who was home from work that day worrying about his wife and his *ameh* Fatemeh Bibi, threw a few things in a bag for them knowing there would not be much room for luggage. When the bus arrived, Yassaman made Mina put a coat on over her dressing gown and, still wearing her slippers, she was guided her into the truck by the handsome Seini.

The bus was already filled with the wives and children of my various uncles, not to mention Fatemeh Bibi's nieces and their children, and the noise of the kids revived Mina as soon as she got on the bus. They drove to Ahvaz, pausing long enough to pick up Shirin and little Cyrus, and Seini drove and drove, heading north to another part of Khuzestan not yet threatened by the Iraqis, to the house of a distant relation.

They stayed in that house for a few days while their men came and joined them when they could. All of my uncles worked for the Company and it was so important that the oil industry should continue running and producing the oil that was going to finance this war that they were forbidden from leaving their posts. The best they could do was reassure their wives and confused children. Those days and night were terrifying, but as always when the clan was together, the children played and the women cackled, despite their circumstances, unable to stop themselves from telling stories and teasing each other. Slowly people started to make arrangements. Fatemeh Bibi's nieces went to Tehran to join their husbands' families and the day Abadan was besieged by

Saddam's army, Seini reappeared again with the same bus and they started the long drive east across the great desert to Shiraz, where Parivash had begged them to come to her for shelter.

The next day Khorramshahr fell to the Iraqis. Mina was never to live in her spick and span house again.

The first real act of God's government (as it called itself) when it had settled down in 1980 was to repeal the Family Protection Law of 1975, taking away the rights that women had won. The legal marriage age for women plummeted to nine and soon high-ranking women were banned from continuing in office. With the country in chaos, the administration in tatters, towns and cities being run by tightly localised networks of armed vigilantes killing who they pleased and taking whatever house and lands they fancied from their rightful owners, God's government had decided that the most urgent matter it had to deal with was the rights of women in the divorce courts and the legal age of marriage for girls. The issue of Islamic *hejab* was discussed, but as yet the women of Iran were not ready to capitulate.

The war proved very useful for the new Islamic regime. As nationalistic as Iranians are, such a bald-faced incursion into their territory could not be countenanced and everyone united under the government to fight the Iraqis. What Khomeini had not been able to achieve in the early days of his rule – such as the enforced veiling of Iran's gutsy women – was now ushered in among a raft of measures that tightened the Islamists' grip on the nation. Opponents were wiped out and any protest or dissent was labelled a threat to national security, an act of treachery against the nation, and ruthlessly repressed. The jails were groaning with political prisoners once more and the executioners were kept busy dispatching yet more souls to that other world.

For the first two years of the war, the regime also sent its troops into Kurdistan to quell the rebels that had taken over many of the major towns, bombing first Sanandaj then Saqqez and anywhere else that had been taken by the *peshmergas* intent on establishing an autonomous state. Ten thousand Kurds were killed by firing squad alone, the executioners hardly having time to break for lunch or tea, the only respites from the gunshots coming at the times for prayer. Morality police roamed the streets of Iran checking on the appropriate dress for women and among their ranks were many black-*chadored* women, so keen to keep their 'sisters' in check that they were even said to hide razor blades in the sponges they used to wipe made-up faces clean.

In Tehran Pars my *amoo's* house was filled with our extended family from Kurdistan, fleeing the fighting in their homeland and flocking to safety like a flight of exotic birds, decked out in their long colourful robes. Mehry, who had protested so vehemently against the veiling, covered her head with a scrap of the flimsiest fabric in order to be allowed to enter work. In those early days, she later told me, she and her female colleagues would leave their scarves unknotted, shaking their hair free as soon as they entered the building, the fragments of fabric dancing to the ground in a pile of chiffon and cotton as they stepped lightly away.

Soon they were stopped even from this small act of rebellion and the only acceptable uniform for working women who did not don the *chador* became a long, loose black coat reaching almost to the ground, topped off with something called a *maghna'eh* – a sort of black wimple that was elasticated around the back of the head and cupped the whole head and under the chin, with no danger of sliding off or allowing a stray hair to escape. Soon, Mehry told me, it became easier to comply than to face the endless harassment that not doing so entailed and so every day she left her house, filled with her multi-coloured cousins, and stepped out into the day shrouded in black. They wore black, she told me, 'because we were mourning the death of our freedom'.

Colour had been bled from my land as had so many other pleasures, and Iran became a country of monochrome. Music and dancing were banned and all that could be heard above the din of the car horns and roar of planes flying overhead was the insistent and regular call to prayer and the mournful notes of religious songs invoking the glories of martyrdom.

In London I had fallen in love with British pop music. Something about the beats and rhythms, the careful coiffeurs (this was the early eighties after all) and the plaintive sometimes untuneful melodies captured me and soon I was living for my Saturday afternoon visits to the local record shop where I would pull out the allowance I had saved to buy a seven-inch single. Each weekend I bought a record and a copy of *Smash Hits*, a music magazine that gave me another world to be part of. I would pore over the reprinted lyrics of hit songs, learning them by heart, and the features with their in-jokes and irreverent attitude planted in me the seed of my love for magazines and pop-culture journalism. At school where television was strictly forbidden, we were allowed on alternate Thursdays to watch *Top of the Pops*, and I would excitedly spend all the homework time beforehand wondering which pop groups would be on and which videos I could sing along to. My greatest ambition was to be a pop star.

Despite my unhappy beginnings at boarding school, over the next few years I settled in and thrived. I shared my mother's love of singing and at school I joined all the choirs and even sang solos in church. I wrote the school magazine and headed up the school debating team. I knew by then that if I didn't get my big break as a pop star I would happily settle for journalism and I even managed to get myself two weeks' work experience at the local newspaper – a heady fortnight of chasing police cars through the village and grappling with typewriters back at the office. Once released from boarding school and studying for my A levels in London, there was the lively underground of nightclubs blaring out the new beats of hip-hop and rap to be discovered. Every Friday and Saturday night, dressed in Levi 501s and a shiny bomber jacket like a fifties American teenager, my friends and I were at the front of every new hip nightclub queue.

At the same time, my cousin Ebby was at the front line, fighting for Iran along the border with Iraq, at Khuzestan's notorious no-man's-land called Shalamcheh which had once been an oasis of palm trees but was laid waste by the war. Ebby was *Daiey* Shapour's son and had been my favourite running companion in the dusty back alleys of Abadan. He was just a few years older than me, but while I saved my money for my ever-growing record collection and lost myself in the dark thumping nightclubs of London, he was lying in rat-infested trenches near the border, the dark night thumping to the rhythm of guns and artillery fire. Ebby was not my only cousin to be conscripted to the war, but he was the only one who fought on the front line, spending the two last years of the war in the border areas.

Saddam Hussein's decision to invade my country was intended to exploit Iran's post-revolutionary vulnerability, as well as allay fears that Iran's new Shia leadership would upset Iraq's delicate Sunni-Shia balance and exploit Iraq's geostrategic weaknesses – Iraq's only access to the Persian Gulf is via the Shatt al-Arab. The historic animosity between the two countries had only worsened with Ayatollah Khomeini's ascent to power in 1979 and his vow to avenge Iraqi Shia victims of Baathist repression. Baghdad planned a swift victory, expecting the native population of ethnic Arabs living in Khuzestan to rise against the new Islamic regime. Saddam also knew that despite the Shah's stockpiled arsenal of the latest weapons, Iran had just executed or lost to exile all its top military personnel – some 12,000 senior officers were purged during the revolution, a purge that only stopped with Iraq's invasion. The Iranian air force was only able to fly half of its aircraft by the start of the war. The Revolutionary Guard was led by clerics with little or no military experience and often armed only with light infantry weapons and Molotov cocktails.

But the Arab minority remained loyal to Iran and the war dragged on for eight long years, the longest war of the last century, a war in which trench warfare was seen for the first time since the First World War and a heinous cocktail of chemical weapons was used by Iraq in combat operations for the first time ever, in direct contravention of international law. This was allowed to pass unpunished by a world which wanted to castigate this frightening new Islamic Republic, no matter that it was not the aggressor.

What Saddam underestimated was the passion of his opponents for their land alongside the strength of Khomeini's ideology and propaganda – and the usefulness of war in helping the regime entrench itself in power. Iraqi forces were repulsed from Abadan by a small unit aided by its fierce inhabitants – including my *daieys* – and Khorramshahr was only captured after a house-to-house fight so brutal that it earned the town its bloody nickname of *khunistan*. Seven thousand Iranians died or were seriously wounded in the battle for Khorramshahr.

Another unforeseen factor was the *Basij*, the people's militia, the force Ayatollah Khomeini called the 'Army of Twenty Million'. The regime used aggressive recruiting techniques, particularly in mosques and schools in lower income urban and rural areas. Iranian television broadcast round-the-clock pictures of young men – boys – with their red *Basij* headbands and guns, telling viewers how wonderful it was to be a soldier for Islam. Women were shown declaring pride that their sons had died martyrs for the cause. By the end of November 1980, some 200,000 new *Pasdars* were sent to the front, accompanied by the *Basij*, troops so ideologically committed that some carried their own shrouds in expectation of impending martyrdom along with plastic keys worn around their necks – issued by the regime for entry to paradise.

In July 1982, after two years of fighting and after Iraq had been repulsed from Iranian soil and Saddam proposed a ceasefire, the clerics instead decided they would not stop until they had taken Baghdad. Iran launched Operation Ramadan on Iraqi territory, near Basra. Although Basra was within range of Iranian artillery, the clergy – who had taken charge of operations earlier that year – used human-wave attacks against the city in one of the biggest land battles since 1945. Ranging in age from boys of only nine to men over fifty, these eager soldiers swept over minefields and fortifications to clear safe paths for the tanks, using their own bodies and sacrificing their own lives to explode the mines. Chanting *Allah-o akbar*, these ecstatic young soldiers for Islam were so fired up with zeal – and many said drugged into such a state – that terrified Iraqi soldiers trembled with fear and tried to run away from their stations.

It was my cousin Ebby who described these human-wave attacks to me, when we met again as adults. I saw Ebby just once; when I first returned, he had come to Shiraz to visit us and when he had walked into *Khaleh* Mina's tiny flat, it was as if my *daiey* Shapour had come to life in front of me. After leaving Iran in 1979, I never saw *Daiey* Shapour again. He survived the war working in Abadan, but he didn't survive the sudden death of his seventeen-year-old son Abbas (named, of course, after our grandfather) in a car accident. After that he got cancer and literally wasted away. *Khaleh* Mina once told me that Abadan had never seen anything like Shapour's funeral, '*Vaaay*, it was like a national holiday, Kamin-*joon*. We couldn't cope with the crowds who came to give their condolences to Ashraf-*khanoum* and Maman-*joon*. We were like slaves in the kitchen making sure the *sholeh zard* and *halva* didn't run out.'

But Ebby's face, unlike my uncle's, was stamped with hardship. That night we sat up late, fogging the room with the smoke of our cigarettes. Ebby was in his thirties, no longer the snotty-nosed kid of my memories but a man with a family and a job. He told me about the war and that he still had nightmares about his time in Shalamcheh: the chanting, the horror of the attacks, of seeing the children running towards Iraqi tanks in waves, their white shrouds flapping behind them.

'There were the Iraqis, large men you know, much bigger than us, and they had the latest arms, brand-new Kalashnikovs, shiny tanks.' Ebby took a deep drag of his cigarette. 'There were bigger powers against us – the West was standing behind Iraq, giving them weapons – and we were so disorganised and poor.' He shook his head, the deeply etched lines dragging down his mouth testifying that he saw no glory in this. 'In the end, it was just stalemate.' He advised me to go and see Shalamcheh with a bitter laugh, 'It's still full of trenches and burnt-out tanks. It's mined to hell but they are making it a tourist attraction now, well, you know, a place of pilgrimage for all the martyrs . . .'

Ebby was still living in Abadan but he wanted to leave. Since the war two members of our family had died of cancer and Ebby fretted about the water, the soil, the health of his children; his brow was never unfurrowed. It was sadly clear to me that he was one of Iran's growing army of heroin addicts. In the morning Ebby kissed me fondly as we said goodbye, pasting on a wide smile for my benefit, but I am still haunted by his hollow eyes.

The war claimed a million casualties before it was over, and still more over the years that followed.

18

Displaced

IN THE EARLY 1980s, Shiraz, capital of the province of
Fars – the cradle of the Persian race – saw its numbers
swelling with refugees every day. This beautiful city, with its
gardens and poets and famously romantic inhabitants, could
hardly cope with the Khuzestanis arriving in droves every day.
Shiraz, where the grape was transmuted into wine long before
being transported to the soils of Australia and California,
long before Iran became the teetotal Islamic Republic, was
now struggling to feed and house the shell-shocked refugees
thronging there. Luckily for my family, *Khaleh* Parivash had a
large house and she turned over the top storey to her siblings
and their families. They were overcrowded and tempers were
short, but at night, when they threw down a row of mattresses
on the floor to sleep side by side, Parivash would come up
and join them and they would gossip into the night like they
had as children. But before too long, the rations that Parivash
was eeking out to feed them fell short and the tension that
sprang from so many families piled in together overflowed.
As good as the Abbasians are at loving, they are even better
at fighting and when the men visited from Abadan on the
weekends, exhausted and wrung out with working every day
in a war zone, they found their women caught in their own
private wars.

The government had set up refugee reception areas in
the cities and eventually all the refugees were registered
and given ration books and accommodation. Yassaman and

her fiancé had been officially transferred to Shiraz to work and the Company provided them both with rooms in the airline's hotel – the Homa, the smartest in town. Mina's very sensibility was insulted by the idea of moving into a refugee camp – '*Akhe,* Kamin-*joon*,' she explained to me years later. 'Your *daiey* Shapour insisted on taking his family there, but they were awful places, and we counselled him against it. But you know Ashraf-*khanoum*, well, it was her idea and you know she had a different, er, culture to us . . .' So Mina went with Yassaman to the Hotel Homa, and she insisted on being accompanied by Shirin and Cyrus, and of course Bush-eiry came too. In the suite provided by IranAir, Yassaman made a temporary home for her sister and her brother's wife, and they were relieved and happy to be in such comfortable, relatively luxurious lodgings.

Somehow a letter reached us in England at this time, bearing the news of *Khaleh* Yassaman's marriage, along with two photos of the happy couple. It was not so long since we had left Iran, perhaps two years, but *Khaleh* Yassi already looked different from the girl I had known. Her once-straight hair was now styled back in flicks, her eyebrows, once so bushy, were narrow and long, and she was wearing scarlet lipstick. My mother framed both these pictures and put them on a side table in the sitting room. For Sedi it was the first time she had not been present at the wedding of one of her siblings, and this impossible separation that she endured, unable even to visit her country for her sister's wedding in these days of war and the Islamic Republic, sat heavy on her heart. She was relieved at least to see signs that her family were not just unsettled and in despair, but going on with their lives, falling in love, marrying, celebrating. But the evidence that life went on without her saddened her as much as the pictures gladdened her, and the reality of our exile hit her with a thud.

Khaleh Mina told me the story of how, in those early days of war and displacement, the first thing they had done was plan Yassaman and Seini's wedding. Mina, Shirin and Fatemeh Bibi set about spiriting up a beautiful *sofra aghd* from their pooled rations, dieting for weeks so that could spend their rations buying the symbolic sweets for the *sofra*. They found Yassaman a white dress with tiers of lace falling to the floor and a delicate net to cover her head, and she was dispatched as was customary on the morning of the wedding to the beauty parlour.

Seini wore a dark brown suit and looked so handsome sitting at the top of the *sofra* that *Khaleh* Yassi told me years later, with a wink, that she thought her heart would stop. Sitting under the canopy of netting held at each corner by a female member of the family, Mina rubbing over the top the two large sugar cones, the two of them grinned at each other as the mullah asked the customary questions. Finally they were married and the two lovebirds fed each other honey from their fingertips and Seini gave Yassi gifts of gold and eventually, after much celebration and posing for photos and eating of *shirin polo* – the rice dish sweetened with sugar syrup and layered with orange zest, slivers of green pistachio nuts and saffron-infused chicken – Yassi and Seini retired to their first home together, a modest double room in the Hotel Homa in refugee-stricken Shiraz.

That first year in Shiraz was tough for my family. The Shirazis were growing impatient with the new mouths they had to feed, with their city being overrun by destitute Khuzestanis, and they started to grumble. Shirin, whose worry for her husband Pardis knew no bounds, found herself fighting in the ration queues with the Shirazis when she heard them complaining about the refugees. When she heard them wonder out loud what a war that was being fought over in

Khuzestan had to do with them, her blood boiled and she gave them all a tongue-lashing which struck the whole queue dumb. 'You should be welcoming us,' she screamed. 'Our men are fighting for you too and all you can do is begrudge us a piece of bread, when we have lost everything. *Tof be roo'etoon*, I spit in your faces, *khejalat bekeshin*, you should be ashamed of yourselves.' With that she had resolved to leave Shiraz and join her husband back in Abadan just as soon as she could. 'He needed me,' she explained to me simply many years later, 'and I was busy, I was the only woman in Abadan. I had all the men to cook for! Everyone had sent their wives away. They couldn't fight a war on an empty stomach.'

New Year came round and Shiraz burst into flower. After a winter that was colder than any of my Khuzestani family had ever known, Shiraz's spring garb was so beautiful that even their war-ravaged eyes could only behold the blossoms and flowers in wonder. The town was filled with orange trees and the blossom that now bloomed on every tree sent out a scent so sweet, so heady, that their senses reeled. Mina, Shirin and Yassaman, drinking in the all-pervading aroma of the flowers, scrabbled around town to lay the best Nowruz table they could manage. They did their best to have fun, as Shirin told me later, 'Oh, how we laughed. Those days were difficult but we tried to be happy.'

Laughing became a little easier when one day Mina discovered her friend Haydeh was also in Shiraz. Haydeh's husband, being a military man, had been in and out of jail since the revolution, but now that his services were needed in the war, he had been restored to his rank and he had moved his family too to Shiraz. The two women resumed their daily coffee drinking routine, joined by Haydeh's mother, Maman Doh, and it was on a tip from Haydeh that *Khaleh* Mina got her new apartment. One day she had rung Mina excitedly. '*Khanoum* Busheiry, they are holding lotteries for new apartments that are being built,' she had explained. 'You should see what you can get, you are homeless after all.'

It was around this time in 1981 that a law requiring every woman over the age of nine to comply with the Islamic *hejab* was passed and, since there was a war and since the Islamic regime now had a firm grip on power, Iran's women could no longer refuse. Protests were no longer countenanced and all dissent was labelled not just un-Islamic but also against national security, against the war effort and against all those being martyred for the cause every day. Soon women were shrouded in black and the Revolutionary Guard enforced the law. *Khaleh* Mina told me how one day, going about her business in Shiraz accompanied by Busheiry, clad in a long, loose coat and with a black headscarf knotted at her chin, cursing the outfit in the heat, she was stopped by one such *Pasdar*, who told her in no uncertain terms that she was failing in her *hejab* and that she should go home and change immediately. Mina looked down – she was wearing open-toed sandals and her long, painted toenails could clearly be seen.

'*Khahar*, sister,' he said, not looking her in the eye as was the proper Islamic way, 'you can wear those shoes but you should be wearing thick black socks. I can see your ankles and your toes and that is forbidden.'

My *khaleh* Mina, always so elegant, always so polite and so effusive with her courtesies, suddenly snapped. Who was this boy who was young enough to be her son? How dare he tell her what to wear, she who had lost everything, her precious home filled with all her household goods. She heard her own voice rising to a shout as she told him in no uncertain terms that she was a refugee and had nothing, that she had only narrowly escaped death by the grace of God and that, having survived all that, having complied with the dress regulations as best as she could, she was certainly not going to spend her meagre rations on socks so she could sweat even more. 'If it is such a problem for you to see my ankles and my toes,' I imagined her pulling herself upright, 'then may I suggest, *baradar* – brother – that you simply don't look.'

There were punishments for such things and women had been carted off to the *Komiteh* and flogged for less. Busheiry who, much to her exasperation, was always with Mina these days, stepped forward as if he really was Clark Gable and, pulling his wife away, explained to the astonished *Pasdar* that they were displaced, they were traumatised, they were upset and yes, of course she would comply, he would take her to the *bazaar* right away. Regaining his authority a little, the *Pasdar* looked down at the dapper little man with his Bryl-creemed hair and pencil-thin moustache and waved them on, muttering, '*Baradar*, you should control your wife. You are the man after all, and the boss of her.'

The *Pasdar* probably heard Busheiry chuckle at that as he led Mina away.

By the time Khorramshahr was liberated in 1982, little was left of Mina's house. The windows had been shattered and everything inside it had been looted. There was a huge family of Khuzestani Arabs squatting inside and their goats were roaming the courtyard. With a heavy heart, Mina accepted that she could not go back there and put her name down for the lottery for a new housing estate being built on the edge of Shiraz. When she found out that she had won a one-bed apartment the size of her living room in Khorramshahr, she had already learnt to be grateful for what fortune had decided to bestow on her. Once the buildings were complete, she and Busheiry moved into their new home and Mina set about rebuilding her life.

Yassaman and Seini had rented an apartment in town and *Khaleh* Yassi had already given birth to a baby girl, one of the first generation of my new cousins, members of a huge club – the children of the revolution – who were born around that time. Khomeini had urged the people to procreate, to create armies for Islam, knowing that in order to strengthen and spread his ideology he needed numbers more than anything else. With the withdrawal of the family planning facilities that were available in the shah's time, and despite the vast numbers who had fled the country and the even greater numbers being mowed down daily by the war, Iran's population exploded. The war had now come to the cities and Shirazis who had been so sceptical of the war's threat were now getting used to nightly blackouts and bomb shelters, as they were in Tehran and other cities.

Life had started to settle for my family. Shirin had decided that she would rather be in Abadan with her husband despite the war, and she had scooped up Koochooloo and they had moved back home to Khuzestan. Everyone else, including Fatemeh Bibi, stayed in Shiraz. She had been living in the Hotel Homa with Mina and Yassi and now she moved with Yassi into the small downtown flat she rented for her growing family. There, apart from the regular journeys she made to visit her other children, Maman-*joon* stayed until her dying day, moving only when Yassi and Seini moved to a bigger apartment, Yassi's children her last true great loves. She never tried to move back to Abadan and the house that had held the heart of the Abbasian family was lost.

Haydeh bought a rambling house just a few minutes away from Mina's new apartment. Here the women learnt to live with not only the war, but also the regime which was now interested not just in what they wore outside the house, but also what they did inside it. Haydeh, who refused to give up her social life, had many parties that were raided and was carted off to prison overnight and more than once was fined and threatened with flogging for being caught in mixed

company and playing music. The punishments for drinking alcohol or even being found with some in the house
were heavy, but none of this stopped Iranians from doing as
they wished. They brewed liquor at home and learnt who
to pay off to have their parties ignored. Ideological though
the morality police were, they were fond of money, and the
war and its attendant economic hardship meant everyone
had a price. Nonetheless, the intrusion and sense of invasion
followed the women home every day and they had to learn
to live with the constant lack of safety that had become their
reality, with these new laws from which they were not even
safe inside their own homes.

The horrors of the Iran–Iraq war burst their way through
my teenage Western concerns when *Daiey* Pardis and Shirin
came to stay with us on their way to make a new life in
North America. I didn't really want to hear anything about
the war, but I loved my uncle and his small, sweet wife, and
so I sat at my mother's *sofra* night after night and listened to
them tell their story.

Shirin told us that she and Pardis had decided, after endur-
ing six years of war, that they could not stay for the sake of
their children. She had an exquisite little girl now, Nazanin –
the delicate one – whom I sat cuddling as Shirin talked. Cyrus
was growing up and she had noticed that, although he tried
to be brave during the air raids and bombings, every time
there was a loud noise, he would make as if to run, his eyes
searching out the nearest table that could be propped against
the wall and crawled under for shelter. He was in secondary school now and he often came home and told them that
the teachers had asked them if their parents prayed, if they
spoke well or badly of Imam Khomeini and whether they
supported the war. They knew they could trust Koochooloo
to say what was expedient but it sat heavy on her heart that

her little boy was being used to spy on his parents, that he had to learn duplicity and dissembling at such a young age. But the day he had come home to report on the *mullahs* that had visited the school and spoken so passionately of the glories of war, of the honour of fighting for your country, of the way that martyrdom guaranteed entry into paradise, that day was the day she and Pardis had decided the line had been crossed. It was too much to recruit children for their unholy war, this war which should have finished four years ago when the Iraqis had been chased from Khuzestan but which had ground relentlessly on. And knowing that the children would be used in human-wave attacks, used to walk over minefields, giving their lives for Khomeini, brainwashed into thinking that it was sweeter to die, to reach that place beyond death than to live. '*Va!*' she exclaimed to herself, still unable to believe such things were going on all around her. The regime had made life difficult but she was still sure that life was for living and no amount of promises of paradise could convince her otherwise. Cyrus was coming to an age when, if the war dragged on as it seemed it would, he would soon be drafted to the front and she and Pardis owed their children a life. They loved Iran and everyone they cherished was there in Khuzestan, but Iran was now in love with blood, with mourning, with death. It seemed the only thing their land now offered was for their children to die and they were not prepared for that. They would have to go to another place where they could be sure that life, not death, was their inalienable right.

She had explained to us that in Iran now people were too scared to say anything to anyone that could be misconstrued and avoided conversation with casual acquaintances, shunned the sorts of interactions that had always made going about daily chores so pleasurable. The obligatory head-scarf made it impossible to swing your hair as you ran your errands. She had seen so much in those last few years in Iran – with the war and the reverberations of the revolution that seemed to go on and on, the way it had changed society and people, her friends even, but one brief visit from one of the Islamic brothers still haunted her. He had walked into her garden, opened the gate and let himself in as if it was not her house but his, not her private property but common land, as if he had a right to everything that he beheld, and a person could no longer have any entitlement to privacy of any sort, whether made of bricks and mud and water or made of beliefs and ideas and thoughts, the old customs of courtesy and manners swept away by this new regime. He had told her, bold as you like, 'Sister, it is better that you cover yourself. A *chador* would be best.'

She had been heavily pregnant, the baby was pressing on her bladder and she was hot and uncomfortable. The doctor had told her to walk as much as she could and she was doing just that, in the privacy of her own garden. She could hardly control herself. She nearly swore at him, but forbore, merely pointing out that she was in her own house and perhaps he had failed to notice that she was heavily pregnant. He had repeated his request, his eyes averted so pointedly that she thought, *Maybe he doesn't see that I am pregnant? Maybe these new men, these Basijis, these young boys burning with zealotry for God are so obsessed with the shine on our hair, the turn of our ankles, the line of our necks that they see nothing else, not even the walls of our houses. Not even that we too are human and deserving of some peace and quiet.* Just to be left alone, that was what she wanted. She had wanted to scream at him, 'Ever since you people came you have been obsessed with us women, covering us up, shutting us away. "Wear this, don't do that, look like this, don't look like that." Just leave us alone, can't you, just, in the name of God, leave me alone to be pregnant in my own garden.'

But no matter what she said to him, he insisted that she needed to cover herself. In the end she stopped arguing and from then on, she paced about in the house, confined to the hallway, chafing at the confinement. Now her garden no longer felt like the sanctuary it had always been, and the vulnerability she felt as a woman on the streets of this newly Islamic state had snaked its way into her home. Now the only chance she had of rebuilding her home, now that even the walls could no longer keep them safe, was to build a new life in another land.

Khomeini finally accepted a ceasefire in 1988 when he could no longer refute the fact that his war was bankrupting the country. The cost was estimated by Iranian officials to be $300 billion – money that the illiterate masses that had brought the ayatollah to power had expected to come to them, not be spent on killing their young. The priest who had wanted to topple Saddam and raise the black flag of Shiism over Baghdad's domes, 'drank the cup of poison' and accepted the truce and finally hostilities between the two neighbours ceased. Khomeini was unrepentant, however, writing, 'We do not repent, nor are we sorry for even a single moment for our performance during the war. Have we forgotten that we fought to fulfill our religious duty and that the result is a marginal issue?'

Although Khomeini declared the stalemate as a victory for Islam and for Iran, after eight years of such horrors the people could no longer be fooled into seeing this inglorious episode in their country's history as anything other than an atrocious mistake.

An old man with heart trouble and plagued by illness, Khomeini held on long enough to see the war end. Six months after the truce was accepted, after an unsuccessful operation to stop internal bleeding, Ayatollah Khomeini died of a heart attack on 3 June 1989, exactly ten years to the day after we had landed in London to start the exile he had forced on us. He was in his late eighties.

People poured on to the streets, beating their chests in unison, pounding their heads to a deadly rhythm, dressed in black and bearing large posters of the dead leader's face, implacable to the last. It was a mass outpouring of grief that soon became a bacchanal of mourning, the people storming the funeral procession and grabbing at the shrouded body to pay their last respects, to tear off a piece of the shroud which was now considered holy. Nearly destroying his coffin in the process, the people reached for him in a mass frenzy, carried away by the electric energy of the day, just as during the revolution they had been inspired by this same energy to commit unthinkable acts of defiance and bravery. The dead man's body nearly fell to the ground and eventually Revolutionary Guards managed to disperse the crowd, the funeral hastily cancelled to give officials time to rethink.

A few days later, encased in a steel casket and surrounded by heavily armed security, Khomeini's body was once again paraded through the streets. Iranians again spilt into the streets, making this the biggest funeral in recorded history with eleven million people washing the streets in a sea of black, undeterred by the searing hundred degree temperatures of midsummer, beating their chests and heads, jumping up and down in a delirium of grief. The whole country filled with the sound of wailing, of religious mourning songs and the frantic chanting that Khomeini always inspired. Fire trucks sprayed water on the crowds to stop them fainting in the heat and helicopters had to swoop down to collect more than 400 people who were injured in the crush. Eight people died.

Khomeini's body was eventually taken to a purpose-built mausoleum on the edge of Tehran's huge Behesht Zahra cemetery, an outsize complex of gold domes and minarets intended to accommodate thousands of pilgrims. Fast food joints and souvenir stalls proliferate here now, an Iranian version of the sort of consumerist Western culture that Khomeini so frowned upon. In the cemetery itself, which I visit on every trip to pay respects at my *amoo*'s grave, there are acres of land devoted to the boys and young men 'martyred' in Khomeini's war, the tricoloured flag of my country flapping above thousands of graves in the shadow of the gold minarets of Khomeini's shrine.

In the struggle for power that followed Khomeini's death, Ayatollah Khamenei was finally chosen by the *mullahs* of the Guardian Council as the country's new Supreme Leader. More of a career politician than a revered spiritual leader, Ali Khamenei brought neither Khomeini's peculiar charisma nor his spiritual authority to the role, and he failed to inspire the sort of devotion in the people that kept them allied to Khomeini throughout his bloody reign. Nonetheless, he still holds the final reigns of power in Iran.

Ten years after stepping forward to lead my people's anguished struggle for freedom, democracy and autonomy from Western powers, Ayatollah Khomeini, who promised the poverty-stricken masses of Iran oil wells in their back garden, had failed to bring them either freedom, equality or economic prosperity. Instead of delivering them a paradise on earth, he instead made their lives such hell that thousands preferred to die as 'martyrs' to reach that other paradise instead.

'We do not worship Iran, we worship Allah. For patriotism is another name for paganism. I say let this land [Iran] burn. I say let this land go up in smoke, provided Islam emerges triumphant in the rest of the world,' declared Khomeini in a speech he gave in Qom in 1980. While his brand of Islam has failed to emerge triumphant in the rest of the world, he did succeed in letting our land of Iran burn. In the process, he managed to drive the children of his revolution – the new generation born since his ascent to power – away from Islam in droves.

19

The Mask of Englishness

GROWING UP IN Britain in the eighties, I had slipped on the mask of Englishness, had declared Britain my country, had stuck my flag in her soil and given myself to her, denying Iran at every turn, refusing to speak Farsi until I had forgotten my language, and rejecting my relations every time they rang, not knowing how to speak to them, what to say, how to carry out *ta'arof*. I ran away from my parents' parties, from the tight community of Iranian friends they had gathered about them in London and spurned any advances of friendship from their kids. I wasn't looking for people who had shared my experiences, who were also expert at navigating the vastly different cultures we all inhabited, the one at home and the one outside our homes, cultures so opposed to each other that we had all become masters of disguise, brilliant chameleons able to change colour and even shift shape as we moved between our two worlds. I only wanted friends from my new life, only wanted to speak English, as if with every word swearing my allegiance to the country that had taken me in, that had given me sanctuary and allowed me to be safe. My parents' efforts to stop my sister and me from forgetting our culture and language were also summarily dismissed: they would speak to us in Farsi only to have us reply in English, they would try to enrol us at Farsi Saturday school only to have us flat refuse to go. Over the years, I became so good at wearing the mask that eventually, the mask became my face.

No matter how hard I tried, and how many times I was given the dubious honour by my British friends of not being considered Middle Eastern but 'one of us', inside our home there was no getting away from my roots. We lived in a distinctly Iranian environment, Persian carpets covering the floors, Persian miniatures decorating the walls and Persian smells issuing from the kitchen. I hesitated always to take friends home – I was too embarrassed by the gap in culture between their behaviour, their casual and informal manners, and what my parents considered correct comportment. Bagher and Sedi were breathtakingly liberal and modern compared to their parents and their own upbringing, but compared to the parents of my British peers, they were old-fashioned and strict. At seventeen, while my best friend was taking boyfriends home to spend the night in her bedroom, I was haggling my midnight curfew and conducting clandestine afternoon meetings with boys in Holland Park.

As a teenager in London I walked the tightrope between my two cultures – entirely Iranian and Muslim at home and outside, where I spent the greater part of my time, British and growing up in the age of Thatcher. I was sucking up ideas of equality and sexual liberation while at home I waited on my parents' friends and pretended I had never kissed a boy. I couldn't imagine telling my mother that I was interested in boys now that I was a teenager and I had left behind my passion for ponies. I wanted to indulge my desires, be like everyone else, but not telling Sedi was probably my failing rather than hers. I don't know what I thought she would do, I couldn't contemplate broaching the subject of sex before marriage, a great taboo in my respectable Iranian family – I was as surely held in place by these strong social conventions as if I had been living in Iran.

I was not quite subjugated to the rules to the point that I eschewed the pleasures of being a teenager in London, but I was sufficiently conditioned into making an internal schism, splitting up my life into two distinct parts – and lying to my parents and torturing myself with my wrongdoing in the process. I lost years of my life to being dishonest which, unlike most of the other Middle Eastern and Asian kids I knew who moved smoothly between the two realities of their lives, made me intensely uncomfortable. My parents managed to fill us with their values even though we lived mostly at school – six years of boarding school where I effectively grew up, living there for eight months of the year. But now I think I underestimated my mother. Had I told her the truth about my life as I partied and smoked my way through London's hippest nightclubs, her reaction would probably have been as cool and unexpected as it was when she discovered I had started smoking at sixteen.

She took me and my friend Jenny out to tea at Barkers, and pulled a packet of cigarettes out of her bag and placed it on the table. In those days she sometimes smoked socially and I thought nothing of it as she reached for a cigarette, but then, in a stroke of genius, she offered the packet to Jenny. Jenny had been my partner in sneaking smokes behind the pet shed at school and now she looked confused, her eyes darting from the proffered packet of cigarettes to my mother, then to me, and back to my mother again. She eventually reached forward and pulled out a cigarette with a muttered thanks. My mother calmly lit it for her before offering me the packet and, encouraged by her non-reaction to Jenny's acceptance, I also accepted one. Had she offered me the packet first I would have whipped myself up into a state of fake indignation at being accused of smoking. We sat there and went on with our tea, Jenny and I puffing self-consciously, all smoking together. As time went on it was also silently accepted that I could occasionally smoke in my room and while my parents let me know they didn't like the habit, they did not try to force me into stopping. They preferred the openness but I was too dumb perhaps to give them the opportunity to know me fully by being open about my other life, my British life, until much later on.

My parents wore their exoticism like a cloak, enhancing them in and also obscuring them from foreign eyes. When we brought home friends from school, my mother was invariably so glamorous and exotic that my friends were stunned into silence. Bagher was always formal, dressed in suits and perfectly mannered, but quiet, distant and remote, not trying to engage in conversation. Sedi was invariably dressed to go out, to a party or a lunch, and whether smart or formal, her designer outfits and perfectly coiffed hair set her apart from the mothers of my friends, who were so cosy and plain in comparison. Sedi exuded charm but her warmth battled with her command of the language – my mother has always been convinced, despite all evidence to the contrary, that she can barely speak English. So in interactions with our friends, she preferred always to rely on my sister and me to be the bridges between her and them, their language, their culture. My parents inhabited a different planet to that of my friends' parents. They were formal and ritualistic in their social interactions in a way that in modern Britain was just not the norm. My sister and I delighted in laughing at them in private, especially at my mother's occasional English malapropisms, but we were fiercely protective of them – and their exoticism – in public.

As a teenager I regularly needled my father to apply for our British passports, many years after we had been resident in the UK long enough to qualify. For fifteen years after leaving Iran and applying for asylum in the UK, we had made do with Travel Documents, temporary papers that allowed us to travel anywhere in the world in the same way as a British passport – except back to Iran. Although after four years in Britain we were eligible for citizenship, my father never applied and I, in moments of heightened teenage passion, called him lazy. I see now that it was a function of Bagher's silent grief; he did not want to accept that we were really here, that we had left Iran for good. Britain had been the country that he had loved, he had so chimed with its reserved, quiet ways but nevertheless, something in Bagher was unwilling to take citizenship, to finally give up on Iran, even after everything that had happened to us and that continued to happen to the country after our departure.

The Travel Document never gave me a sense of security and I hated feeling singled out by its flimsiness every time I had to use it. When I tried to join a school trip to Paris at seventeen and found myself barred from France because I was Iranian, my worst fears seemed realised. Supposedly the Travel Document was just a British passport in waiting, but in reality, after a spate of bombings in Paris that were attributed to an opposition Iranian group, France decided it would prefer not to welcome an Iranian teenager on to its soil and I was refused permission. I was furious and terrified all at the same time, and I longed for the sense of security that having a British passport – so civilised, so acceptable in the world – would give me.

It took my father another five years after that to capitulate but, after another raft of nervous visits to the Home Office in Croydon, I finally got the small burgundy booklet that gave me my freedom, and peace of mind. Along with the British passport I got the right to possess once again my Iranian passport, and so, after so many years away, the ability to return home.

My first visit back in 1996 only lasted three weeks, twenty-one precious, bewildering days that passed in a whirl. On my return to London after my first journey back I cried for a week and I couldn't bear to return again until 1998. I found letting go of my newly discovered Iranian self extremely painful, and the impossibility of explaining everything I had experienced in my country to my friends made me feel alienated all over again. As time passed and my English persona slipped back on like a well-worn cloak, Iran receded and the distance between the two countries I am from created a gulf inside me that was hard to bridge. It was as if the only way I could live comfortably in London was to forget Iran; the coping strategy I had learnt as a child had soaked deep inside me and it was hard to change.

Over the decade after my first trip, I made several journeys to Iran, soon travelling without my mother, going alone and my stays growing in length until I was staying a couple of months at a time. My visits spanned the two terms that President Khatami was in power, a period of greater social openness and debate in Iran, and I became more comfortable there, with my language improving daily, my English accent lost. I was beginning to like the Iranian me, a creature infinitely more polite and, when occasion demanded it, sharp-tongued than the girl who marched around London huffing at tourists on the underground. I had cracked the codes of *ta'arof* at last and had learnt to haggle, overcoming my reserve and feeling triumphant the first time I beat a carpet seller down to my price. My mother and *Khaleh* Mina were experts and I knew my father was a world champion – I had once watched him haggle down a second-hand car salesman so persistently and patiently that the man had nearly wept in relief when the deal had been concluded, turning watery eyes on me and declaring he had never met anyone like my father before. But of course, my father had taken the Iranian art of haggling on to a world stage when he had worked for the oil company, and the time he bought me that car was the first time I had seen him in action.

In Shiraz I stayed with *Khaleh* Mina in her tiny flat. Recently bereaved – Busheiry had shuffled off this mortal coil the previous year – Mina was finally free to live her life as she chose. What she chose was to clean her flat every day, to pour her energy into making her small space as spotless and shiny as she could manage. Suffering from back trouble and all sorts of problems with her legs, she would hoover relentlessly even when she could barely stand. Her first act on getting up in the morning, after washing her face, was to apply her blusher and lipstick, laughing as I watched her. She told me she had latterly turned down a marriage proposal from an elderly relative of Maman-*joon*'s. She had been shocked to receive the offer from the white-haired man and she had turned him down in the politest terms, but she said to me as we drank Nescafé and blew smoke rings late into the night, '*Va*! Kamin-*joon*, imagine the cheek of it. That after a lifetime of being nursemaid to Clark Gable, I should choose now to marry another old man so I can nurse him through his last years!' She puffed like a champion on her cigarette, her hands drawing arabesques through the air as she gesticulated. 'No, *azizam*, I am finally free and I don't fear being alone. I gave Busheiry my life, I was a good wife to him, discharged my obligation. *Baste*, enough!'

Khaleh Mina was not alone. Two of *Khaleh* Yassi's children belonged to her and they practically lived with her, moving with ease between their two homes and their two mothers. *Khaleh* Mina poured her immense energy into them now her husband was gone.

Khaleh Yassi lived right in the heart of town with her beloved Seini and four children as well as Maman-*joon*. Having retired from IranAir after eighteen years of service, she had set up her own travel agency – no mean feat in this country in which more than 80 per cent of all industry is controlled by the government. We went to see her sitting behind her managing director's desk, perfectly turned out in modest *maghna'eh* topped by a voluminous *chador*, her face caked in 'no make-up' make-up. She grinned as I proudly snapped pictures of her posing behind her desk, her employees rushing to bring us tea. One day, when *Khaleh* Mina and I dropped in to see her, we found the three women that worked for her sitting at their desks with newspapers piled high with mounds fresh herbs spread out in front of them. They were cleaning the herbs for the dinner *Khaleh* Yassi was planning to make that night. They looked up at us and smiled and when *Khaleh* Mina raised her eyebrows quizzically at her younger sister, *Khaleh* Yassi dropped her voice and said, 'Well, it's a quiet day and they have nothing else to do. I am paying them, they might as well help me.' *Khaleh* Yassi had wanted to have it all and she had got it all, and the small matters of revolution, war and the Islamic Republic had not stopped her.

For all that *Khaleh* Mina's home was spotless and shiny, *Khaleh* Yassi's home was chaotic, filled with children, the smell of cooking and Fatemeh Bibi's scratchy-voiced outpourings. Yassi and her husband were still madly in love. When he got home from work or a basketball match, *Khaleh* Yassi, tripping girlishly around the flat in her tight sexy clothes, would wait on him hand and foot. The genial Seini was the only man who ever tried to explain the relationship between the sexes in Iran to me. One night, as I sat and practised English conversation with one of his sons, he came and joined us, and as our talk turned general, he tried to explain to me the mentality of Iranian men. 'Look, Kamin-*jan*, we Iranian men are *gheiraty* – possessive,' he said with his customary friendly tone. 'I love my wife and I enjoy her body. I like nothing better than to see her dressed like this.' He indicated *Khaleh* Yassi who was skipping around the flat in a negligée. 'But she is my wife. And her body is for my enjoyment – I don't want other men looking at her the way I do.'

Perhaps the most *gheiraty* man in Iran's history was Ayatollah Khomeini himself. After all, did he too not try to enforce
all our women to cover themselves from the prying eyes of
'strange' men? But Iranian men's mixture of Persian sensual-
ity and Islamic prudery has not confused our women at all;
Iranian women are a tantalising combination of the sacred
and the profane. They can be seen dancing the night away
at parties in décolleté dresses and made up like supermod-
els, and the next morning found at the mosque covered in
a *chador* weeping for one of our imams, their faces washed
by genuine tears. It was like this in my mother's time and,
I soon discovered, it is like this in Iran now. The outfits
the women wear on the street are different but underneath
they are the same as they have always been. This duality
presents no problem to Iranian women, whose natures easily
encompass the two seemingly opposed desires – to party and
to pray – but the men of Iran, long privy to the best-kept
secret of the country – the incredible calibre of its women –
have always been jealous of their womenfolk, scared of their
strength and too enamoured of the quality of their loving and
caring to want them to have too much freedom. Iranian men
have tried, ever since Islam gave them a legitimate excuse, to
keep us at home for their own enjoyment, knowing as they
do that, should Iranian women be given a free reign and not
hampered with negative conditioning about themselves, they
would march out of the kitchen and rule the world.

Whatever else the shah did to Iran, he undoubtedly gave
women more freedom than ever. At the time of the revolution, Iranian women were marching around the country
– the world – holding jobs and university positions and
they could choose whether they wore high heels or *chadors*.
Iranian men, *gheiraty* till the last, panicked, worried they
were going to lose us to careers, modernity and freedom,
stricken with the unthinkable notion that their elaborate

dinners would not be waiting for them when they got home, that there would be no feline creature attendant to soothe their brows and help solve the issues of their day and raise their children. Sometimes I think that the whole revolution was just a reaction by Iran's men, an attempt to stop women shedding their traditional roles and that Ayatollah Khomeini, with his insistence that women should embrace the 'feminine' values of housework and childbearing, helped our men find a reason within Islam to usher us back into the home.

It didn't work. Now over thirty years after the revolution, Iranian women are more visible in public life than ever. Economic necessity has driven this as much as anything else – the war decimated Iran's economy and the mullahs' mismanagement of the oil wealth and tough new sanctions imposed by the West means that only the very wealthy can afford to have their wives sit at home waiting to stroke their brows when they get in at the end of the day. The gap between rich and poor yawns wider than ever, and into this chasm have tumbled the middle class, whose members have found their standards of living slipping every year since the revolution until they now can barely manage to survive.

Many of my cousins – all educated and professional people – have at some point held two jobs to make ends meet, and most still do. The girls in my generation of my family have all been to university and have all worked, many after having children. What Iranian women snatched out of the jaws of the repression was education, and 65 per cent of university entrants are now women. So alarmed are the *gheiraty* men who run the country that they have had to pass a law to equalise the numbers of the sexes that enter university. Thirty years after the revolution tried to take away so many of Iranian women's rights, the Islamic Republic is having to positively discriminate in favour of the men to make sure they are not left trailing behind the girls as they stride forward.

After the revolution, many devout traditional families who had refused in the shah's time to send their daughters out to school or college in the miniskirted, liberal, and – to them – decadent and permissive society of the time, felt safe in sending their girls out into a covered-up and segregated Islamic world where the school books had been thoroughly revised by the Islamic regime during the Cultural Revolution. Universities sprang up where there had been none before, as Iran's population became more literate – now at 89 per cent, the highest literacy rate in the Middle East. The baby boom of the revolution and war years has given Iran an overwhelmingly youthful population and these young people – Khomeini's armies for Islam – have needed facilities.

What the Islamic regime has given them is lots of new universities to go to, and for those who are not successful in the country's notoriously difficult and stressful university entrance exams, there are 'open' universities which have less exacting criteria and higher fees. Universities are scattered all over the country and Iranian students have no choice over where they attend – their grades dictate which universities offer them places – so young Iranians are, for the first time, living away from home in residential dorms en masse, girls leaving home before marriage – unheard of in my mother's time under the shah, when a girl only left her father's house to move into her husband's. Now almost all girls, from the lower-middle classes upwards, can expect their education to take them all the way into their early twenties. Of course, there are still traditional and conservative fathers who believe that too much education will spoil a girl for marriage – still regarded as the main objective of a woman's life – but they are not as numerous as they were.

★　　★　　★

My cousin Noosheen always travelled to Shiraz to see me when she could. She was a true child of the revolution, born in the first years of the war to the comedian half of my twin uncles, *Daiey* Reza. Unlike my other female cousins and her contemporaries, Noosheen did not have a face vividly and expertly painted with make-up, she had not plucked her eyebrows into the latest fashionable shape and she showed no great interest in clothes or pop music and dancing. A modest Iranian girl, Noosheen was possessed of a quiet humour and a lively mind that I adored and we became firm friends.

My *daiey* Reza is a man of modest means, living with his family of four children in just three rooms, his wife Leila a broad-hipped woman of deep affections who is constantly busy in the kitchen. A generation ago Noosheen would have been married off to some distant cousin in her teens, but the last time I saw her she was headed to university far from home where she lived first in a dorm and then in a shared flat with other girlfriends. She is now a graduate with a good job – but her job in the university town is too far to allow her to commute from her parent's small flat in Esfahan, so she lives in a flat of her own with another girlfriend. Thirty years after the revolution sought to shut women back up in the home, ordinary girls like Noosheen are leading independent lives of financial autonomy away from their family homes, living alone – something that my mother and her sisters didn't dare dream of.

Noosheen and her ilk are my great hope for Iran's future, the women jumping forward through loopholes in the system. Only one thing can still set them back inexorably – another war.

Noosheen lives her independent single life in Natanz, now notorious in the West as the site of one of Iran's nuclear reactors and likely candidate for Israeli or American bombing with nuclear-tipped weapons. Should those bombs one day fall, they will wipe out not just the fabled domes of Esfahan and poison the land for thousands of years to come, they will also obliterate my sweet modest cousin and her quietly modern life.

20

Returning

M Y ONLY TRIP back to Khuzestan was for Ebby's funeral. I joined the other Abadanis heading to the graveyard; they had come bearing flasks of rose-water for washing the graves and boxes of sweets to hand around to other mourners. The graves were raised stone platforms topped by a gravestone or, more often, a picture of the deceased set in a glass case.

It was January and rain had turned the marshland into fields of mud, palm trees swaying in the breeze. I stood by my other cousins, Ebby's brother and his sisters, holding the trays of homemade *halva*, honey biscuits, and fruit we had brought. In the martyrs' section of the cemetery there were special prayers taking place, the flags placed above each grave flapping in the wind that circulated the scent of the rose-water. But we were not in the martyrs' section, because, although Ebby was a veteran of the war, he died not on the battlefield, but over a decade later in an abandoned slum in Abadan, a homeless heroin addict with AIDS and hepatitis.

His sisters – my cousins – leapt sobbing into my arms when I arrived and his wife, a moon-faced woman in a volu-minous black *chador*, muttered quiet words of gratitude for my presence. After years of feeling alone in their struggle with Ebby and his addiction, they were touched that I had made the journey from England. Neither Ebby's sisters, his wife nor his brother had seen Ebby for years before his death, his addiction had tried all their love and patience and even his wife, who had stayed with him through everything else, had finally had to listen to her parents and move out for the sake of their children. She told me that she had always loved him, they had all always loved him and, even though Maman-*joon* had never judged Ebby for his drug addiction and had still wanted him included, there was a sense of anger and recrimination by the time everyone abandoned him to his fate. Now they could lay aside their anger and grieve. Not just for his death, but also for his young life which was destroyed by the war.

I crouched in the mud by the grave, washed off the dust of Abadan and set a table like at a party: white gladioli in the centre surrounded by dishes of dates, *halva*, fruit, sweets dripping with honey. I ate some obligatory *halva*, and passed on the sweets to other mourners at other graves. No one talked about Ebby's ignominious death, the drug addiction that soared out of control after he came home from the front line and which took his family and everything he had before taking his life.

Khuzestan had never recovered its pre-war importance and Abadan was no longer the sophisticated city of pre-revolutionary days. The grand Abadan Hotel where my parents had danced the night away was a broken-down shell of a building. The oil refinery was still at work – in 1997 it had reached the same rate of production as before the war – and the waters of the Shatt still flowed gently between the town and Iraq's palm fields – but the main town was a dusty relic of its former self, the pavements broken and streets with their neon shop fronts a mix of new buildings, shambolic old buildings, and gaping holes where bombed-out ruins had not been rebuilt. Ebby had died in one of these, down the street from Fatemeh Bibi and Abbas' old house, where his father had grown up. That night I strolled through town with my cousins, who pointed out the old Cinema Rex, scene of the horrific fire. Recently there had been another fire on the site and now it was being prepared to become a new shopping mall, selling shoes. They told me that several sets of bones had been unearthed since the work started but the regime's new gift to the people – consumerism – was quickly replacing such relics, driving them from people's minds.

The next day I boarded a bus for Ahvaz. It was 2003 and at the grand age of thirty-three I had screwed up enough courage to go back to the last place we lived before the revolution drove us out. Approaching the city from Abadan, through the expanse of desert still mined in some areas, I recognised the road we had been driving along when I had first seen Baboo. The scenary brought back memories which I had long kept suppressed.

Hiding behind large sunglasses, I alighted nervously from the bus in Ahvaz and fell into the arms of my cousin Mahnaz, one of *Khaleh* Mahvash's daughters and one of my particular childhood friends. Mahnaz was no longer the teenager I had remembered, but a middle-aged woman with two children of her own. Nonetheless, the Hayat Davoudy grey-green eyes were the same, the beaming smile wide and she held me tight to her and then held my hand affectionately, never letting go until we reached her home.

I settled into Mahnaz's family – she had taken a few days off work, and we went everywhere together, her children soon calling me '*Khaleh* Kamin', much to my delight. Mahnaz was, like *Khaleh* Mahvash's other children, academically brilliant, but the revolution and war had thwarted her ambitions. Mahnaz graduated from high school just after the revolution but, instead of going to university as planned, thanks to Khomeini's Cultural Revolution, she found herself cooling her heels at home for two years. 'We had nothing to do,' she told me, 'nothing at all. Every day we sat at home with nothing to do. We could barely go out – all the hassle over the *hejab* and what you could wear was too much – and so we sat at home with nothing to do.'

Mahnaz had eventually returned to studying and had become a high school physics teacher. Alongside her full-time job and looking after her two children and husband, Mahnaz was now studying for a PhD at Tehran University, making the long journey once a week to Tehran for two days of tutorials. Transport connections were not what they had been, planes were often cancelled and the journey to Tehran could be arduous. Perhaps it was the early exclusion from the realms of the intellect that had driven her back to the class-room, but Mahnaz's determination to complete her studies grew with each difficulty and she never missed a class, even when it meant going cross-country on an overnight bus. Her husband supported her, although it meant that for two days of the week he was left to his own devices with the children, but he bore it to make his wife happy.

Mahnaz had not grown up in Khuzestan – her parents had moved away soon after getting married – but the pull of her Abbasian roots had made her feel instantly at home when she had moved there with her husband for his work. 'It was supposed to be for a year,' she confided, 'but you know what they say, Kamin-*joon*, Khuzestan has this habit of getting under your skin. We have been here fourteen years now.' The land of her ancestors had not only claimed Mahnaz back but had given her two Khuzestani kids; both Mahnaz's chil-dren were born in Ahvaz and, unlike their mother, they had the sparkling black eyes and thick black hair of natives of the region.

It was Mahnaz who accompanied me to find our old house, who insisted when I prevaricated and who pushed me when I had procrastinated until I was nearly out of time. On a moonlit night, on our way to the airport, we drove into the

Company's compound, circling the streets until we found
the right one. It took a while but we eventually located our
house, there in its cul-de-sac opposite the house where the
Armenian boys had lived. As we parked in the drive and got
out, a young guard approached us, and Mahnaz explained
that this had once been my house, that after more than
twenty years away I had come to see it again. The guard,
regarding me with curiosity, explained that the house was
empty and, suspicious, suggested we should probably leave.
I would not have argued but Mahnaz sprang into action, all
her Hayat Davoudy charm and her Abbasian quick-witted-
ness coming to the fore as she persuaded the guard to let
us stay a while. I chimed in, walking around and describ-
ing what had changed. I pointed at the little booth that had
housed our Arab guards which now stood at the end of the
driveway, rather than up by the gates of the wall of the house
as it once had done.

With this a light came into the guard's eyes. 'You are
right!' he declared. 'It did used to be there. It was moved a
few years ago . . .' And with that, convinced that we were
not thieves, he took out a key and opened the gate for us. 'I
don't have keys to the house,' he called out over our shoulders, 'but you can look around the garden.'

The garden was enough. I stepped in gingerly, comforted
by Mahnaz's hand that was clutching mine once more.
And there it was, bathed in moonlight, the garden with its
tall palm tree, the stump where we used to tie Baboo, the
fragrant flowers of Khuzestan releasing their scent into the
night, the walls we had scaled tumbling with bougainvillea
and the rooftops we had raced over. I walked around, holding Mahnaz's hand, telling her stories, leading her here and
there to show her where we had skateboarded and where
the fluffy chicks had turned into the hens that laid our eggs.
Together we peered through the curtainless windows at the

parquet-floored rooms; they seemed so vast now I was used to the small proportions of London flats. Mahnaz never let go of my hand.

As we stood back by the gate, inside the tall walls that had enclosed our own private paradise, she smiled at me and said, 'You know, Kamin-*joon*, your memories are of your games, all the mischief you got into, all the fun you had.' I loved her for reminding me that beyond what had happened here, there had been fun and laughter. My childhood, I remembered, had been very special and the revolution had not changed that.

She took me to the airport after that, collecting a flask of tea on the way 'just in case'. Sure enough, Mahnaz, a veteran of Khuzestan's internal flights was well-prepared; my flight was cancelled and we were obliged to sit out the night in the provincial airport that had not so much as a teashop open. We retreated to her car and drank the tea and talked all night. We spoke of our family, our mutual aunts and uncles and cousins and of how life had been for them, why they were so often in *ghahr* with one another and how the hardships of war had split them into factions.

The Abbasian children were always close, even though that closeness and love was as often as not expressed by fighting, squabbling and bickering. It's been a hard habit to shake, just as they can't resist talking over each other, each raising their voices higher and higher to be heard without slowing down or missing a beat. They were all – with the exception of the sweet-tempered Pardis – capable of unleashing their tongues with a vengeance if they were crossed and, even now, as my aunts and uncles grow old in Iran, they fill their time with fighting and falling out. Having watched them now on my trips back over the years, I have realised that this is a sort of hobby for them and I have spent uncomfortable hours in the midst of family arguments, trying desperately

not to catch someone's eye when my aunts and uncles are
airing decades of hurts and slights. Every time I visit, I have
to acquaint myself with who is talking to whom and who is
in *ghahr* with whom.

Ghahr is a word that I have long sought to translate into
English, and failed. Its closest meaning is 'sulking' but that
implies altogether too petty and childish a thing, whereas
ghahr is a formalised ritual that is so much a part of the honour-
bound and proud Iranian system of interaction that it carries
a kind of epic quality. We Iranians are a thin-skinned lot, we
hold our honour dear and are sensitive to it being slighted. I
was at first alarmed by such disharmony in my family, until I
realised that it was something that existed alongside and quite
apart from their love for each other. In the last few years,
for example, my oldest *khaleh* Parivash and youngest *khaleh*
Yassi have been in *ghahr* with each other and so they won't
visit each other's houses. With immense tact, *Khaleh* Yassi
would sidestep all the gatherings at *Khaleh* Pari's house and
I found out that it was because *Khaleh* Parivash had hosted
a religious party at her home (with so many imams whose
births and deaths must be commemorated, religious holidays
and parties proliferate in the Islamic Republic) and had not
invited *Khaleh* Yassi. Probably this was in retaliation for some
kind of slight from Yassi towards one of Parivash's children,
but its origin is not important and nor is it remembered;
Khaleh Yassi was offended and therefore refused to visit her
oldest sister. It made the logistics of my visits more complicated as it obliged me to go and stay with everyone in turn
(in order not to offend them). But I soon noticed that it did
not in any way indicate a cooling of the feeling between
these two sisters: they spoke on the phone for at least an hour
every day, *Khaleh* Parivash giggling uncontrollably at *Khaleh*
Yassi's irreverent humour and they were the first to ring to
enquire after the health of the other when there was heart

trouble (as *Khaleh* Parivash was prone to having) or a slipped disk (with which *Khaleh* Yassi suffered for a while). I was tempted to put this all down to the peculiar mix of impertinence and formality that characterised my mother's side of the family, this bickering love they had developed in that house in Abadan, until on my visits to Tehran I heard also of many different varieties of *ghahr* that bounced between the branches of my Kurdish family, those people I had considered always so reasonable and logical.

But reason and logic have nothing to do with it. So formalised are Iranian interactions, so highly developed and refined the culture in this respect that you are obliged to react with *ghahr* should someone insult you in a certain way. My relations no longer take a gun to shoot those that have shown them disrespect, as a great-aunt of mine did many years ago when the Hayat Davoudy still had their lands in Bushehr and a servant served her tea with a teaspoon standing up in the glass (terribly disrespectful, I was assured. What choice did she have? my mother still shrugs), but they do enthusiastically practice their *ghahr*. We laughed about it now, Mahnaz and I, as we talked under the Ahvaz sky.

I realised I had always felt that no one in Iran could possibly appreciate my experience of exile, so slight did it seem compared to everything they had lived through, and so I never tried to talk about it. But Mahnaz's cleverness was matched by her sensitivity and she turned to me, fixing me with the same green gaze of our grandmother, and gently said, 'It wasn't the same you know. After you left. It wasn't the same. Everything changed, the revolution and the war, they changed us. We,' she indicated sweepingly, meaning the generations of cousins our age, 'we were lucky. We had amazing childhoods, we were close, although we lived all over the place. Remember all those family parties? I learnt to swim in your pool in Tehran . . . That all stopped. The war scattered us and it made everyone a little crazy. Look at our new cousins,' she meant the generation born after I had left, the children of the revolution, 'they didn't have the same kind of upbringing we had, belonging to everyone in the family. They are not bonded to each other – to the family – like we are.' Fat tears rolled down my face as she took my head in her hands, kissing my cheeks. 'Iran changed then, it became a different country. Don't think that you missed out on anything.'

21

Saying Goodbye

M AMAN-*JOON* WAS DYING and her last wish was
to see Pardis again. He had not returned since leaving for America during the war with Iraq and she would
throw up her skinny hands and, in her scratchy voice when
she could catch her breath enough, say, 'I want Pardis, bring
me Pardis, *naneh.*'

In January 2004, I found myself back in Iran accompanying my mother and her two American-based brothers for this
journey to say goodbye.

We found the family in disarray, at war with each other
now that Fatemeh Bibi, the glue that kept them together,
was so unwell. Recriminations and accusations had taken
the place of parties and jokes, the stress of watching their
mother dying turning in on the family, eating it from inside.
They had settled into factions and although they tried to pull
together for Pardis' first visit to Iran in more than a decade,
the tension often boiled over into ugly fights and confrontations which had me and my cousins cowering.

The war had not only dislocated the Abbasians physically,
it had gone deep to the heart of the unit. Perhaps it was
because Maman-*joon* no longer had her own house and there
was nowhere for Fatemeh Bibi's children to gather without
the hierarchies of the family getting in the way. *Khaleh* Yassi's
modest apartment could not be expected to house the Abbasian hordes and while Maman-*joon*'s love bore no difference
for one member of the family to the next, her heart refusing

to love even one iota less just because of personal failings, my uncles and aunts, with the wellbeing of their own children to think about, were much quicker to judge. And so the factions formed during the war had hardened and several sets of the Abbasians were at war with the others.

Maman-*joon* had become a slip of a thing; tiny and skeletal, unable to walk and hardly able to breathe, but still possessed of bright green eyes and all her faculties. She lay on a small mattress in the corner of the one bedroom in *Khaleh* Mina's flat – where we were all staying – and she tried to catch her breath. Sedi and I shared that bedroom with her while we were there and Maman-*joon* spent the majority of her time lying there, though more in that world than this. When she was awake, she fought so hard for each breath that she constantly emitted a small noise – '*enk*' – which Yassi's kids, who loved her and played with her as if she was just a little girl, imitated when they came to visit, teasing her in a way none of the rest of us would have dared. She brightened and laughed girlishly at their teasing, at Amin – *Khaleh* Yassi's youngest – who sat with her, now a tall twinkling teen- ager, and said, 'Maman-*joon*, *enk enk*!' until she dissolved in giggles.

Fatemeh Bibi, always so jolly and courteous throughout her life, had given up all pretence of caring for others' opin- ions of her in deaf old age. At family parties and gatherings she would loudly pass comment on those around her, saving her most virulent criticism for her daughters-in-law. '*Va!*' she would say to Ali, *Khaleh* Yassi's other son, 'what's she done to her hair? It's ugly. And just look at her, why does she look so like a man?' Ali told me that he would shrink in his seat, mortified. When it fell, as it inevitably did, to Mina to scold her – 'Maman, *baste* – enough. *Zeshteh, khanoum* – it's not appropriate!' – Fatemeh Bibi would raise her chin defiantly and answer in the loudest voice she could manage,

'Why not let them hear? I am only telling the truth after all.' She could not resist arguing with Mina till the last.

Maman-*joon* lay on her bed on the floor in the corner of the room and received us as we sat with her one by one and stroked her hair and kissed her hands. I would often catch her with a faraway look in her eyes, but I soon realised she was not contemplating higher things – she was looking at her left wrist which she was holding aloft, and jingling her gold bracelets. She had no other possessions except her well-guarded stack of photographs, and she made sure to tell all her daughters that after her death they were to have two of her bracelets each. She seemed often on the edge of death – one night her breathing became so laboured, her struggle to catch another breath so intense, that I could feel her slipping away. My mother got out of bed and went and sat by her mother, stroking her hair and raising her up a little so the fluid that collected on her lungs had a chance to disperse. Fatemeh Bibi would hate to go while her children were still around her, Sedi knew. She was not ready yet to leave the party and Sedi stayed up all night with Maman-*joon*, helping her to grasp at each breath until the danger was past.

Eventually we left Iran and Fatemeh Bibi, having got her last wish to lay eyes on her beloved Pardis one last time, to see with her own eyes that he was fine in the new life he had chosen, only managed another two months, and I am sure that those were only for the love of *Khaleh* Yassi's children, who kept her laughing until the end. After our departure she had moved back to Yassi's, where she had been looked after and cared for by a hired nurse, a sweet girl also called Fatemeh, *Khaleh* Yassi herself now in bed with a slipped disk. One morning in March just two weeks before Nowruz, *Khaleh* Yassi rose before the rest of the house, as was her habit, and she went to take tea to her mother. Fatemeh Bibi looked her in the eye and cupped her cheek. '*Khodahafez, azizam*,' she said – goodbye, my darling. She then closed her eyes, and with a last '*enk*' let go of life. I imagine that she was satisfied with her lot.

Sedi was bereft and jumped on the first plane to Iran, arriving in time to help her brothers and sisters make the funeral arrangements, buy and cook all the food that would be needed to feed the many people who would come in the following week to pay their respects. They wailed and wept and beat themselves when the pain got too much, releasing their grief in the way that Shia Islam gifts its followers – blessed relief. My cousin Alireza's eldest daughter Maryam – Maman-*joon*'s first great-grandchild – was chosen to lead the prayers at her funeral. A sweet, moon-faced girl who looked like her mother Shahnaz, and who had grown up with the same firm faith in the divine, she chanted the verses from the Qur'ān beautifully.

Maman-*joon*, had always been concerned with the appearance of things – she always said that she did not care what people said behind her back as long as they were charming to her face – and had often said in those last months to anyone who would listen, 'When I die, I expect you all to cry a lot. I don't want any dry eyes or brave faces. I want rivers of tears, *ghorbonetam*, and don't think I won't be watching . . .'

Fatemeh Bibi's funeral was all she could have wished for, the last big party that she attended. And attend she did – at the end of the first week of mourning, she appeared to Maryam in a dream, young and beautiful, her figure full and her white arms chubby and she said in the rich voice that had been hers before the operation on her larynx, 'Maryam-*joon*, you have done well. You prayed beautifully and everything was perfect. Go and tell the others that I am pleased. But you have all cried enough now, *baste*, it's time to get on with your lives.'

When Sedi arrived back at Heathrow, dressed in black and her hair striped by dark roots, we all rushed at her, taking her in our collective arms. She was crying, her face bare of make-up as was the custom, her hair undyed. She was still in mourning for her mother and tradition dictated that she wear black and eschew make-up and hair dye for another year. We all knew Sedi would never see out the year in black, she found it too depressing, and it had been she who, on our first visit together back to Tehran, had urged Mehry and Guity to quit mourning their father after three months, and had harried them into putting on lipstick again and doing their hair. She kept to her mourning uniform for another week, which she marked by receiving her friends who came to pay condolences. She gave me Maman-*joon*'s bracelets and they joined the six gold bracelets that I was given as a child and I still wear. Sometimes, in a distracted moment, I find myself holding aloft my left wrist and jangling the bracelets; it's a strangely comforting gesture.

For Maman-*joon*'s wake in London, I drove Sedi one morning to New Covent Garden flower market where we arrived late and bought up all the white flowers still left. We decked out the flat in with vases of white blooms and made the traditional dishes of *halva* and *sholeh-zard* and for the next week, all Sedi's friends came to cry with her, including her British boss Cherie, a woman with whom she became life-long friends. She didn't have her family around her, but the collection of Iranian friends – and Cherie – she had in London flocked around her like her sisters and gave her comfort.

My parents had not prospered in Britain. They had lived at first as if they were still in Iran, seeing the same people they had known there, moving in the same circles and rarely coming out of their Iranian bubble. My mother devoted herself to us and she continued to be a consummate hostess and the life and soul of all parties, her kitchen producing all the elaborate and delicious dishes we had been used to in Iran, her table always overflowing with the wealth of the choices on offer.

But as the years wore on, my father's age excluded him from work and he was increasingly a fixture on the sofa, where his piles of newspapers and stacks of books caused my mother no end of annoyance. The changes that had started in Iran did not stop over the next decades in Britain and they required my parents to change too, and, in order to survive, they too bent to the wind, reshaping themselves. My father officially retired and my mother instead started to work and so, late in her life, she got all the financial independence and autonomy she had craved in her youth. It required her to give up her carefully constructed image of herself, the status and respect she had enjoyed in Iran because of my father's job, and to finally accept her new life in Britain, a decade after we had arrived, to integrate into British society.

My mother integrated but she has never lost her Iranian ways. English friends of mine get confused when, on seeing them, she enquires after the health of every family member by name, and she treats authority in such a deferential way that it used to make me cross, this constant effacing of herself, calling people 'sir' in English, as if they were the king and she was so much less. As I grew up I realised that she was just being Iranian, translating literally into English the consummate Iranian art of humbling oneself, of treating others with such elaborate respect that every phrase that we utter that is not to do with sacrificing yourself for the beloved, is about denigrating yourself in front of the other.

When I started to have my own friends in Iran outside the family, this was one of our favourite games, the exaggerated niceties and *ta'arofs* of our culture, and with men, it was our favourite way to flirt. It would go something like this:

Me, answering the phone: 'Hello, where are you?'

Him: 'Look at the ground, Kamin-*khanoum*. I am there, the dust beneath your feet.'

It was not just amusing, but also breathtakingly romantic, a return to the sort of courting language not used in the West for centuries. I have never so often been referred to as a lady and never before or since has my beauty been compared to the rose and the nightingale. The more I occupied my culture, the more I liked it, the more it amused me, such a playful language made so absolutely for amusement and love.

After being so disappointed by my rejection of Iran as a child, my parents were at first thrilled that I wanted to redis-cover my roots and reconnect with my family. But after I started travelling back to Iran on my own for work, they were less thrilled. They were uncomfortable with me writ-ing about Iran, even when those articles were printed in the travel section, and they hated that my name accompanied these articles. They have never lost their suspicion of the regime and, being Iranian through and through, reasoned that to be known was to be, sooner or later, in trouble and that the only way to survive unscathed is to stay anonymous, unknown.

Every time I boarded the plane for Iran alone, my mother rang every one of my relations to give them strict instruc-tions to never leave me alone, let me go anywhere alone, or in fact, to let me out of their sights. Luckily, Mehry and Guity had grown too practical to chaperone me thus – their gruelling daily life gave them no choice but to leave me to my own devices, and Mehry would reassure my mother on the phone while waving me off as I skipped out of the door. Sedi and Bagher had not reconciled themselves to the Islamic Republic; my father has never been back and my mother's own visits are made, she repeatedly assures me, purely for the sake of her family.

I, however, had other ideas. By the end of Khatami's second term in 2005, I wanted nothing more than to move back home. It became my battle cry, one that I repeated often to anyone who would listen. Sitting in the car with Mehry in Tehran, I would glance up at the sunny winter skies, and declare that I had spent long enough under England's drizzle and it was time for me to come home. Sitting at *Khaleh* Mina's kitchen table chewing over the possibility, I promised her that I would soon be back. So determined was I that I left my own slippers in the houses I considered home: *Khaleh* Mina's in Shiraz and Mehry's in Tehran.

I was not the only one. In my travels back and forth to Iran, I had made some friends, other Iranians my age who had been brought up either in America or Britain, and they too declared the same thing. We were all pulled back to our homeland, intoxicated by the rediscovery of our country and our Iranian selves, and desperate to have a stake in Iran again, to feel in some way involved in its present and in planning its future. Some made it back, buoyed by Khatami's victory and the promise of better times and more openness, and there was some effort to lure us back too.

One day I had gone to visit to the press attaché of the Iranian Embassy in London. I was involved in writing a radio documentary that people at the BBC were interested in commissioning, but before they would take it further, they wanted to know that we would be given visas and permissions. The press attaché, a particular friend of President Khatami, could not have been more charming, offering me tea and chatting easily, erudite and refined. It was like sitting in an elegant drawing room in Tehran with aromatic tea and a fine Persian carpet under our feet. He assured me that of course we would have permission and soon moved on to talking about me, enquiring about my work and praising my loyalty to Iran.

'An educated lady like you, *Khanoum* Mohammadi,' he said, 'you could have chosen to do anything. And it is a matter of pride to us that you have chosen to write about your country. There are so many misunderstandings about Iran, and we need people like you, *Khanoum* Mohammadi, who are well educated and know how to communicate, to help explain.'

I never made the radio documentary and so I never went back to see the press attaché nor took him up on pitching the various subjects he had suggested the BBC might be interested in. I stuck to uncontroversial topics because, while I too wanted to explain Iran, I really didn't know how I could explain the Islamic Republic in a way that he would find praiseworthy – charming as he was, he was in any case a scion of the regime.

I found myself finally in a community of Iranians who, like me, had spent their lives split between two places. They also passionately wanted to bridge the gap between their two cultures. We engaged with the Islamic Republic because we love Iran and our families, and so we all found ways to reconcile ourselves to the mullahs in order to be part of our country. My Iranian being no longer stayed in Iran when I flew away, and I felt much more whole not having to endlessly explain one or the other of my worlds.

We all had grand plans to move back to Iran, to set up projects, to discover our families, our country, to transmit our privileged education to our countrymen. But then later that year, Mahmoud Ahmadinejad was elected president and once again, all our plans changed.

22

Back Home

I AM SITTING ALONE in a taxi, sweeping over the futuristic loop of highways that encircle Tehran. Everywhere around me are massive billboards bearing the faces of Ayatollah Khomeini and current Supreme Leader Ayatollah Khamenei. The sides of Tehran's ever-taller buildings are painted with huge images of the 'martyrs' of the war, but they now compete with billboards advertising home-grown movies, mobile phones and leather jackets worn by the male heartthrobs of Iranian cinema. The north of the city is packed with glossy shopping malls filled with shops selling glossy goods – from the latest BlackBerries to the hottest fashion in headscarves and *manteaus*. The brands are familiar – Zara, Mango and Benetton are just three of the fashion retailers I know so well from Europe, and electronic goods are stamped with the insignias of Toshiba, Sony and the like. In the malls, there are New York-style coffee shops with sofas to lounge on and an array of coffees with flavoured syrups on offer. The girls and boys who frequent these places are like creatures from another world – young, beautiful and fashionable, their hair coiffed and styled, the girls wearing tons of make-up, their haircuts expertly cut to fall forward out of the scraps of silk scarves that flutter off the back of their heads, their *manteaus,* which barely skim their bottoms, so short and tight that it is clear they are wearing nothing underneath. Boys wear aviator shades, their hair gelled into the kind of styles that trendy Western advertising executives can only dream of. These are the wealthy young people who live in the north of the city, frequenting the new cafés and chic restaurants with minimalist interiors that would be equally at home in Paris, New York or London.

As I am driven through the city's mesh of motorways, I reflect on the last six months that I have been living in Iran and I feel that I am in a science fiction novel. These have been the first six months of Ahmadinejad's presidency and, despite all our reservations, there have, as yet, been no real changes. This society, so young – 70 per cent of the population is under thirty-five – and so lively, so modern and forward-thinking no matter whether in Tehran, Shiraz or Sanandaj, so overwhelmingly itching for change, controlled by men such as the two whose images puncture the skyline so frequently, dressed in robes and turbans, their beards white, their shrewd eyes cold, from a different world from the one occupied by the young people. I cannot reconcile the two, despite my frequent trips back over the past ten years, despite the six months I have spent living here, travelling the country, staying in different provinces, taking in the most deprived villages in Kurdistan as well as the most privileged lifestyles in the breezy north of Tehran. My overwhelming sense is of a ruling regime madly out of step with society, of a country in which the culture has evolved far beyond the structures of the law, and of a system defunct and irrelevant but determined to hold on to power at all cost.

So much so that they are willing to turn a blind eye to the transgressions that are almost unavoidable if you wish to lead a normal life in Iran. Go to a party and you have broken the law – unless that party is full of only your close relations, and both men and women are correctly attired in Islamic dress – even the husband of an aunt is counted a 'stranger' when it comes to Islamic modesty. If that party has alcohol, mixed company and thumping pop beats, you have broken several more laws. Go out in a tight, short *manteau* with your hair spilling out of your headscarf and you have transgressed. Walk down the street with a man not your husband, brother or uncle, and you have violated another rule and so on until even I, with my careful and paranoid Western ways, soon stop bothering to toe the line and do as my friends and relations do – just as I please.

There are at least two societies operating concurrently in Iran at any given moment – the one papering the surface, which complies to rules and laws, and then the one hiding beneath, what actually happens. In between there are a multitude of nuances and subtleties, and the way people negotiate all these different realities with such ease fascinates me. Everyone wears so many masks – the regime forces them to – that it can be hard to know who anyone really is, and I now understand the old adage I was brought up with: 'Never trust anyone except your family'. The paranoia and distrust that has always existed in Iranian society has made us Iranians masters of dissembling, our very genes encoded with the ability to appear to say one thing while meaning something completely other. The response to the Islamic regime is, sadly, nothing new.

Nonetheless, the culture has evolved and continues to do so, no matter how much the regime tries to control and direct that evolution. In the information age, it is hard to keep the veil over the face of Iran, and no matter how many Internet sites are banned, there is always a clever hacker who will break the codes and post the information somewhere easy for others to find. Mobile phones are ubiquitous and vital now not just in the ever increasing hook-ups between the sexes, but for planning parties, underground gigs, fashion shows, film screenings and private views that are so easy to tune into in Tehran.

Life, I have found throughout my years of returning to Iran, always goes on. The Iran that I am living in now is a

different place to the shell-shocked Iran that I returned to
ten years ago. Reformist President Khatami's overwhelming
sweep to power in 1997 and his re-election for a second term
was a sure indication of the people's desire for change. Seen
as a liberal, Khatami was carried to the presidential position
on the crest of a wave made up of young people and women;
he spoke of reform and liberalisation, although he is also a
mullah and at no point suggested any change to the system of
Islamic rule. But he did point out that 'whenever in history
a religion has faced freedom, it has been the religion which
has sustained damage,' understanding in his canny way that
the rule of the mullahs was turning a whole generation – nay
a whole nation – off religion en masse. Indeed, the Iran he
inherited had the lowest mosque attendance of any Muslim
country in the world.

His efforts were to prove unsuccessful, and Iran's complicated political system, which encompasses democratic elements
with autocratic controls, made sure that Khatami's attempts
at reform were blocked. The Supreme Leader holds the real
power in the country and so the people grew disillusioned,
and all those young people who had worked so tirelessly to
canvas for Khatami and the reformers, turned their backs on
the political process so determindly that the next presidential election was won by a surprising candidate – Mahmoud
Ahmadinejad, the anorak-wearing former Revolutionary
Guard and war veteran who, despite his conservative poli-
cies, was favoured by those who voted for him because,
ironically, he was not a mullah in religious robes.

Whatever else he failed in, Khatami's era did usher in
greater social freedoms. My own journeys to Iran over the
years bore witness to this. Blanketed in a baggy black *manteau*
reaching almost to the ground, with a black headscarf and
a constant nervous twitch adjusting it during my first few
visits, my *manteaus* too gradually got shorter and tighter, and

my headscarves became more colourful and slipped further back, my hand no longer flying up to push away stray hair every few minutes. I learnt from my young cousins not to treat the *hejab* as outerwear, as I had been doing, but instead to build it in as part of my outfit – the key to being as stylish as these exotic colourful creatures that fluttered around Tehran looking so chic. They schooled me in the fashions of each season, pointing out that since what was in vogue changed almost monthly, there was no point in my investing money in my own *manteaus* and headscarves when I could just borrow theirs. I would arrive every time from London in a long baggy coat and black cotton headscarf and, once home, my teenage second cousins would lay out all their *manteaus* and scarves on their beds, and help me pick a few for my trip, explaining to me that the twenties drop-waisted style was acceptable now but on its way out, to be replaced by the nipped in waists and full skirts of *manteaus* inspired by Christian Dior's New Look of the late forties. My scarves went from plain black squares knotted under my chin to fine wool shawls in pastel paisley patterns picked out with elaborate embroidery, to Hermès-inspired silk squares with bold patterns, to chiffons splashed with bright flowers. I too finished off the look with the obligatory pair of outsize designer sunglasses perched on my head, the logo prominent, and I tripped around town with this new species of butterflies flitting through Tehran.

Thirty years after my mother and her sisters marched through the bazaar in their miniskirts and Biba eyeshadows, coming home 'pinched black and blue' as they told me, I accompanied my young cousins to parties and movies in tight Capri pants topped by figure-hugging *manteaus* and rainbow scarves, our lips glossy and eyelashes curled and lengthened by mascara, followed as we went by a convoy of admiring men. The colour is back in Iran.

The taxi driving me through the surreal landscape of modern Tehran with its contrasting billboards urging both consumerism and the values of 'martyrdom', drops me at a soaring tower block in the north of the city. For a few weeks now, I have been living alone in one of Tehran's most distinguished tower blocks. With its doorman, 24-hour security, tinkling fountains in the front garden and clocks announcing the time in Tehran, London and New York in the lobby, it is clear this skyscraper's spiritual home is Manhattan. However, unlike the Park Towers of Manhattan our Tehrani towers are not just known by their street numbers. The delicacy of the Iranian sensibility is evident even in the midst of these most modern of edifices: our towers are called things like 'Tower of Light', 'Tower of Shadow', 'The White Tower', 'Tower of Rain' and most common of all are names of flowers. All over the north of Tehran bloom skyscrapers such as 'Lily Tower', 'Tower of Poppies', 'Tulip Towers' and my current favourite, 'The Fragrance of Roses Tower'. Most famous of all is the Koh-i-noor Tower, 'The Mountain of Light Tower', named after the famous Iranian diamond the Koh-i-noor which now resides in the Tower of London as part of the British Crown Jewels.

Life in my tower is comfortable. Living in Tehran is not exactly like living in London, where I have a variety of ways to entertain myself any given minute of the day. It may be that a simple desire to go for a swim on a hot day here is attended by the hassle of finding a pool which allows women to swim on the day and time I wish to go (swimming pools are strictly segregated); and going out to the latest hot restaurant, movie or concert may mean having to stay dressed in my *manteau* and headscarf throughout the evening, but at least there are some options. At least, of an evening when my date comes to pick me up to escort me to a party, I feel safe in the knowledge that the doorman of my very posh tower block is not going to ring the religious police to report me for being alone with a man, and as for his opinion of me – this foreign Iranian who has gentleman callers – I care not a jot.

The cultural life of Tehran is rich, with private art viewings, secret screenings of controversial documentaries and movies, underground rock concerts, officially sanctioned classical concerts, and even illegal fashion shows on offer almost every night, as long as you know the right people. Alternatively there is the party circuit with Tehran's rich and beautiful, those expensively suited men and their glossy, whippet-thin wives who live in penthouse suites of marble towers or behind the walls of sprawling villas in the north of Tehran, right in the lap of the mountains. Although I have been a guest at one or two of these parties with one of my well-to-do cousins, I am much more comfortable in the circle of foreign journalists, diplomats and NGO workers who observe life in the city with a wry detachment, always amusing when I am missing the dry British sense of humour and longing to party in jeans with a face bare of the thick make-up that is de rigueur in society here.

When I get bored during the day, I slick on some lipstick and ring my most glamorous cousin who screeches up at the gates in her huge white SUV, a pair of massive Chanel sunglasses perched atop expensively streaked hair and the season's latest silk headscarf knotted loosely at her throat. She takes me off to a number of very shiny shopping malls in the north of Tehran where we browse designer boutiques and drink coffee in wannabe coffee shops. We swap gossip about the family, discuss the best shape for me to train my eyebrows into and laugh at the fashionistas who have taken the summer's tanned look a little too far and are glowing bright orange. She drops me off when she has to pick up her son from his round of classes, always leaving me with a party invite. I love my cousin and I enjoy dipping into her yummy mummy routine once in a while, but after attending several of her parties, I feel life is too short for the vapid conversation and hot competition that characterises the interaction of these women when they are gathered together with their husbands. With a sinking heart I realise it reminds me of the lives of the yummy mummies of Notting Hill.

Most of all, I like spending time with my family, with Mehry and Guity, who live close by. Although I have learnt to acclimatise to life in Iran and in Tehran I could almost pass for one of the chi-chi ladies whose concerns stop at owning the latest espresso machine and having the best tai-chi teacher, the reason I am in Iran is because, after all these years, I am still crazy in love with my family. In Shiraz I live with *Khaleh* Mina, the two of us squeezed into her little flat laughing and gossiping into the night. *Khaleh* Yassi's kids are grown-up now and no longer stay with her – Ali is at medical school and Yassi's eldest daughter is now married and living in Tehran where she works during the day and works out in the gym on the evenings her husband is out of town.

After so many years of confusion about my identity, with the twin blessings of getting older and increasing familiarity with and ease in my homeland, I realised then that the mask had been shed – in both Iran and London, I wore the same face, just one that spoke different languages. My Farsi now fluent and my manners playful, I was, if anything, enjoying life in Iran more than my life in London. Increasingly the siren call of Iran was getting harder to ignore and so, here I was again, this time for six months.

Tehran had changed too since my first visit ten years ago. With a huge population, the city had exploded, inching up the skirts of the Alborz more and more every year. Our old house in Darrus, which had once had nothing in front of it, was now practically in the centre of town. All over Tehran, skyscrapers and tower blocks rose with alarming alacrity, replacing lovely old houses built behind brick walls which harboured nightingales and rose gardens. Even new-build villas like ours at Darrus were being razed and replaced, or having floors added to them – land was scarce and Iranians, so used to living in large proportions, were now squeezing themselves into tiny apartments with small dimensions, their rose gardens reduced to a few flower pots on high-rise balconies.

Mehry never got her wish to travel. Iran was refashioned but not in the shape she had imagined in 1978. Concern for her parents kept her in Iran long enough for it to become impossible for her to leave the new Islamic Republic that was unwilling to give her – an unmarried woman – any independent rights without the guardianship of her male relatives, so she established herself instead in a career as a scientist. Through those hard first years of the new Islamic regime when women were being intimidated back into the home, she held fast to her job and eventually, with the war taking so many men away, her talent was allowed to shine despite her gender and she rose through the ranks. From the first time I returned to Tehran, I would spend hours sitting with Mehry, talking to her of my travels, pouring over maps and planning the journeys we would go on when she took early retirement.

Mehry and Guity had resisted the onslaught of the exploding city as long as they could. Every year more of the houses that surrounded theirs were knocked down and replaced by blocks of flats. Their house was not an old Persian house but representative of the modernity of another era, with two storeys and the garden in the back set behind a long stone patio and they were determined to hold on to it. Behrooz and his family had still lived upstairs and Mehry and Guity

had cared for their mother, Mehry working while Guity
took care of the house and fed all the stray cats of the neighbourhood as was her wont. Slowly they were surrounded,
besieged by the buildings rising around them every few
months, blocking their view of the sky and casting their
garden, once so verdant and filled with fruit trees and bushes
of bright flowers, the patio lined by pots of jasmine that I
would find scattered over my pillow at night, into shadow.
The fruit trees suffered, the flowers no longer bloomed as
bright and Guity would say to me sadly every time I visited,
'Look, they have taken our sun . . .'

Eventually they gave in and sold their land to one of the
many developers that had been aggressively pursuing them
for the past few years. Clearing out the old house took
months, and they held long conferences with my parents on
the phone about what to do with our Persian carpets which
had been with them since the revolution. Too large for any
house we were likely to inhabit in London, my father asked
Mehry and Guity to do with them as they would, and their
soft hearts, still so hopeful of one day seeing their beloved
uncle again, could not bear to let them go, just in case. So as
well as having to move fifty years of their own possessions,
they also moved some of the relics of our old life. Somehow
they managed too to transport Sa'adat-*khanoum*, who was
now entirely reliant on them for getting around, unable to
walk even to the bathroom by herself.

The last house of my childhood had finally disappeared,
razed to the ground to accommodate modern Iran. By the
time I returned for my long stay, Mehry and Guity and
Sa'adat-*khanoum* were installed on the fourth floor of a
modern apartment block in a busy neighbourhood in the
northern reaches of Tehran. Their kitchen was open-plan
and their living room windows gave views of the hills that
were pretty at night, when the lights lining the mountain

roads lit up, but they had no jasmine pots and Guity stood disconsolately by the windows, scattering stale bread and seeds down on to the street for the birds, no longer able to feed the cats she so loved.

By the time Mehry was retired, her father, my *amoo*, had died and her mother, the redoubtable Sa'adat-*khanoum*, had buckled under her bereavement. She practically lost the use of her legs overnight and for the next decade she gradually lost the use of her faculties as well. Mehry and Guity's life became an unrelenting round of nursing their mother, their freedom eroded from year to year as their mother slowly got worse. Sa'adat-*khanoum*, who had been so hale and hearty and had loved to hike out into the countryside dragging us all in her wake, became virtually housebound, so difficult was it for her daughters – themselves now in their sixties – to manoeuvre her down the stairs and into the car. Mehry, despite her growing weariness, submitted herself to her fate with some grace, but it cost her dear, I could see that. We nonetheless continued to spread out the map of the world and enthusiastically planned epic overland journeys that we now knew we would never go on.

I had stayed with them for months, skipping off on my travels to visit the Abbasian clan who were now scattered all over the country, and striding off on my own to Kurdistan, unable to have Mehry join me. Unbeknown to my mother and her worries, I lived an independent life in Tehran, moving into my own flat when a friend leaving for Europe gave me her keys. While *Khaleh* Mina and the other Abbasians still tried to protect me as if I was a lone child, Mehry and Guity, seeing my discomfort in living with them, giving them so much more trouble than they could really cope with, let me go. After years of being trapped inside family homes, I was living in Iran as I chose.

★   ★   ★

One cold February night, I donned my most conservative *hejab* and piled into a car with one of my Kurdish cousins, grandson of Sa'adat-*khanoum*, alongside some friends, other British-Iranians who were living in Tehran, and we headed downtown to Javadieh, a neighbourhood in conservative southern Tehran. It was the night before Ashura and we wanted to see the religious festival firsthand in a traditional area.

Ashura marks the moment that the two main sects in Islam irretrievably broke apart, a chasm that had opened after the Prophet's death when disagreement about who should succeed him had split his followers. There were those who believed that the Prophet's cousin and son-in-law Ali was his rightful heir, and those who believed that the new leader should be elected from those companions of the Prophet most capable of the job. The Prophet Mohammad's first successor was Abu Bakr, his close friend and father of his wife Aisha. He became the first caliph and his followers adopted the word Sunni – meaning 'one who follows the traditions of the Prophet' in Arabic. Those however who believed that the leadership should stay within the Prophet's own family (he had no sons) became known as Shia, an abbreviation from the historical 'Shia-t-Ali', or 'the Party of Ali'. Imam Ali, the first Imam – or saint – of Shia Islam's Twelve Imams, was eventually given the leadership of the caliphate, becoming the fourth caliph.

In the endless series of battles and struggles that followed between these two sects, Imam Ali had been killed by one of his own followers for murky political reasons – and when his grandson Hossein, the third Shia Imam, had taken on the powerful army of the Caliph Yazid with a small band of hopelessly outnumbered men at Kerbala in AD 680, facing certain death, the gruesome slaughter that ensued gave Shiism its first martyr and set the two sects apart for good.

As Catholicism is to Christianity, so Shiism in to Islam, a cult of devotion in which pain and passion opens a way to connect with God, its rituals based on mourning, its genesis a rebellion against the established order.

I had seen images of Ashura in the Islamic Republic where it was marked lavishly, with its long processions of black-clad men flagellating themselves with chains and beating their chests. In some places, the chains wore little spikes that tore through the flesh, mortifying the body, as the chants rose rhythmically. I expected it to be a time of heightened fervour and zealotry but, of course, I was wrong again. In the week leading up to the day of Ashura itself, I saw many processions as they snaked out of mosques, the chants and sounds of the chest-beating echoing through Tehran's noisy streets. I saw people gathered around the processions, crying with great emotion, ostensibly mourning the loss of Imam Hossein all those hundreds of years ago. I saw friends in some of these gatherings, weeping openly when, only the night before, they had been partying with great passion. This was all accompanied by an unexpectedly giddy holiday atmosphere – Iran was on vacation and the streets of Tehran were clear of heavy traffic.

Everywhere we drove there were roadside stalls giving away steaming hot cups of tea and the various traditional sweets that are distributed at religious festivals. Mosques handed out free food, and we took to joining any queues that we passed just to see what was on offer. That night in Javadieh, the atmosphere and the processions seemed to me something like a carnival, the rhythm and the beat reminding me of hip-hop, and in the melee of bodies and the sizzling feeling of anticipation, it was all I could do not to dance. Even in the conservative neighbourhoods of south Tehran, boys and girls were busy using the freedom that Ashura gave them to be on the streets all together to flirt and have fun.

It is tempting to see this seamless combination of Islam and flirting as a symptom of the Islamic Republic, but Mehry told me later that Ashura in her day was the same. Iranians have always had an irrepressible sense of fun, and growing up in sixties Iran girls were sheltered, and they too took advantage of religious festivals to flirt with boys. She told me that, if eye contact was made with a handsome boy in the procession and smiles were returned, then the boy would announce the digits of his phone number in between the chanting and chest beating, so that she could memorise it and call him later. It would go something like this: '*Ya* Hossein − 7 − *Ya* Ali − 6.' In those heady days of the shah's supremacy, women had little more freedom than they do now and the necessities of chastity and modesty that haunt women still were just as strong in pre-Islamic Republic Iran.

As I was growing up, I was familiar with the brightly coloured images of Imam Ali hanging everywhere, depicted as a handsome man with a thick black beard, a bright green headdress (green being the colour of Islam and worn also by *seyyeds* − those who can claim direct descent from the Prophet Mohammad), radiating the light of *aql*, the light of God which Shias believe was transferred directly to the prophets and saints. At the time of Ashura these would be joined by portraits of Imam Hossein, also poster art in style, the colours bold, almost naïve, another handsome, black-bearded man, though often depicted with grey or green eyes.

Although the shah was keen to secularise society and in fact his own portraits hung everywhere, ubiquitous, looking down on all Iranians as they went about their business, in offices, in government buildings, classrooms, university buildings, nonetheless, the faith of the Shia Iranians was too deep-rooted, and as I was growing up, even as I moved through our mainly secular world, I came to be as enamoured of Imam Ali's image as I was with the shah's, whose pictorial omnipresence made sure his image was burnt into our brains.

I survived my six months in Iran, even thrived, but mostly by accident. As a journalist I went on a government trip to a remote province. I was ill-prepared, taking with me a selection of brightly coloured, patterned silk headscarves as was the fashion in Tehran, while all the other women on the trip were wearing *maghna'ehs* to all the official functions the trip turned out to involve. I went to visit government offices in high summer wearing high-heeled sandals and cropped trousers, only realising my gaffe after the eyes of every man I talked to travelled silently to my painted toenails and bare ankles. Nonetheless, no one ever said anything, always treating me with deference and respect, and often with good humour. I felt immense freedom in navigating this society myself, at home in Iran finally, as an individual as well as tied to my great family.

When I finally left Iran, Mehry's younger brother *Amoo* Parviz drove me to the airport. As we sat and had a final tea together, he started to talk to me about life in the Islamic Republic. This man, now a grandfather, for me will always be the handsome youth at whose wedding I was a bridesmaid in the late seventies. He had a thick moustache then and wore a white suit like John Travolta's in *Saturday Night Fever*, his bride had cascading honey-coloured hair, their wedding reception was held in the glitziest disco in Tehran. She died during the Iran–Iraq war, leaving him with three small children and, after a decade alone, he married again and seemed happy in his life. He had come to Europe the year before for business and had managed to take a few extra days to come to London to see us. It had been his first trip west since the revolution and the first time in as long that my father had seen his nephew, but it had been short.

Now, as we sipped our teas at Mehrabad airport, he started to confide in me, much to my embarrassment and no doubt his too, proud man that he is. But confide he did, in that way I have become accustomed to Iranians doing with me; to them I was trusted family or old friend and yet also an outsider who would take their secrets home with me rather than sit and gossip in Tehran. No one really wants to do this but their hearts are so full they must spill out some of the worries lodged there in order to go on. He told me that on his visit to Europe, he had felt like an alien. Looking, walking and talking just like all the other people but, after thirty years of Islamic rule, after all the daily compromises he had had to make with his soul, his conscience, his very being in order to survive the regime and even prosper, he felt so different to all the people living as people should – in freedom – that he had felt locked up inside himself, unable to break the mask, unable to relate to anyone or allow himself to be understood.

'Kamin-*jan*,' he said to me as I tried to contain his confidences, 'we are not like other people. I realised this in Europe. There is a gulf because they simply cannot understand what we go through every single day of our lives in order to survive this regime.'

Back in London I was no longer heartbroken. Unlike every other time that I had left Iran, when I relived some of the buried grief of that first most sudden of partings, this time, I felt contained. I was sad but also happy to be home – in my other home, the country that gave me free air to breathe and where, after so many months in Iran, I saw everything through two sets of eyes, noticing for the first time the shapes and sizes and colours of all the people here and how little attention they attract, the casual individuality we take for granted in the West. When, in the streaming crowds of West

End workers, lovers paused to fall into each other's eyes and steal a kiss, I wanted to cheer for love and for freedom.

Soon after my return, and throughout Ahmadinejad's presidency, my flat in London became a refuge for Iranian friends on the move. My rickety sofa was pulled out time after time to provide a bed for those hyphenated Iranians like me who were seeing the hopes engendered by Khatami's presidency souring, who were fleeing the pressure of being always under scrutiny. As American–Iranian academics were jailed in Iran, more friends bowed to the inevitable and left before they too became inmates of Evin prison. When the last of these friends left my flat, bound for yet another new life in the US or Dubai, I went and sat at my mother's kitchen table. My heart was heavy and we sat and drank tea, Bagher, Sedi and I, while I talked and tried to ease the aching sense of déjà vu. I told the of the despair I had seen in my friends, of how we had sat up into early hours, talking and listening to Persian music, sometimes dancing, sometimes crying.

'I mean,' I said, carried away by my own emotion, 'can you imagine, they have left everything behind – their houses, businesses, families.'

Silence fell as my parents both looked at me, blinking. Of course they could imagine. We have been here once before. We are here again.

Now in London, during the holy month of Ramadan, I help my mother cook *shole zard* and *halva*. We take the vast trays of food to the Shia mosque in Kilburn, an Iranian place built with money provided by the Supreme Leader. London's population of Iranians has also exploded since we arrived and they are no longer just those who escaped the revolution like us, but also those who left during the war, and have been leaving ever since, people looking for better opportunities, for freer air to breathe, many former revolutionaries among them, their own lives a testament to the curdling of the dream. The Shia mosque caters to the most recent arrivals and going there is like entering a little bubble of Tehran. Coloured lights are strung outside and in the courtyard mill the young butterflies I had most recently seen in Tehran, their colourful scarves falling off the back of elaborate hairstyles, the boys gelled and clean-shaven, all standing about in groups, throwing loaded glances at each other, giggling.

Inside we enter the women's section and, when prayers are over and we have all wept as much as we need, everyone bringing their own private griefs to spill out in the ritual mourning that so lightens our hearts, long *sofras* are thrown down in rows from one end of the room to the other, and everyone sits down cross-legged to break their fast together, the mosque handing out food provided by an Iranian restaurant nearby, girls taking round vast pots of tea from which they charge our glasses. Sedi and I work our way down the rows, offering the trays of food to the assembled women who help themselves to mouthfuls for themselves, for their children, even to take home for their men, muttering blessings as they do so. The faces in front of me are an anthropological study of Iranian ethnicity – we have the broad cheekbones of the Turkoman, the dark tattooed skin of the ethnic Arabs, the heavily accented Farsi of the Azerbaijanis who speak their own Turkish dialect. My mother and I return to our places, in turn accepting food being offered by others, joining the women of my country as we chat and pray and laugh and eat the blessed food that everyone has cooked with such love.

My mother anchors me to my culture. Visiting her house I am returned to the Abbasian bosom, and her kitchen with its smells of saffron, rice and freshly washed herbs, the table groaning under a large basket filled with a cornucopia of fruit, is my haven. Sedi goes on supporting us with her indomitable strength, her ability to be flexible as circumstances require and to stand upright in the face of adversity. She sings to us and fills us with her love and her wicked humour and her food into which she pours all that is in her huge heart. After all these years of living in exile, Sedi is so much more to me than my mother – she is my mother tongue, my motherland, and to me, she is also my beloved Iran.

Iran itself will go on, of this I am sure. The rule of the mullahs will one day be wiped from the pages of history as have the eras of the Achaemenids, the Arabs, the Safavids, the Qajar and the Pahlavi shahs before them. But Iran, with her refined Persian culture and her strong women and poetic men is, I am sure, a survivor. She will survive the post-modern era as she has survived the terror of the Greeks, Mongols, even the machinations of the *farangis*. And, if needs be, she will even survive the weapons of the Israelis and the Americans, no matter how much devastation is wreaked on our beautiful land and on our innocent people. Our culture and our history continue to enrich the souls of new Iranians born to families far from home, and from Los Angeles to Perth, a new generation of Iranians are growing up with a longing they can hardly understand, a heart beating with the yearning to visit the land of our ancestors, to lie under a tree in the soft sunlight and become intoxicated by the fragrance of jasmine and orange blossom – to repossess our own personal paradise.

Epilogue

WHEN AHMADINEJAD WAS first elected, I asked Bagher what he thought. I may have berated him for not returning to Iran, but I know that he follows all the news from Iran on the Internet and I rely on him to have the sort of in-depth knowledge and insight that I, in my dilettante fashion, lack. In trying to form an opinion or understand some peculiar aspect of Iranian culture or literature, I always turn to my father, and together we attend Persian classical concerts and lectures about art and conferences on modern Iranian identity. My sister and mother sometimes join us for the concerts, but mostly my father and I go alone. One such conference was filmed and televised in Iran, and I only found out when one day in Tehran, Guity called me into the sitting room where, there on the television, was my father. Sitting in the audience of a lecture at the British Museum, the camera had caught him in passing, and his niece thrilled to see him. Mehry had been to visit once or twice over the last decades when her work had brought her to Europe, but Guity, fixed always inside the house, has not seen her uncle in three decades. I watched her as she stared at the television intently, standing in the middle of the room, the remote control poised in her right hand, hoping for another glimpse of him. She turned to me and said, almost pleading, 'But Kamin-*joon*, why don't you bring him back?'

Mehry understood my father's stubborn nature better but Guity seemed to think that my mother or I could influence him in some way, talk him round, change his mind. But we had no effect on him. Our entreaties would be met with a muttered, '*Inshallah*, next year' and so every time I went back to Iran I failed my cousins in not bringing them their uncle.

When I heard that Ahmadinejad won the election again in 2009, the first person I called was my father. He had predicted four years ago that Ahmadinejad's ascent would mean a tightening of the power of the Revolutionary Guard, a step towards a military dictatorship. Now, given all that has happened, he seems to have been right all along.

What followed Ahmadinejad's victory – the demonstrations, the chants of *Allah-o-akbar* from rooftops at night-time, the beatings, killings and arrests – hit me like a recurring nightmare. Current affairs enthusiasts were excited but I couldn't share their exhilaration, the sight of the violence on the streets blinded me to any historical perspective, and all I was concerned about was my family and my country once again. In the first few days after the election, when demonstrations seemed vast and unrelenting, I was phoned by a British newspaper that wanted to put me on a plane bound for Tehran so I could report from the demonstrations. I demurred, saying that given the number of my friends and acquaintances already in jail, I didn't think it would be safe for me to go. The prospect of being imprisoned or even questioned does not attract me and I am certainly not brave. But the newspaper insisted and, exasperated, asked me outright: 'But aren't you *interested*? Don't you want to *help*?'

I laughed out loud at the irony. Was I not interested? Well, I was interested in more than the news story, more than the fact that Iran had become the latest hot snippet and more than trying to report the anguish of the Iranian people. What I was – *am* – more interested in is that Mehry should not have to find herself frequenting government buildings looking for news of me, that her and Guity's well-earned sleep should not be disturbed by the arrival of *Basij* in the middle of the night, that *Khaleh* Mina's little flat not be forcibly mortgaged against my release from jail and promise of good behaviour in the future. The regime ruthlessly strikes at the heart of what Iranians hold dear – their family ties – in order to control them. Often activists, journalists and other political prisoners are not released until the deeds of the family house have been taken as guarantee against 'good behaviour' in the future. I may be bold enough not to mind what happens to me, but I would never want to risk the peace and anonymity of those I hold dear in Iran. The web of love that ties us all together is what is used even to control those of us living outside the country.

In these days that Iran has changed her image a little, now that the world has finally seen something of the true face of Iran, of all those ordinary people who are unsatisfied and unhappy with the regime, there is slightly less to explain. Now we are all cyber warriors protesting by posting online, disseminating information, gathering in our cyber communities as if on the street corner as I had as a child in Ahvaz, spreading video clips that have reached us on wave after wave of technology across the globe. And we are there waiting, us Iranians in the outside world, in the diaspora, waiting, praying, and ready to do so much more than pray. Our distress, guilt and frustration for not being there, the helplessness that those of us who lived through the revolution have become used to feeling in regards to Iran, the pain of it all repeating again, an endless repetition of history in different costumes, we can at least offset, or hold at bay, by being there, at the end of the cyber cord, waiting. We are ready to receive the images, to set up portals and websites and post codes to break locks on banned sites, any way to help the countrymen that suddenly we are linked to in this faceless but totally united way. There is exhilaration to it, and it undercuts the sadness.

Because there is an elation to finally being seen, to finally being recognised. But the sadness remains when the elation wears off.

Just as the *shabnamehs* appeared on the streets overnight during the Constitutional Revolution, leaflets that informed and mobilised the masses, and the revolution of 1979 was the first of the media age, so the protests that have made green the coolest colour utilise the latest in modern media and communications. It seems that we are destined to always be at the forefront of the latest technology in our bid for freedom and democracy.

I call my *daiey* Pardis in America on the computer, both of us putting on our video cameras so we can chat face to face. He is babysitting his daughter Nazanin's two small children while she works – the two latest additions to the Abbasian clan are the apples of *Daiey* Pardis and Shirin's eyes – and he tells me, while jiggling a toddler on his lap, 'There is no ideology here in this Green Movement, Kamin-*joon*, and that's better, it's about much simpler things. We had our bellies full, so we had time for ideology, but look where it got us.'

My country, having reeled from one form of tyranny to another throughout its history, is not well. Brought up by neglectful, deceitful and selfish fathers, it is a child that has learnt to cope but its survival strategies are neurotic to say the least. These neuroses will take many generations to unravel.

My dearest wish is for my country to be free. I don't know what freedom will look like under the Iranian sun, whether it will wear a short skirt or have pink hair or hold peaceful demonstrations where no one chants death to anyone and no flags or effigies are burnt and no one is shot or beaten or intimidated. I don't know if it will hold hands in the street with a handsome dark-haired boy with eyes the colour of honey or whether it will cast its eyes modestly to the ground, but I know it will swing its hair in the breeze (if it so chooses) and wear its strength lightly. I hope it will mean female wisdom steps out of the home and into public office and I hope it will mean a ceaseless growth of our peculiarly Iranian charm. I know it will still hand out *shole zard* on the street as blessings and get misty-eyed at the recital of Persian love poetry. I know it will still be in love with Islam and laughter and want nothing more than to lounge on elaborate carpets in the embrace of a walnut tree watching the butter-flies dance in the dappled sunlight, drinking hot black tea and eating fruit filled with sunshine.

We clamber uphill in the summer heat. The wind whips up clouds of dust and throws them in our eyes as we struggle up the sheer hillside, our faces scrunched against the day. The strangely rounded shapes we are climbing over were once houses, made of mud, houses that after heavy rains were abandoned and allowed to dissolve into the hill, where in years to come, more houses were built of mud, and so on and so on until the melted village became a hill with sheer sides and the villagers moved their houses into the valley and started to use materials that withstood the rains when they came.

At the top, standing on hundreds of years of housing, on kitchens, bedrooms and on homes filled with love and dreams and struggles, I lean into the wind. Below me stretch fields of gold, heads of wheat nodding in the breeze, patches of ploughed land glow rich brown against rows of green crops. A stream winds through the valley, edged by bamboo, the fields a patchwork of cypress and cedar trees, copses of fruit trees all the way to the khaki peaks engraved on the Kurdish horizon, layer upon layer, separating this land from its neigh-bours, enclosing it, untouched and remote from the world in a state of grace, like the Garden of Eden.

The village is poor. Houses that are not made of mud are constructed of breezeblocks, the edges softened by a layer of light brown mud. Dust blows through the streets, and here and there an old, wooden door still exists from the days before metal kept the world out of the inner courtyard. The wooden doors are massive, thick and dignified, even in their weathered state; double doors with iron knockers, one side a solid knob on which men would knock, and on the other a heavy ring which women would use, so the lady of the house knows by the quality of the knock whether she should answer the door covered up or not.

Somewhere in the village there is a wedding celebration and the sound of reed flutes pierces the air, soaring out above the jumping rhythms of traditional Kurdish wedding songs. Soon a group will gather in a circle, men and women linking hands to start the tripping steps of Kurdish dances, their shoulders shrugging to the beat, led by a man waving a white handkerchief. I have seen my father skip his way through complicated steps with a nimbleness that belies his advanced years when we gather in our flat in London and form a woefully constricted circle of four, with my mother, sister and I unable to follow my gazelle-like father properly. He may not have visited Kurdistan in nearly sixty years, but the dances are branded into his memory, and I know that whatever else his youth was full of, dancing must have been a favourite pastime.

The women are wearing long dresses in brightly coloured fabrics, with sequins and dazzling flower prints, reaching to the ground over ballooning pantaloons. Around the waist is wrapped a cummerbund of clashing flowers and a sequinned net hangs around their shoulders. Some are wearing head-scarves in observance of the rules of the Islamic Republic of Iran but some are just wearing the netting over their hair. It is a wedding after all.

All this I know as I lean into the wind and survey the land. Ancient, ripe and forbidding, its people poor, uneducated and living lives close to the poverty line, little changed for centuries save for some blessings of the modern age – electricity, cars, paved roads. Outside the houses are mounds of dried cowpats, fashioned into bricks, which will be burnt to heat houses in the harsh Kurdish winter, still the villagers' most reliable method of fuel in this country bursting with oil and gas. A group of young boys are racing up the hill to examine the strangers, the baggy folds of their Kurdish trousers flapping as they stumble up the slope. Soon they will be at the top, full of questions and giggles, but I know they won't address me directly as I am a woman and this is the Islamic Republic of Iran, and I am glad as I want to be alone with my thoughts in the wind, and I am unexpectedly grateful for the space that this imposed separation gives me. Sometimes in busy places, I am happy to disappear under my headscarf and not have to participate. The Islamic Republic, in seeking to make its women invisible, has opened up for us also a space to think, a space to be, that is not available in family life. For women in Iran, that room of one's own must remain a metaphysical space, but at least it vaguely exists. This personal encounter with the unexpected benefits of the *hejab* is how I know that in those women for whom thinking is as necessary as breathing, this Islamic Republic has nurtured the means of its own destruction, little may it show now. It may not be tomorrow or next year, but I know that the women of Iran will one day take what is rightfully theirs, powered by nothing other than their huge hearts, fierce intellects and sharp tongues, as long as they have this space to think.

I lean into the wind once more and I wonder again at how a boy born here eighty-five years ago, in a time before electricity and surnames, made it out of this half-forgotten land of Kurdistan to be sent to Britain to be educated, then to take one of the country's top jobs, travel the world to negotiate and oversee multi-million pound international oil projects in the heady days of Iran's OPEC power, and end up growing old in a modest flat in London studying Rumi, Hafez and Sa'adi, locked out of the homeland that he so loved by a bitter mixture of circumstance, disillusion and pride. My father has not been back to Iran since the first days of the Islamic Republic when he fled with his heart in his mouth and a stash of cash hidden in the lining of his briefcase. Unlike many others in his situation whose overwhelming sentimentality for their land eventually forced them to make some sort of peace with the Islamic Republic in order to be able to go back to Iran, my father's obstinacy in the face of such hurt overrode what sentimentality he had for his country. I call it obstinacy and pride, but of course, it may simply be heartbreak.

We are scattered now. The fruits of those seeds planted by Shokrollah and Kowkab, by Mirza Esmael Khan Hayat Davoudy and Ali Abbasian, we are scattered in ways that not even Abbas Abbasian could see when he cursed his children with *ghorbat*. From Kurdistan to Tehran to Canada to Australia are strewn the proud, quiet Kurds that carry in them still the memory of the cool air of Sanandaj. From Abadan to Shiraz to London to California to Holland to Sydney are dispersed the garrulous, hot-blooded descendents of the house of Hayat Davoudy, hiding in their reasonable twenty-first-century breasts the same pride that made our ancestor shoot her servant over a misplaced tea spoon, all champion chatterers and masters of the belly laugh.

There in her little flat in Shiraz is *Khaleh* Mina, finally able to please herself, as she compulsively cleans her home and infuses those around her with her own brand of unconditional love. She still teaches me, across all these miles, what it is to live the life you are given without regrets and painful struggle. She twirls her beautiful hands with their long, manicured nails which somehow miraculously survive the assault of cleaning products every day and says to me, 'Happiness is inside you. We have all lost a lot, but here is life. You have to look in front of you, *ghorbonetam*, not back.' And she pushes her glasses up her nose, takes a drag of her cigarette and, blowing out the smoke, she throws her head back and laughs, her right hand instinctively coming up to cover her mouth, trying to contain the spirit of that laugh.

Mehry is in her tower in Tehran, spending her retirement taking care of her elderly mother, the Sa'adat-*khanoum* of upright posture and brisk walks replaced by a woman with no memory, slumped in her chair and unable to will her legs to straighten so she can walk, asking throughout the day, 'Who is that?' as her granddaughters strut about the flat, midriffs bared. Mehry is still the man of the family, dragging her weary body up and down to her car several times a day to brave the traffic of Tehran to run errands and take care of the multitude of chores that running a household involves, while Guity is still the woman, leaving the house only to shop, and staying in to cook and wash and iron and make endless pots of tea. Yet Mehry still smiles her laconic smile, drops light kisses on her mother's forehead like benedictions and keeps on going without complaint.

Whether it is my cousins making good their new lives in Europe, North America or Australia, bringing up their children and stitching new identities on top of the old one, or the cousins still in Iran living in the big city or a small town, trading clothes or erecting skyscrapers, showing off or falling out, studying and marrying and negotiating the curious mixture of old and new that Iran now is, or whether it is us, our own mini-village of Mohammadis gathered around my mother's kitchen table in London, we have all survived. Like the cypress trees of our land that have grown for thousands of years and weathered all the storms of Iran's changeable history, we have all learnt to bend to the prevailing winds, but we are not broken. And nor is Iran.

Acknowledgements

THIS BOOK HAS been a true labour of love and I have been blessed with the support of many people over the years I have been grappling with my family story. First and most resounding thanks must go to my agent Judith Murray who has always walked the line between encouragement and pressure with infinite grace, and all at Greene and Heaton, especially Elizabeth Cochrane and Ellie Glason for protecting me from grim reality. My wonderful Bloomsbury commissioning editor Katie Bond was a fan of this book long before I was ready to write it and cleverly managed to convince Bloomsbury to take a chance on an unwritten story from an unproved writer – she has been a joy to work with, full of insights and indefatigable enthusiasm. Others at Bloomsbury have helped turn this book into a physical object, namely Anna Simpson and copy editor Clare Hey whose sensitive and intelligent edit made me believe I could actually write.

Of course this book could not have existed without my prodigious family who have so generously shared their stories with me from every corner of the globe. Special thanks go to my cousin Sara Parhizgari who brought all the might of her fine brain to spotting and correcting my mistakes, but my biggest thanks go to Bagher, Sedi and Narmin who have stood shoulder-to-shoulder with me on this – as in every other – endeavour in my life; how lucky I am to have you . . . My friends have given me sustenance and succour all; special mention must go to: Kicca Tommasi for weeping over every draft, Clare Naylor for imagining the kitten heels in Abadan before I could, The J Sisterhood with whom I have shared ideas, belly laughs and the best dances ever, and Christobel Kent for sharing her tower. Nassim Assefi lent me her indomitable spirit when mine dipped, and Yurek Idzik helped me get through the labyrinth unscathed.

Special thanks go to my love Bernardo Conti who has given me a home and a hearth, not to mention the vast spaces of his heart to dwell in. If life has to be a circus then thank God you are its ringleader . . .

A NOTE ON THE AUTHOR

Kamin Mohammadi was born in Iran in 1969 and exiled to the UK in 1979. She is an experienced journalist, travel writer and broadcaster who has written for the British and international press including *The Times*, the *Financial Times*, *Harper's Bazaar*, *Marie Claire* and the *Guardian* as well as co-authoring the Lonely Planet guide to Iran. She is currently living between London and Italy.

A NOTE ON THE TYPE

The text of this book is set in Bembo. This type was first used in 1495 by the Venetian printer Aldus Manutius for Cardinal Bembo's *De Aetna*, and was cut for Manutius by Francesco Griffo. It was one of the types used by Claude Garamond (1480–1561) as a model for his Romain de L'Université, and so it was the forerunner of what became standard European type for the following two centuries. Its modern form follows the original types and was designed for Monotype in 1929.